T0303759

BLOSSOMS IN THE GOLD MOUNTAINS

Copyright © 2018 Lily Chow

01 02 03 04 05 22 21 20 19 18

All rights reserved. No part of this publication may be reproduced, stored in a retrieval system or transmitted, in any form or by any means, without prior permission of the publisher or, in the case of photocopying or other reprographic copying, a licence from Access Copyright, the Canadian Copyright Licensing Agency, www.accesscopyright.ca, 1-800-893-5777, info@accesscopyright.ca.

Caitlin Press Inc.
8100 Alderwood Road, Halfmoon Bay, BC V0N 1Y1
www.caitlin-press.com

Text design and cover design by Vici Johnstone
Cover photo by Roland Chute, courtesy J.A. Chute
Printed in Canada

Caitlin Press Inc. acknowledges financial support from the Government of Canada and the Canada Council for the Arts, and the Province of British Columbia through the British Columbia Arts Council and the Book Publisher's Tax Credit.

Library and Archives Canada Cataloguing in Publication

Chow, Lily, 1931–, author
    Blossoms in the gold mountains : Chinese settlements in the Fraser Canyon and the Okanagan / Lily Chow.

ISBN 978-1-987915-50-1 (softcover)

    1. Chinese—British Columbia—Fraser River Valley—History.
2. Chinese—British Columbia—Fraser River Valley—Biography.
3. Chinese—British Columbia—Okanagan-Similkameen—History.
4. Chinese—British Columbia—Okanagan-Similkameen—Biography.
I. Title.

FC3850.C5C546 2017   971.1'004951   C2017-904596-2

Blossoms in the Gold Mountains
花朵盛开在金山

Lily Chow

CAITLIN PRESS

To my grandchildren, Colton and Magnus Wallin

CONTENTS

ACKNOWLEDGEMENTS   11

INTRODUCTION   14

YALE: THE HEAD OF NAVIGATION   24

LYTTON: THE SECOND GOLD TOWN   51

KAMLOOPS: THE RAILWAY TOWN   80

VERNON: THE PAST COW TOWN   113

KELOWNA: HOME OF OGOPOGO   144

ARMSTRONG: THE "CELERY CITY"   180

AFTERWORD   204

ENDNOTES   209

BIBLIOGRAPHY   218

LIST OF MAPS

Chinese Settlement Locations in BC   9

Yale Chinatown   30

Guangdong Province   37

Lytton Village   66

Location of Fur Trading Forts near Kamloops   80

Vernon Ranches   116

Vernon Chinatown   125

Kelowna Chinatown   146

Armstrong Chinatown   181

Lum Lock and his wife, Lee Quon Ho, and their family settled in Kelowna after the gold rush. Kelowna Public Archives KPA #2194.

CHINESE SETTLEMENT
LOCATIONS IN BC

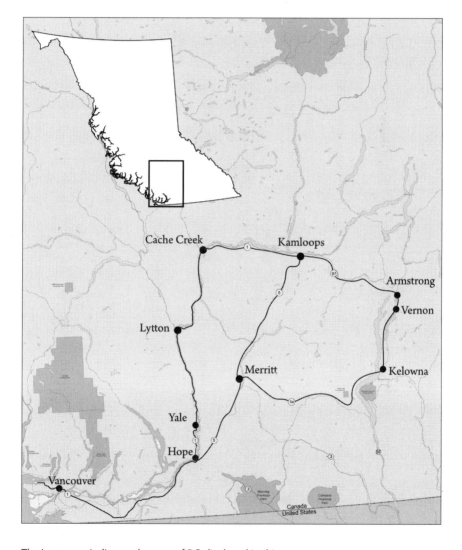

The inset map indicates the area of BC displayed in this map.

Girl and boy in traditional dress taken in North Kamloops. c.1907. Photo by Spencers Studio. Courtesey J.A. Chute.

ACKNOWLEDGEMENTS

Many kind and wonderful individuals, institutes and organizations have provided support and assistance to me while I was carrying out research for this book. I am thankful to them for sharing with me historical information and some family stories that reflect their lives and those of their ancestors.

To begin with, I would like to express my heartfelt thanks to Vici Johnstone, the publisher of Caitlin Press, for encouraging me to write about the early Chinese settlements or Chinatowns in the British Columbia Interior and for publishing my work. I am also thankful to Catherine Edwards, the editor who fine-tuned my writing, and to all the staff at Caitlin Press who worked on the layout and design of this book. To Richard Mackie and Shari Yore, I offer my appreciation for their invaluable suggestions and comments about the manuscript. I am grateful to David Chuenyan Lai for sharing his reference map showing the different counties in Guangdong and his studies of the Chinese cemeteries in Kamloops and Kelowna, which I used for my research.

Today the Chinatowns of the past no longer physically exist; they have been abandoned, demolished, burned down or replaced by city or highway development. Since many of the early settlers have passed on or left the settlements, and their descendants have also moved away to other locations or to other provinces, it has been quite a challenge to trace Chinese-Canadian history directly from the earliest Chinese families who once lived in the villages, towns and cities of the Fraser Canyon, the Okanagan and the Spallumcheen regions. But—thank goodness—many of the seniors and long-time Chinese-Canadian residents remember the Chinese settlements of the past. Many historians, researchers, teachers and students have also collected and written about some of the history of the Chinatowns in their local areas, and their findings have been one of the sources for my own writing. For these efforts, I would like to acknowledge the following people: Debbie Zervini, Irene Bjerky, Darla Dickson, and Darwin and Susan Bearg in Yale; John Haugen, David Chong, Peter and Alice Chong, the late Rita Haugen, Kenny Glasgow, Bernie and Lorna Fandrich, Jim Steer and Dorothy Dodge in Lytton; Elsie and George Cheung, Joe Leong and Scott Owen in Kamloops; Linda Wills, Barbara

Bell, Liz Ellison, the late Walter Joe, Harry Lowe, Law Kum Onn, Chan Yue Zhuan, and Gillian Hwang in Vernon; the late Ben Lee, Tun Wong, Lee Shui Dong, Ursula Surtees, and Wayne Wilson in Kelowna; and Ben Mahan, Ralph Lockhart, Mrs. Hughei Jong, and Mary Jong in Armstrong. Each and every one of them has been very helpful and generous, willing to share with me their understanding and knowledge of the early Chinese immigrants and the Chinese Canadians who were and are living in their areas in the past and present. Some of these individuals allowed me to interview them and have given me permission to quote them and include the information they provided in this book. To them, I am very grateful indeed.

Besides these individuals, I am also very grateful to Andrea Laforet for sharing her interview with the late Elder Annie York and to Chris Lee and Douglas Quan for their interview with Bevan Jangze. I also obtained some historical information about the lives of early Chinese settlers in Yale and its vicinity from the collection of Imbert Orchard interviews. He was a CBC Radio journalist whose interviews can be found in the BC Archives.

Many government records and documents, journals and periodicals, and historical magazines and directories were obtained from various museums and archives and from the special collections of this province's universities. These institutions include the Anglican Diocese of British Columbia Archives UBC, the City of Vancouver Archives, the Royal BC Museum and BC Archives, the Yale Historic Site and Museum, the Lytton Museum and Archives, the Kamloops Museum and Archives, the Greater Vernon Museum and Archives, the Okanagan Heritage Museum, the Armstrong Spallumcheen Museum, the Nlaka'pamux Nation Tribal Council, and Rare Books and Special Collections at the University of British Columbia and Special Collections at the University of Victoria. The curators and staff at these archives and libraries helped me find statistics, documents, maps, images and audio and video recordings. To them, I extend my sincere thanks.

Furthermore, I would like to thank the branches of the Chinese Freemasons society and the Dart Coon Club in Kamloops, Vernon and Kelowna. The leaders of these Chinese organizations generously shared with me three of their anniversary publications (in Chinese) for 1988, 1998 and 2007 respectively. Last, but not least, I would like to extend my sincere gratitude to the Okanagan Historical Society, whose annual reports, which began appearing in 1926, contain numerous articles about Chinese immigrants, Chinese Canadians and Chinatowns in the Okanagan and the Spallumcheen Valley. These articles are interesting and informative and their authors' efforts commendable.

Without the kindness of Gord Rattray, the executive director of the New Pathways to Gold Society, who took me in and out of the Fraser Canyon and the Okanagan to meet with local community leaders, historians and residents over the past ten years, I might not have been able to find out so much about the Chinese settlements. Many thanks, Gord and the New Pathways to Gold Society.

I apologize in advance if anyone has been unintentionally missed out in these acknowledgements.

Lily Chow
April 2017

INTRODUCTION

In February 2007, Chris O'Connor, then the mayor of the Village of Lytton, invited many people from different communities in the Fraser Canyon and the Cariboo to a meeting held to prepare for a celebration of British Columbia's 150th anniversary. Governor James Douglas declared BC to be a crown colony in November 1858, so BC would be 150 years old in 2008. It was therefore time to prepare for a celebration to commemorate the significant history that led to the birth of the BC crown colony.

Out of curiosity, I asked Gord Rattray to take me to the meeting so I could find out what the communities in the Interior were planning for the celebration. When I arrived at the Kumsheen Secondary School gymnasium, I found a large blue screen with the BC flag—a setting sun over mountains—set up in the middle of the auditorium. Below the BC logo was a brilliant yellow poster proclaiming "150th Anniversary in 2008." In front of the screen was a sturdy, small, rectangular platform representing the historical "stump" on which Governor James Douglas stood in 1858 to deliver his speech to a crowd of over ten thousand people in Yale at the height of the Fraser gold rush. On five rows of risers set against one side of the auditorium, facing the blue screen and the stump or platform, sat people from many Interior communities. The assembly included representatives of the BC Heritage Branch, Chief Byron Spinks of the Lytton First Nation, Chief Robert Hope of the Yale First Nation, and many Indigenous people and members of other ethnic groups—in short, people from all walks of life. It was heartening and encouraging to see such a large crowd at the gathering.

In his opening remarks, Mayor O'Connor stated the purpose of the meeting and invited people in the assembly to share stories of their ancestors and other pioneers and describe their deeds and contributions that have shaped BC's history. He also requested suggestions and ideas about how to celebrate BC's 150th anniversary. After his speech, many people went up onto the platform, told their stories and offered suggestions for the celebration. Notably, several miners shared their gold-mining experiences and told stories about some of the pioneer gold miners in the Fraser Canyon and the Cariboo. They described mining tasks and challenges and successes and failures in gold mining in the past and present. Many people in the audience nodded their heads, some sighed, and others laughed after each story was told.

But no one mentioned the Chinese gold miners and their endeavours. How could that be? The Chinese gold miners cannot be left out of BC history! Bold and naive as I have always been, I stepped up onto the platform and pointed out that the lives of Chinese miners and their mining ventures were an integral part of BC history and that their efforts and endeavours had contributed to the development of BC in its formative years. Every head turned and stared at me, a tiny old Chinese-Canadian woman. I could hear my heart pounding and feel the heat on my face. After I had delivered my brief talk, I bowed and left the platform.

At break time, John Haugen and Janet Webster, members of the Nlaka'pamux Nation, told me there were Chinese characters written on the boulders and cliffs at Van Winkle, a Chinese mining site in Lytton. This information aroused my interest. Immediately I asked if they could take me to the mining site so I could look at the Chinese characters. They generously agreed to do so. Then we exchanged addresses and phone numbers.

I was positive that the early Chinese miners and labourers had reached Lytton and its vicinity. At the height of the Fraser gold rush, Chinese miners arrived in Yale but couldn't find accommodation there because this boom town was packed with ten thousand people. So they migrated to Big Canon, Boston Bar and Lytton. During the construction of the Canadian Pacific Railway (CPR), Andrew Onderdonk, the chief contractor, hired about seventeen thousand Chinese labourers to work on the line in BC that passed through Lytton. Historical documents and old newspapers also state that some enterprising Chinese merchants followed the Chinese miners and labourers to set up small businesses along the way during these two important historical events. Therefore, I believed that early Chinese immigrants must have passed through and left their footprints in Lytton. Now that these two First Nations people had told me of the existence of Chinese characters on the cliff, my assumption was proved correct.

Actually, I had visited Lytton prior to this meeting. When I started research on Chinese history in the Interior, I went to Lytton hoping to find a museum where I could look at Chinese artifacts and documents and meet people in the village who might be able to tell me the history of the early Chinese immigrants in Lytton. Unfortunately, I found none, and drove away from the village disappointed.

Now that these two wonderful First Nations people had agreed to take me to the Chinese mining site to see and read Chinese writing on the cliffs, how could I refuse? Etchings and carvings of Chinese writing and calligraphy on walls, boulders and cliffs have been found in many famous mountain resorts in China, Taiwan and Southeast Asia, and in Chinese temples all over the world. They are elements of Chinese culture. In Canada, many Chinese temples have written or carved Chinese calligraphy on the walls of their buildings. In BC, Chinese writing was even found on the walls of the Dominion Immigration Building, once located on Dallas Road, Victoria. Between 1907 and 1957, thousands of Chinese immigrants were detained in this building, sometimes for months, before they were permitted to land in Canada. Those miserable, frustrated and angry Chinese detainees wrote messages and verses on the walls of their cells to vent their pent-up emotions. When the building was demolished in 1978, Dr. David Chuenyan Lai salvaged pieces of the walls with Chinese writing and donated them to the Royal BC Museum. In 2007, when Shanghai TV crews visited the museum, Dr. Lorne Hammond, the curator, showed them the writing. I was with the TV crews and therefore had the privilege of reading the writing. I was deeply touched by the verses and empathized with the feelings of anguish and misery, despair and despondency, loneliness and isolation they expressed. Therefore, I anticipated the Chinese writing on the cliffs at the mining site in Lytton might reveal something important that would reflect the lives and experiences of the Chinese gold miners living there. In the fall of 2007, I asked John Haugen to take me to the mining site.

The trip was fruitful. Besides taking me to the mining site, John gave me a tour of Lytton. At the mining site, I could hardly see the writing, because it had been eroded with the passage of time. But in the village, John showed me the location of the Chong Wah Chinese Merchant Company, once a famous Chinese general and grocery store, and the vacant lot where there had been an early Chinese joss house. Imagine, a Chinese joss house in Lytton! These two important Chinese landmarks suggested that Lytton had had a sizeable Chinese population in the past.

The following summer, I went to Lytton again. On this trip, John Haugen introduced me to his mother, the late Rita Haugen, and two of his sisters. Rita was a sweet and gracious lady who allowed me to interview her. She told me about the friendship between her family and the Chongs, the owners of the Chong Wah Chinese Merchant Company, and about the marriage between a Chinese labourer and an Indigenous woman in Lytton. In the meantime, John connected me with the Chong brothers, the sons of the Chinese merchant Chong Wah, who were then living in Burnaby.

A month later, I visited and interviewed the Chong brothers in their home. They were very kind and generous, sharing some experiences from their childhood days growing up in Lytton and their business dealings and friendships with the Indigenous people in the area. The information provided by the Haugens and the Chongs, plus findings from the Royal BC Museum and various archives in the Fraser Canyon, have enabled me to compile a fairly comprehensive history of the Chinese in Lytton.

Lytton, however, was not the very first place in the Interior that the early Chinese passed through or settled in. During the Fraser gold rush of 1858, Chinese miners and merchants arrived in Yale before they migrated to other cities, towns and villages. The first group of Chinese gold miners came from California. They were soon joined by their countrymen, who came from various counties in the Zhujiang (Pearl River) Delta of Guangdong Province via Hong Kong. The gold miners dispersed to their mining claims along the Fraser River near Yale, and merchants set up stores and businesses in Yale. A few of these merchants sent for their wives to join them in this period. The first woman to arrive was Mrs. Kwong Lee, who landed in Victoria in 1860, and went to Yale to join her husband. A year later, in 1861, the first Chinese baby was born in Canada: Won Cumyou (温金有) was born in Port Douglas at the head of Harrison Lake. Cumyou's parents were Won Ling Sing (温连胜-译音) and Wong Shee (黄氏). His father was a store and restaurant owner who emigrated from Hakka in Guangdong to San Francisco and later moved to Port Douglas.

When gold was depleted in the Fraser Canyon around 1862, the Chinese miners followed the white miners to the Cariboo in the north and the Similkameen Valley in the southeast of BC. Chinese merchants followed and set up businesses at certain central places in these regions to serve the miners.

Some of the early Chinese immigrants found wealth in gold mining and returned home to China, but many did not. The remaining Chinese gold miners continued pursuing their search for the glittering metal. When they found that gold mining was risky and not always profitable, many Chinese miners took up working at odd jobs and providing services such as carrying water or chopping wood for local residents and working as

domestic servants and cooks in private homes. Some set up small businesses such as laundries and bathhouses in Yale and its vicinity. A few grew
vegetables on leased land, selling their produce to local grocery stores or
door to door in Yale and the surrounding area. Others migrated to nearby
regions and worked on farms and ranches or in orchards.

In 1880, when Andrew Onderdonk won the contract to construct
the Canadian Pacific Railway in BC, he set up the railway headquarters
in Yale. All the Chinese labourers had to report to the headquarters before
they were dispatched to work on the construction at various sites. The
arrival of the Chinese construction labourers increased the Chinese population in Yale, and their settlement became a well-known and busy Chinatown in the Fraser Canyon. Unfortunately, many labourers died due to
accidents and illnesses during construction of the railway. In the fall of
1884, almost all the Chinese labourers were laid off except a few that the
company retained to do maintenance work in the winter. The labourers
who had been laid off were not provided with return passage so they could
go home to China. Many were stranded in the Fraser Canyon, especially
at Spences Bridge, while others went to the Chinese communities in Victoria and Vancouver for assistance and support. Those who were stranded
in the Fraser Canyon gradually migrated to the Okanagan, the Spallumcheen Valley and the Kootenay to pan for gold in creeks and streams, to
work as cooks and servants in private homes, and to find labourers' jobs on
farms, orchards, and ranches—just as the earlier Chinese miners who had
given up mining had done.

Although the Chinese had been disenfranchised in Canada in 1872,
these two influxes of Chinese immigrants were not affected by the Canadian immigration policies when they entered BC. The head tax was enacted in 1885 immediately after the CPR construction was completed.
At first, the head tax was $50.00 per entry but it was increased to $100.00
in 1901 and to $500.00 in 1904. Consequently, many Chinese immi-
grants who came to this country after 1904 did not bring their wives and
children with them or send for them later, because they could not afford
to pay the head tax for their families to enter Canada. The intention of
the head tax was to stop Chinese immigration; however, it did not apply
to consular officials, merchants, clergymen, tourists, scientists, students
and teachers who sought entry to Canada. When the hefty levy failed
to deter the Chinese from coming, the Dominion government passed
and enforced the Chinese Exclusion Act on July 1, 1923, which more or

less stopped Chinese immigration. Between 1924 and 1949, when the act was repealed, no more than three hundred Chinese people immigrated to Canada; many of these were students, clergymen and refugees with Chinese ancestry from other countries. The negative impacts of the Chinese Exclusion Act on the Chinese community in BC were enormous; many of these consequences will be illustrated as each chapter unfolds.

Several causes stimulated the Chinese to immigrate to Canada from Guangdong Province despite the heavy head tax. During the nineteenth century, many peasants in Guangdong did not own farmland but instead rented it from landlords to cultivate crops. They had to pay rent or supply a high percentage of their harvest each year to their landlords. Arable lands were scarce, and crops were often affected by drought, floods and locust attacks. Frequently, crop production was insufficient for the peasants to pay the rents and taxes to the local government. Consequently, many peasants were in debt, living with poverty and starvation. Banditry, robberies and thefts were common. Over the past three decades, I have visited four or more counties in the Zhujiang Delta several times. In each village, I found tall watchtowers. The farmers told me that every family in the village took turns sending a man from each family to stand sentry in the tower at night. When bandits, robbers and thieves invaded their community, the man in the watchtower would alert the villagers so they could prepare to defend and protect themselves. This practice began around 1850 and lasted until 1950, showing how unsafe the peasants were and how vigilant they had to be. Living under such adverse and oppressive conditions, some impoverished peasants took up arms and rebelled against the Qing government. For example, in 1850, the Taiping Rebellion (太平天国起义) was one of the peasant uprisings that set out to destroy the Qing dynasty. The Taiping reformers were people from Guangdong and Guangxi provinces.

The Second Opium War (1856–60), fought by the British against the Qing government, actually started in Guangdong. In October 1856, several Chinese workers in the port of Guangzhou (Canton) were allegedly accused of lowering the British flag on a vessel anchored in the port. Shortly after, a British warship sailed up the Zhujiang River estuary and attacked Guangzhou. Several battles between the British and the Chinese were fought in Humen (虎门), a town on the eastern shore of the estuary in Dongguan County (东莞县). Meanwhile, the French joined the British in their military operations and they captured Guangzhou. After this, the United States, Russia and other western countries joined the British and the French in their military campaign. The war spread to Tianjin and Beijing, forcing Emperor Xianfeng (咸丰) to leave the palace in Beijing and take refuge in Rehe (热河), a summer resort. On October 18, 1860, British troops rushed into the Beijing Summer Palace (圆明园) and set fire to it. In brief, many skirmishes and negotiations between the Qing government and the eight foreign powers took place. Finally, the Qing government was forced to sign the Tianjian Treaties with the British and the French, which benefitted the eight foreign powers in trade, established foreign envoys in major cities, and allowed foreign merchants and missionaries to travel freely into the interior of China. The Qing government also had to pay indemnity of six million teals of silver to the British and the French. In 1860, the importation of opium into China, one of the terms of the treaties, was legalized. The Tianjian Treaties were a most humiliating settlement for China.

Emperor Guangxu (光绪), who ruled the country from 1879 to 1908 under the thumb of Dowager Empress Cixi (慈禧太后), realized the weakness and incompetency of the imperial government and the poor education system, which mainly benefitted the mandarins and other elites. With the support of his trusted advisors, the emperor initiated a reform movement. Dowager Cixi imprisoned him and halted the reformation, which lasted only 103 days. Political turmoil erupted, followed by military campaigns among the warlords in various provinces. The Chinese people, then, were living between hell fire and deep water, facing poverty, assaults and violence in the villages, the dangers of warfare, and the uncertainty of political turmoil. Many Chinese, especially those in Guangdong, wanted to capture every opportunity to leave the country.

As mentioned earlier, some of the gold miners in Canada had been successful. They returned home, bought land for cultivation, built houses and improved the standard of living of their families. These individuals encouraged young men to leave their villages and immigrate to BC. They loaned money to their young relatives to pay the head tax and told them that job opportunities were always present in BC as long as they were willing to do any kind of labour. Meanwhile, new immigrants could still pan for gold in the rivers and streams, because it was believed that the mother lode had yet to be found.

My father-in-law, Chow Loy Chung (周来松), was one of those young men who borrowed money from a relative to pay the head tax to gain entry to BC in 1916. He worked hard as a labourer on the construction of the

Grand Trunk Pacific Railway, then on farmlands, and finally in the Domtar cement factory in Powell River. In summer, he panned for gold in the streams and creeks. Gradually he paid off his debt for the head tax, went home, and built a large and modern house in Kaiping, which gave me the excuse of visiting "home" every two years over the past few decades and enabled me to visit museums in various counties, especially Humen in Dongguan County.

This book, however, focuses mainly on the processes of Chinese settlement, the features of the places where they settled, namely, the early Chinatowns, and the development of the existing Chinese communities in the Fraser Canyon, the Okanagan and the Spallumcheem Valley. It begins with Yale and Lytton in the Fraser Canyon, followed by Kamloops, Vernon and Kelowna in the Okanagan, and then Armstrong in the Spallumcheen Valley. Each chapter is introduced with a brief history and geography of the place, the location and the features of Chinatowns in each area, and the occupations of the Chinese residents. To a certain extent, their occupations mirrored the changing landscapes in the places where they settled and made a living. For example, the rock piles at the mining sites in Lytton are evidence of a changing landscape in the Fraser Canyon, as is the cultivation of celery in Armstrong, where the Chinese vegetable gardeners had turned bog into farmland. The employment of the Chinese immigrants also reflected the immigration policies in effect at the time and the widespread racist attitudes towards the early Chinese and their descendants that emerged sporadically as late as the 1960s. The determination and stamina demonstrated by the early Chinese immigrants to make life work showed their strength and resilience despite the hardships and struggles they faced. Their ways of life illustrate the influence of Chinese culture and traditions, and their values and beliefs.

The road to settlement was often rugged and challenging; therefore, the Chinese immigrants formed or established organizations in their communities to offer assistance and support, as well as security and protection for one another. These organizations and the roles they played are described in the following chapters. Also, accidents and incidents that occurred and affected individuals or the community are recorded to show the kinds of hardships and suffering that settlers had to endure. But the lives of the settlers were not always dark and cloudy, antagonistic and characterized by drudgery. A few of the interviewees I spoke with shared the amusing and joyful days of their childhoods with their siblings and peers, their loving relationships with their parents, and their efforts to gain acceptance and recognition in the community at large. Actually, a couple of the interviewees turned the rejections and dismissals they encountered in their younger days into a force driving them to achieve and succeed in gaining the respect and admiration of people in both the Chinese community and Canadian society at large. Their stories also reveal how they reached out and established friendships and relationships with the mainstream community and different ethnic groups, especially with Indigenous peoples.

During interviews with key people and on-site research in the various communities, I discovered that some Chinese Canadians were known by the names of their businesses instead of their personal names. For example, the name of the owner of the On Lee Store in Yale was Zheng Huan Zhang, but the people in the community called him On Lee. As a result, all his children were registered with On Lee as their surname at birth and in school. The tombstones of Zheng's two deceased sons are inscribed with James On Lee and David On Lee respectively. And very often credits and acknowledgements were given to this family under the name On Lee. Therefore, I have used both surnames, On Lee and Zheng, whichever seemed appropriate. For instance, if their official registrations in government departments or school districts was On Lee, I made no attempt to change this. I point out Zheng as the surname because other Chinese publications, such as the *Chinese Times*, published Zheng as their surnames instead.

Confusion in Chinese names also arises from the different English spellings for surnames. For example, the children of Cheng Ging Butt use Tsang or Jangz as their surnames. To show that they are members of a single family, I insert a Chinese character within parentheses beside their surname; for example, Cheng (郑), Tsang (郑) and Jangz (郑). Similarly, Zhou, Chow, Chou, and Joe have the same Chinese character (周). It may be interesting, if not alarming, to note that both Zheng and Cheng are referred to by the same Chinese character. Zheng is the pronunciation in Mandarin, whereas Cheng is Cantonese—the language of Guangdong. The variety of different spellings for the above surnames (郑) and (周) might have been caused by the dialects spoken by the early immigrants on their arrival in this country and in the hospitals where their children were born. Often, clerks and registrars were unfamiliar with the pronunciation of the different dialects and came up with whatever spelling was similar to the phonics of the spoken word. Again, I make no attempt to rectify the spellings, because they are recorded as such in many government documents. However, I add explanations according to my own understanding and Chinese characters within brackets wherever they are needed.

Also, Chinese names usually consist of three characters; the surname always appears first, followed by the given names, like Low Bing Chong (刘炳昌). But many people, including clerks and registrars in different institutions or government departments, were unaware of the order of Chinese names. The surname of the gentleman Low Bing Chong is Low, but he was known as Mr. Chong in the community, and his children use Chong as their surname. Again, I retained Chong in describing this family, because Chong has become the legal surname and the deeds and contributions of this Chong family have been recorded this way in public and legal documents. Similar cases can be found in almost every chapter in this book.

The system of romanization used in this book is Hanyu Pinyin, a standard writing form in the People's Republic of China. For example, Qing Ming is used to refer to the festival of brightness instead of Ching Ming, which is Cantonese. Similarly, Guomindang, the romanization in Hanyu Pinyin, refers to the Chinese Nationalist League or Party, instead of the word Kuomintang, which is used in the Wade-Giles and other systems. In addition, Chinese characters are written in simplified form unless the traditional Chinese characters are used in original or official documents.

Although I have done my utmost to seek out as many descendants of the early Chinese immigrants and Chinese Canadians as I could, it has not been possible to find them all. The personal history in each settlement recorded here came from those Chinese Canadians and other people from the local community who were willing to generously share with me their past and experiences, and their observations and knowledge. Some Chinese-Canadian families might have been missed in this book, due to limited time and ability to find the sources. In writing history, however, it is inevitable that information is omitted, excluded or misinterpreted, even though time and effort have been made to cross-reference it with all the possible primary and secondary sources. I therefore take responsibility for any possible omissions, errors and misinterpretations.

YALE: THE HEAD OF NAVIGATION

The village of Yale sits on the west bank of the Fraser River in the traditional territory of the Yale First Nation, about 177 kilometres north of Vancouver. It offers a spectacular view of the Fraser River flowing quietly by—or roaring through with fury in late spring when melting snow adds to its volume. In winter, the current slows down and water near the riverbanks freezes, forming sheets of glittering ice. The lofty mountains to the northeast form the backdrop of the village, the beginning of the Fraser Canyon.

A short distance beyond Yale, the Fraser River is forceful and turbulent. In the early days, many steamboats could not travel past Yale but instead had to stop there. This is why it was called the "head of navigation." Both the Fraser gold rush and the construction of the Canadian Pacific Railway (CPR)—two important historical events—began at Yale, BC.

In its earliest days, Yale was a trading post of the Hudson's Bay Company (HBC), a fur brigade that established a fort there in 1848. In 1858, the lure of gold transformed Yale into a busy town that consisted of a gold commission office, hotels, saloons, restaurants, general stores, a pack-train station, stables, blacksmith shops, an Anglican church and many residential houses.[1] The population exploded until accommodations became so scarce that miners had to camp in tents or sleep on the riverbanks or in any open space. At the peak of the gold rush, it was estimated that ten thousand people, including many Chinese, lived in or had passed through Yale.

The Arrival of the Chinese

When the Fraser gold rush began in 1858, many Chinese merchants, prospectors and miners travelled by boat from California to Victoria. The Chinese prospectors and miners then boarded one of the sternwheelers—such as the *Enterprise, Sea Bird, Maria, Douglas* or the Hudson's Bay Company steamship, the *Otter*—to sail across the Strait of Georgia and up the Fraser River to Fort Langley. Some would disembark there and walk the trail leading to Harrison Lake and then continue on foot to Lillooet. Others travelled by sternwheeler up the Fraser River to Fort Hope—an HBC trading post founded in 1848—or via canoe to Yale. Others trekked along the trails from Whatcom (now Bellingham) in Washington State to the Fraser

Valley.[2] On June 3, 1858, the *Victoria Gazette* stated that "a batch of celestials have landed from Oregon and are encamped in the neighborhood of Yale." In July, the same newspaper wrote that "twenty-four wagons, loaded with as many persons as could get upon them, arrived [in Yale] during the day. Of these about one-third were Chinamen... The Chinese are coming rapidly... Of the great number of passengers arriving by riverboat, many are Chinamen..." All these reports indicate that the Chinese took different routes and used various modes of transportation on their way from California to Yale before they advanced to the various goldfields. These Chinese gold seekers were soon joined by their countrymen who emigrated from Guangdong Province via Hong Kong.

By the middle of 1858, thousands of miners, prospectors, merchants and people from all walks of life had arrived in Yale. To reach their claims in the goldfields, the Chinese gold seekers usually hired an Indigenous guide to help them reach their sites. Travelling on foot, they had a special way of carrying their belongings to the goldfields. They carried their loads with a wooden pole about two metres long. They fastened a canvas sack containing their mining gear, a tent and clothing with cords at one end of the pole and another sack with their cooking utensils and provisions at the other. They balanced the pole on their shoulders and carried their loaded sacks to the claims. This was economical because they only had to pay the Indigenous guide for leading them to the claims, and not for packing goods and supplies.

When more Chinese immigrants, especially those who had come from Guangdong or Hong Kong, arrived in Yale, there was no room for them. Many of them had to leave the village and go to nearby places such as Rancherie (Spuzzum), Alexandra, or Big Canon (also known as Black Canon). About three hundred Chinese immigrants migrated to Tranquille Creek at Kamloops Lake to pan for gold.[3]

The Chinese Placer Miners

Many of the Chinese immigrants were placer miners. Once they had reached their destination, they pitched their tents and lost no time in beginning to prospect or digging and mining gold. These Chinese placer miners used a circular pan or a rocker to wash away river sands and gravel to obtain gold particles. In panning for gold, they scooped up a small amount of sediment from a river bed, added a small amount of water to the sediment and then swirled the mixture in a rotating fashion while holding the pan at an angle. The swirling motion would wash the sand and gravel away but prevent gold particles from spilling out. The miners then picked up the gold particles or nuggets from the pan.

A rocker consisted of a stack of two hollow boxes, the bottom one longer than the one on the top. To extract gold from a rocker, miners would scoop up some dirt or sediment and put it in the top box. Then they would add water and shake or rock the apparatus. The finer pieces would sift through a wire mesh between the two hollow boxes, and the sands and gold particles would be caught in the lower box, whose bottom was lined with a piece of cloth or blanket. The residue was then panned out to separate the fine gold from other debris.[4]

Many white miners abandoned their claims and moved on to mine other claims when they could no longer find gold nuggets on their original claims. The Chinese miners often took over these abandoned claims and worked them for any gold flakes and dust that might be left behind. Arthur Urquhart, an Indigenous man from Spuzzum, recalled that the Chinese miners were very thorough in their gold panning. "The Chinese miners spoke a mixture of Cantonese, Indian and Chinook," said Urquhart. "We all liked them when we were just children. They erected little log houses

Soon after they arrived in Canada, many Chinese immigrants followed the gold rush. They worked as miners, alongside the Indigenous men of the region. Courtesy of the Royal BC Museum and Archives D-07865.

adjacent to the [Spuzzum] river, which would be quite convenient for their diggings. And they lived very simply. Most of the time they went to Yale to get supplies."[5]

On July 10, 1858, the *Victoria Gazette* reported that "most of the claims now being abandoned are immediately taken up by Chinamen. The Chinese are coming into the country rapidly, and as many of their countrymen are already here… Chinamen not only 'jumped' claims, but also took possession of the cabins and cooking utensils of [white] miners." The last statement assumes that the Chinese miners had taken over the properties illegally.

On August 19, 1858, Donald Walker, an agent of the HBC, visited Fort Yale to stop the sale of liquor to Indigenous people. "This business of supplying the savages with liquor by the whites has found a counterpart [the Chinese], who also furnished them with arms and ammunition," reported the *Victoria Gazette*. This information implies that the Chinese were competing with the whites selling liquor and that they had supplied weapons to Indigenous people in Yale and the surrounding areas. The *Victoria Gazette* continued its report: "In the early part of last week, a boat loaded with these pestiferous people [the Chinese] arrived at a bar on the lower end of the Big Canon… and proceeded to sell powder and shots to the Indians…" The language of this newspaper illustrates anti-Chinese sentiment and contemporary western attitudes towards both the Chinese and the Indigenous people.

The Canyon War and the Chinese Miners

On August 21, 1858, the *Victoria Gazette* reported that "a fight occurred at the Rancherie, where the Indians were killed and their encampment burnt. Ten Indians (one of whom was a chief) were killed and two whites, a man and a woman, from Hill's Bar died [during the fight]. Two companies, 150 men in each, were immediately formed at Fort Yale… Serious trouble was apprehended." The miners then appointed Captain Snyder to take charge of the contingent. In a letter to the *Victoria Gazette* editor, Captain Snyder wrote: "It is said that the Chinese on a bar close by are in league with the savages… All miners have left the river between Big Canon and the Fork [Lytton] on account of these disturbances."

Prior to taking military action, Captain Snyder and his men went to interrogate the Chinese miners at China Bar to find out whether they had supplied firearms to the Indigenous people; the Chinese miners denied having sold or supplied such ammunition to them. Snyder then asked the Chinese miners to leave their claims, because a battle between the white miners and the Indigenous people would soon take place. The Chinese could return to their claims when the war was over.[6] Fortunately, Nlaka'pamux Chief David Spintlum (Cexpe'nthlEm) successfully intervened, preventing the war from taking place. The Chinese miners then returned to their claims at China Bar and resumed panning for gold.

Chinese Miners and Their Licences

On March 19, 1861, the *Colonist* stated that "there are 4 to 5 hundred Celestials at work... on various bars between Hope and Yale." A year later, the same newspaper estimated that there were three hundred Chinese miners working between the Harrison River and Yale and two hundred between Yale and Lytton. Between 1861 and 1862, the Hope Collectorate entered in its records the names of miners who had applied for mining licences, including some Chinese. Below is the summary of the licences issued to Chinese miners during these years.

Licences Issued to Chinese Miners by the Hope Collectorate in 1861 and 1862

Year/Date	Number of Chinese	Fees
1861, February 27–28	26	£1.92 (pounds)
March 20	3	Same as above
March 29	15	£1.40
April 4–17	100	Same as above
May 8–24	38	Same as above
June 11	1	Same as above
July 18–22	7	Same as above
August 13	18	Same as above
September	0	—
October 8–30	8	£1.40
November	0	—
December 4	6	£1.40
1862, April	1	£1.51
Total	223	

Source: Royal BC Museum, GR0252, Volume 33.

It is interesting to note that the mining licences or certificates were charged in English pounds instead of Canadian dollars. Presumably $5.00 Canadian was equivalent to £1.92, or later £1.40. The collectorate set up in Fort Hope was to make sure that all miners paid their mining dues regardless of their port of entry to the Fraser, since some came overland and others by boat.

The Chinese miners were often slow to procure their mining licences. Mr. Coffee, the police officer at Yale, went to the sandbars along the Fraser near Yale, where twelve Chinese miners were panning for gold. Coffee sailed across the river in a canoe to find the Chinese miners on various sandbars and demanded they show their licences. They were unable to produce them and were taken to Mr. Sanders, the gold commissioner in Yale. They were all made to pay for their mining licences, and four of them were fined $25.00 each.[7]

The Challenges and Costs of Living

Placer gold mining was a risky enterprise that required a maximum amount of work to get a minimal or even at times no return. Spring run-off usually added huge volumes of water to the Fraser and its tributaries, making it impossible for the miners to do any mining. In 1858, David Higgins, a renowned journalist, travelled to Yale and found that "all along the river, wherever there occurred a bench or a bar, miners were encamped waiting for the river to fall."[8]

The cost of living in the goldfields was very high, and food was not always available. Only blankets and beans could be purchased at Fort Yale. In 1858 at Fort Hope, flour was selling for $60.00 a barrel, bacon for 75 cents a pound, beef for 37.5 cents a pound, pork for 33–35 cents a pound, butter for 75 cents a pound and sugar for 50 cents a pound. At the same time, in Victoria flour could be obtained for $15.00 a barrel, bacon for 25 cents a pound, pork for 15 cents a pound, butter for 20 cents a pound and sugar for 12.5 cents a pound. If miners wanted to purchase food and goods in Victoria, the cost of transporting them to the mine sites could be quite enormous. A pack train operated by Indigenous people charged $8.00 to $10.00 to carry a hundred pounds of goods from Yale to the Forks (Lytton).

The shortage of food caused suffering and hardship and even starvation for many miners, including the Chinese. Some starving Chinese miners in Yale could not get provisions and had no means to pay Indigenous people to pack them in for them. A few Chinese resorted to eating dogs and cats, and two Chinese people starved to death at Big Bar. A boat filled with provisions and manned by Chinese was stopped by several white men who forced the Chinese to sell them their goods at 30 cents a pound for flour and other articles at proportionally low prices.[9]

The Chinese Settlement: Chinatown

As the miners arrived in the Fraser Valley, so did merchants who set up businesses in Yale. For example, Kwong Lee & Company established its headquarters in Yale and opened other stores in the area. In 1860, Mrs. Kwong Lee, wife of the company's owner, arrived in Victoria. She was the first Chinese woman to immigrate to BC.

By 1862, the peak of the Fraser gold rush was over, since gold had been depleted from many areas along the Fraser. Many miners went north to the Cariboo or east to Rock Creek and the Similkameen Valley. Instead of following other miners going to the north or to the east, some Chinese miners settled in Yale, and a Chinatown developed there. Chinatown was located at the east side of the town between Rail Road (now Douglas Avenue) and Front Street and bounded by Yale Street on the east and Regent Street on the west.

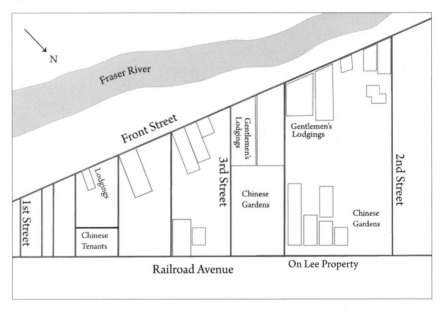

Once there was no more gold to mine, several of the miners decided to settle in Yale and establish their own businesses. Chinatown soon developed on the east side of the town, occupying a section of the economically thriving Front Street.

The Chinese settlers cultivated vegetable gardens and operated small businesses such as general and grocery stores, restaurants, and laundries, or they worked for farmers and ranchers in the surrounding area. A few found employment on pack trains or worked by themselves as individual packers. While they were living in Yale or the villages nearby, they often continued mining on abandoned sandbars between Hope and Yale. But they always returned to Chinatown and took shelter with their fellow workers when they were unemployed, especially in winter. In Chinatown, they found odd jobs at Chinese businesses, or they cut wood and carried water for local residents. Because of this, the Chinese population in Chinatown fluctuated from season to season.

In 1862, Bishop George Hills of the Anglican church visited Yale. He met Wong Chan Yun, a young Chinese man who spoke some English. Hills asked him if the Chinese in the area had a place of worship. Wong told him that he was not aware of one but that he worshipped Shung Ti [God], who was once a man, now in heaven. He continued, saying that when the Chinese prayed, they would kneel down, holding in their hands incense sticks glowing with amber. Hills spoke to him about Jesus Christ and urged him to listen and learn about Jesus.

Some of the businesses in Chinatown included groceries, laundries and restaurants. The residents would gladly house or employ miners who were out of work for the season, or those who were passing through Yale from other villages. Courtesy of the Royal BC Museum and Archives E-00709.

Bishop Hills found a Chinese cemetery in Yale where forty Chinese people had been buried. He recorded that all the graves were neatly looked after, and each had a mound of dirt on top and a painted board with a Chinese inscription at one end of each grave. "They bear testimony to the groaning and travailing of the creature[s] seeking for Rest and Peace but they know not yet the Prince of Peace," wrote Hills in his journal. "At the foot of each grave was a bundle of light papers and each piece of paper had several incisions. A number of incense sticks were inserted at the foot of each grave. At the head [entrance to] of the cemetery three half-circles of stones formed an enclosure and five painted boards with Chinese inscriptions [were] inserted at the entrance. Each board marked the name of the districts in Guangdong where the Chinese came from."[10]

Hills recorded in his diary that the Chinese had three meals a day, mainly rice and tea. Occasionally they added chicken, pork or potatoes to their meals. The Chinese were fond of poultry and would pay $5.00 for a fowl. He also documented the work habits of the Chinese miners in the Fraser Canyon:

> The Chinese are coming up in great numbers and spreading themselves over the bars. They work over again the claims which have already been searched by Europeans. They are content with a dollar or two a day… they have been buying up claims…
>
> At present they are helping us to develop the land. They are conscientious, cultivating gardens out of barren wastes. Mr. Ferrier, a leading miner on Hills Bar, told me he employed them as labourers and preferred them greatly to white men. They worked for $2.50 instead of $4.00, worked longer and more obediently… their labour was a great saving.

On the evening of November 16, 1871, a fire broke out at the house of a Chinese doctor in Chinatown. The Kwong Lee establishment and three Chinese houses nearby were destroyed. The flame raged furiously and spread towards the town centre. Fortunately, Kwong Lee & Company was able to save a great portion of its goods, which were stored in stone cellars or vaults. Total destruction by the fire was estimated at $10,000.00; the Kwong Lee company suffered the greatest losses.[11]

After the Fraser gold rush, the Chinese population in Yale declined, and the village appeared deserted. Due to its prominent position on the

Author Lily Chow visits the remains of Kwong Lee & Company's successful Front Street store, which was was destroyed by fire in 1871. Kwong Lee & Company established several businesss in Yale. Image courtesy of Darwin Bearg.

Fraser River, Yale retained its role as a transportation and distribution centre in the Fraser Canyon, supplying provisions, dry goods and mining equipment to the miners in neighbouring goldfields.

Construction of the Canadian Pacific Railway

Between 1880 and 1881, Andrew Onderdonk, an American engineer and contractor, secured several contracts from the Dominion government to build the stretch of the Canadian Pacific Railway (CPR) in British Columbia.[12] Onderdonk selected Yale as the railway construction head office. He erected a charming two-storey building for his family, several houses for the engineers and other contractors, and machinery shops. His house had living quarters for his Chinese cooks. He designated Emory, a village a little more than six kilometres south of Yale, as a terminus for sternwheelers to disembark and unload equipment and supplies needed for railway construction.

This was because the sternwheelers could not always reach Yale due to the river's strong currents. The main warehouse of the CPR construction company was located in Emory.

In 1880, the first batch of railway labourers arrived in Yale from California. It consisted of 330 white people, 101 Chinese and a few black people.[13] The group was joined by local Indigenous people. The white labourers were accommodated in the company's houses, but the Chinese and black labourers set up tents near the construction sites. The Chinese labourers were housed in Camps 14 and 17 at Yale Creek, a short distance from Chinatown.

Railway construction began the morning of May 15, 1880, at the site of the first tunnel just north of Yale. The Chinese labourers shovelled the granite debris from the tunneling explosions and carried away rocks and stones. If boulders were too large or heavy, they would use hammers, chisels, picks and other implements to break up the rocks. On July 17 the same year, the *Inland Sentinel* reported that "our attention was attracted to a number of Chinamen engaged in handling the drill and hammers; three different parties... were busy at work, and certainly the strokes were regular and drill systematically turned." The tasks of the Chinese labourers included cutting timber and removing tree stumps and loading them into small dumping cars. They also burned and cleared debris.

The arrival of the Chinese labourers breathed new life into Chinatown—about two thousand Chinese from different walks of life arrived. The *Inland Sentinel* reported that "the east end of the town is principally occupied by Chinamen, and they are exhibiting a praiseworthy spirit of enterprise in building and improving their property. Some of the stores carry large stocks." The Chinese merchants in Chinatown renovated their buildings to increase storage space for their stock. New houses were erected as more Chinese merchants arrived in Yale to set up small businesses.

Yuen Wo advertised his "New Wash House," a laundry, in the *Inland Sentinel*. The laundry was located at "the corner of Douglas and Regent Streets where the subscriber is prepared to give satisfaction to all persons who may favour his Wash House." By the end of the month, this business had been turned over to Cho Foo. A new advertisement announced that "The undersigned has disposed of his Wash House and business at the corner of Douglas and Regent Streets to Cho Foo. In returning thanks to my patrons, I would respectfully recommend my successor. [Signed] Yuen Wo. Yale, May 31, 1881."

On October 13, 1881, Kwong On Wo & Co. obtained a railway contract to supply fourteen thousand pounds of fresh pork per month to the CPR company. "We have not been able to learn the price," reported the *Inland Sentinel.*

In 1882, the Chee Kung Tong (致公堂), a chapter of the Chinese Freemasons society, was established in Yale.[14] On October 19 that year, the *Inland Sentinel* reported that "the Chinese residents of this place [Yale] have commenced the construction of a Josh [joss] house. It is situated on the upper side of the railroad track on Douglas Street directly at the entrance of the cut." The joss house was a place for the Chinese with traditional beliefs to worship gods and goddesses or saints whom they believed would bless them.

CPR Needed More Chinese Labourers

The Fraser Canyon imposed great difficulties and challenges to railway construction. The huge and lofty mountains composed of solid granite had to be drilled through so that tunnels could be built. In the first kilometre and a half out of Yale, four tunnels were needed. Labourers spent time drilling through mountains, building galleries to notch into the sides of cliffs, blasting large boulders with dynamite and cutting gigantic trees before they could level the ground to lay railway tracks. By 1881, not a single mile of railway track had been laid.[15] Onderdonk desperately needed a larger labour force with physical strength. He advertised in various newspapers in BC, Ontario and the United States for white labourers, but few answered the call because many accidents had occurred since the commencement of the construction, and that discouraged white labourers from applying for the jobs.

In the fall of 1881, Onderdonk asked the Dominion government for permission to hire more Chinese labourers.[16] Prime Minister John A. Macdonald supported his request and stated in Parliament: "It is simply a question of alternatives: either you must have this [Chinese] labour or you can't have the railway."[17] After he got permission from the Dominion government, Onderdonk immediately contacted the Lian Chang Company (联昌公司),[18] commonly known as the Lee Chuck Company, to recruit labourers from various counties in the Zhujiang Delta of Guangdong to work on the CPR construction. He chartered two ships to transport the labourers. Other companies, such as Stableshmidt, Ward & Co., Tai Chong, Tai Yuan, Kwong Lee, and Tai Soong, among others, also brought

When several difficulties arose with the construction of the CPR, Andrew Onderdonk sent a request to recruit Chinese labourers from counties in Guangdong. With an influx of around 17,000 labourers to BC, business in Yale's Chinatown exapanded and flourished once again. Courtesy of the Royal BC Museum and Archives D-07548.

shiploads of Chinese labourers from Guangdong to BC via Hong Kong. Between 1881 and 1883, about fifteen thousand Chinese labourers came directly from Guangdong, plus approximately two thousand more came from the United States, BC, Vancouver Island and other Canadian provinces. In total, about seventeen thousand Chinese labourers were employed to construct the stretch of railway in BC.

After arriving in Victoria, the Chinese labourers were transferred by steamship to New Westminster, where they were divided into gangs of thirty men. One member in each gang would be assigned as a cook and another one appointed as a bookman who would record the number of hours that each member of his gang worked in a day. Then the Chinese labourers were taken directly to the railway construction line by the *Western Slope*, the *William Irving*, or one of the other sternwheelers that travelled between New Westminster and Emory. From there, the labourers either walked or were transported by small railcars to Yale.

In Yale, a few gangs were housed in tents at Camps No. 15 and 17 in the neighbourhood of Yale Creek near Chinatown, while the others moved along the construction route as far as Lytton or farther as the construction

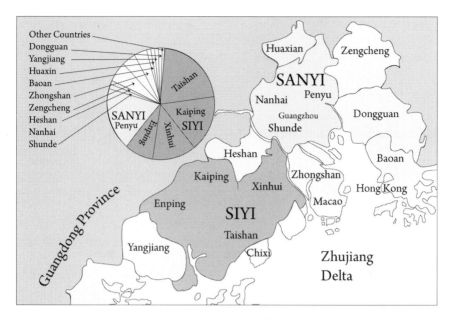

Located on the sea in southern China, the province of Guangdong served as a convenient port of emigration. This map of the Zhujiang Delta shows the different areas in Guangdong from which the Chinese labourers emigrated. The chart indicates the percentage from each area.

progressed. Their tents were always set up near the construction sites for convenience's sake. The newcomers carried out tasks similar to those carried out by labourers who had already started work on the construction. In addition, the Chinese labourers had to fill ravines with rocks from dynamite blasts and flatten rocky mountain ridges to create a path eighteen metres (sixty feet) wide where they laid the steel tracks. In this operation, ties or "sleepers" would be placed at right angles across the grade at exact distances apart. Parallel rails would then be laid on top of them. Usually, Chinese and Indigenous workers brought the ties and rails to the site. White or Indigenous men spiked the rails to the ties and inserted fishplates—rectangular pieces of iron roughly twenty by thirty centimetres (eight by twelve inches)—under the joint to connect one rail to the next. Then the space between the ties would be filled with crushed gravel by Chinese labourers so that the line would not shift when a train passed over it.[19]

As working teammates, many Chinese and Indigenous labourers developed good friendships. Joseph York, an Indigenous man from Spuzzum, claimed that one of his best friends was a Chinese labourer. His Chinese friend was presumed dead when a piece of blasted rock broke through his tent when he was inside. York heard him groaning and thought he must have died. York felt sad. A few days later, though, he saw the Chinese labourer reporting back to work. He was totally surprised.

The influx of thousands of Chinese labourers encouraged merchants from Victoria and Vancouver to migrate to Yale and set up small businesses in the Chinatown. In 1882–83, the *BC Directory* listed the following merchants in Yale's Chinatown.

Chinese Merchants in Yale, BC, 1882–83

Store or owner	Trade	Address
Foo Yuen	Grocer	unknown
He Tie	General merchandise	Front Street
Hong Lee	Shoemaker	Douglas Street
Kai Kee	General merchandise	Front Street
Kwong Lee & Co	General merchandise	Front Street
Lun Sang	Grocer	Douglas Street
Po On	Doctor/physician	Douglas Street
Yen Kee	Washing and ironing	Douglas Street
Sam Sing	Washing and ironing	Douglas Street
Won Comyou	Clerk (Kwong Lee & Co)	Front Street
Ye Hop	Washing and ironing	unknown
Yuen Chong	Restaurant	Douglas Street
Yuen Wo	Laundry	Douglas Street

Source: *Williams' British Columbia Directory, 1882–83.*

The *Williams' British Columbia Directory* of 1884–85 added three more Chinese businesses to this list. They were Hop Wo, a Chinese restaurant at Cariboo Road; On Lee, a general and grocery store; and a Chinese doctor, Yuen Sing Tong, who had a herbalist store on Douglas Street.

Incidents and Illnesses

In May 1881, the Chinese labourers in Camp 17 noticed that 2 per cent of their wages had been deducted as a commission for the Lee Chuck Company. This deduction had not been included in their agreements when they were hired. Already 30 cents had been deducted from their daily wages of $1.00 per person per day to pay for their passage to Canada. The labourers also found that every sack of rice or sugar weighed five to eight pounds less than the quantities for which they were charged. A few of the Chinese labourers representing the group at Camp 17 went to Chinatown to look for the representative of the Lee Chuck Company, but they could not find him. They went back to Yale Creek, where they were joined by more Chinese labourers armed with spikes and spades. They headed to the large warehouse of the company to attempt to get the rice and sugar owed to them. The *Inland Sentinel* reported that "as they were about to chop down the doors of the building the police arrived, intervened and arrested several ringleaders. Whilst Constables Roycraft and Barr were escorting the ringleaders to the lock-up, some Chinese attempted to rescue their comrades, and assaulted the officers by hurling stones at them… During the struggle several shots were fired, and one struck a Chinaman on the neck. After much trouble the ringleaders were eventually caught and locked up… the arrested rioters were then released with a bail of fifteen hundred dollars."[20] At the trial held in the Assizes Court, one ringleader was fined $50.00 and sentenced to one year's imprisonment for wounding another person. George P. White was charged with shooting a Chinese man, but his penalty was not mentioned.

On August 24, 1882, eight Chinese labourers—Cheng Foo, Ah Sue, Ah Him, Ah Tong, Ah Tai, Ah Chuck, Lock Sing and Tie Chueh—went on trial for an unlawful and malicious attack on John Kerrigan, their CPR foreman in Yale. Kerrigan told the judge:

> On the morning of August 14th I had some holes to spring. [While] springing the holes my gang ran away, and knocked off other gangs… I told them I would not allow it, as there was no danger, and that there was no necessity of going away so far. I told the book-man [Cheng Foo] several times… to explain to the gang. Then I went [on]… springing a hole… the gang kept running away, and I told them again I would not allow it any more. Just then Ah Him and Ah Chuck raised their shovels to strike me. From their actions I firmly believe that they intended to strike me… I ordered them… to their camp and told the book-man Cheng Foo to send them [away]… He said they would not go. Then I told Cheng I would not give them time; [immediately] they made a riotous noise, and by their gesticulations I felt alarmed, and went to my camp to get a pistol.

[When I returned] the two men still remained in the cut. A few minutes before noon, I asked the book-man for his book; he felt in his pocket, and said that he had lost it, or some other excuse. These eight men who are in court now attacked me with sticks and stones on my head and body... I recognize them... they belong to my gang.[21]

At the end of the trial, the eight Chinese men were convicted of assaulting the foreman, James Kerrigan. Cheng Foo (the bookman), Ah Him, Lin Chin, and Ah Tai were sentenced to four years in the penitentiary with hard labour. Ah Loun, Ah Chuck, Long Sing and Ah Tong were sent to prison for three years with hard labour.

In 1883, many Chinese labourers suffered from beriberi due to vitamin B deficiency. A good number of the sufferers in Emory died from the illness. No medical facility was provided for sick Chinese labourers, since the CPR hospital would only admit those who were injured on the construction sites. Sam Sing, a Chinese resident, offered his home temporarily to take care of the sick. Some prominent Chinese merchants, who founded a Chinese Benevolent Association (CBA) in Yale, opened a hospital and hired Dr. Po On, the herbalist, to attend to the sick Chinese people.[22] Together with the CBA, the Chee Kung Tong in Yale helped the poor, held funerals for those who died and buried them in Yale's Chinese cemetery.

On January 3, 1884, the *Inland Sentinel* noted "... the Railway Chinamen are in old buildings along Douglas Street, some of them in very poor circumstances. Yesterday a store on Front Street threw out some frozen potatoes and a poor old Chinaman standing in the cold picked out a few that were not decayed and put them into a little box... Persons that witnessed the scene thought the sight a pretty hard one." Obviously, these Chinese labourers either could not handle the hardships of the construction jobs and quit or they were dismissed by the CPR because they were ill or injured to the extent that they were considered unemployable.

The following month, the same newspaper reported on a Chinese funeral and the health of the Chinese labourers. It said "A rough box [containing the deceased was] conveyed upon a pony cart, and two Chinamen accompanied [the cart to the cemetery]... We learn that other Railway Chinamen here were sick at the old structure called a hospital on Douglas Street."

Similarly, another funeral took place in April 1884. The *Inland Sentinel* wrote:

> The occasion appeared to be the funeral of one of their members who recently died at Spence's Bridge. The [deceased] was brought to Yale for burial. At the east end of Douglas Street flags, bunting, and streamers... were displayed, and tables spread along the street contained refreshments, ornaments, and fire crackers. After a long and mysterious ceremony, the wagon [carrying] the coffin moved forward, led by a Chinese band playing, and the Society [members] following behind. They marched around town before burying [the deceased] in the cemetery...

On May 22, 1884, an accident took place in the Acid and Powder Works warehouse (a powder magazine) just over a kilometre away from Yale. The *Inland Sentinel* reported that:

> Mr. Ashworth, the Superintendent, was present when the nitro that was being ground by a Chinaman exploded... and in an instant the Chinaman and Mr. Ashworth were spattered over with burning nitro. The Chinaman ran out of the door, while Mr. Ashworth leaped out of an open window and called out to another Chinaman standing by to throw water on the burning Chinaman... Mr. Ashworth was sent by a hand car to the CPR Hospital where his burned face and hands were properly dressed by the matron, the head nurse. In the meantime the poor Chinaman was suffering and finally reached the Chinese Hospital where he died that night.

Mr. Ashworth resigned as a superintendent of the Acid and Powder Works after the accident. The editorial of the newspaper blamed Onderdonk for using cheap labour to cut costs and allowing Chinese workers to work in the powder magazine.

As the railway construction proceeded, the Chinese labourers left Yale and followed the construction crews to other sites. By 1884, the CPR company had dismissed many Chinese labourers who were either stranded in the Interior or migrated to Vancouver or Victoria to look for job opportunities. Some of the unemployed Chinese labourers returned to Yale. A few of them pre-empted a piece of land on the Indian reserve where the Spuzzum Creek meets the Fraser River, a place referred to as "the point" by the local Indigenous people. "Some crooks sold them [the Chinese] the land at 'the point,'" said Elder Annie York. "The Chinese didn't understand that it was a piece of Indian land and they put a ditch there for mining. The Indians didn't like it, so they started fighting with the Chinamen." The dispute was eventually settled by Louie Antoine, a member of an early police force, and the Chinese moved off the reserve land. "The Indians were mean; they threw the Chinese shovels in the river," continued York. The fighting could have been prevented if the authorities had checked the legal status of the property before the Chinese signed the property transaction document.[23]

Two Well-Known Chinese Merchants

A few small Chinese businesses, like Kwong Lee & Company, followed the railway workers and set up stores at the construction sites to supply goods and food to their fellow countrymen. When they left Yale's Chinatown, they shut down their businesses there. Two Chinese general and grocery stores, the On Lee Store (安利商店), owned and operated by Zheng Huan Zhang (郑焕章), and the Fook Woo Store (福和商店), owned and operated by Cheng Foo, remained in Yale. These two families continued to live in Yale for generations.

Zheng Huan Zhang was born in 1841 in the village of Gu Dou Yi, Zhong Shan County, in Guangdong Province, as indicated on his tombstone in his family's private cemetery. He came to British Columbia in the late 1870s and made his way to Yale. In the spring of 1881, he paid $800.00 to purchase a property on Lot 10, Block 2, on the south side of Douglas Street across from the Oppenheimer Brothers store. In 1883, Zheng established the On Lee Store, a general store, and a bakery on the property. The first advertisement for the On Lee Store appeared in the *Williams' British Columbia Directory* of 1884–85. The Fire Insurance Plan, 1885, shows that the owner of the On Lee Store had four buildings on the property: a grocery, a washhouse and two other buildings.

In 1884, Zhang married Mary Laye (黎玛丽-译音), a young Chinese woman from his village in Guangdong. The wedding ceremony took place in Yale, officiated over by the grand master of the Chee Kung Tong (the Chinese Freemasons society). The wedding was a grand event, with firecrackers exploding, Chinese musical horns hooting and cymbals clashing. Guests were invited to a fabulous Chinese dinner.

Over the years, the couple raised six children in Yale: Thomas, Connie, James, Ola, May and Sophy. The On Lee Store flourished and expanded to include a warehouse in the adjacent building that sold lumber, hardware, feed and other items. The family was well-known in the community as the "On Lee family." All the children and the children of the sons used On Lee as their last name.

"On Lee was not the last name of my grandpa's family," said the late Walter Joe, a son of Connie On Lee, who lived in Vernon. "The name of my grandfather was Zheng Huan Zhang, who opened the On Lee Store in Yale during the CPR construction. After he got married, he and his family lived there for a long time. But everyone called them the On Lee family. I regret to say that my mother and her siblings were registered with the last name On Lee at birth and in schools."

The building of the On Lee store had some interesting features. It was a two-and-a-half-storey wooden building with an overhanging porch at the entrance. The store took up most of the first floor, with a small kitchen in the back. A staircase at the centre of the building led to the sleeping area on the second floor. On the left inside the store was a small shelf or cupboard, which held an altar and incense. Behind the long counters at each side of the store were shelves reaching up to the ceiling. Zheng or On Lee sold groceries on the right side of the store and dry goods on the left side. There was a large wood stove in the kitchen, and the space surrounding the stove served as a gathering place for local Chinese people who would come to the store and listen to Chinese records played on the gramophone during their leisure time.[24]

According to the birth and death register, On Lee (Zheng) passed away on August 2, 1907, but on his tombstone, it is marked 1909. He was buried in the Chinese cemetery, a special plot reserved for the On Lee family. After his death, Mary and her children continued operating the store until she too passed away, on July 16, 1928. Then James On Lee, the second son, converted the On Lee house and store into his private residence. James, however, built a store, service station and hotel complex near the highway and continued to operate the new complex until his death in 1961. Following his death, the On Lee property passed through the remaining children. In 1983, Mrs. Kim Young, the youngest On Lee child, sold the residence to the provincial government, hoping that it could be preserved as a heritage site. Two years later, the house burnt down.[25]

The private On Lee Chinese cemetery is located on a piece of land beyond the railway crossing on the north side of Yale between Highway 1 and the entrance to the cemetery at Chinamen Road, a short alley in the northeast of the village. The cemetery is always kept clean and the Chinese characters on the tombstones of Mr. and Mrs. Zheng, the original On Lee couple, are still very visible. James On Lee was buried next to his parents. Apparently, the descendants of the On Lees come to pay homage to these senior members almost every year and clean up the plots. And a few excavated plots have been found, an indication that the remains have been exhumed. It was a Chinese custom to ship the bones of a person's remains home after they had been buried in the ground for five or seven years. In 1936, the Canadian government prohibited the exhumations for health reasons.

Another popular Chinese merchant in Yale was Cheng (Jangze) Foo, also known as Cheng Ging Butt. In 1881, Cheng emigrated from Xin Hui (新会) County, Guangdong, to work on the CPR construction. While working at his job, he lost a finger and was discharged by the CPR company. He settled in Yale and established a laundry service. His business expanded to include a grocery store known as the Fook Woo Store (福和商店), located on the north side of Douglas Street. In 1903, he was naturalized.[26]

In the early 1900s, Cheng married Leong Lin Heong (梁莲香), a young woman from Xin Jiang Province (新疆省) who was thirty years younger than he was. She had been kidnapped in China, brought over to Canada and sold to a Leong family in Victoria as a housemaid, and thus had the surname Leong. When she was with the Leong family, she worked in the Leongs' tailor shop. In Yale, she was known as Lena Leong. Cheng and Leong had twelve children, but two of the babies were stillborn. The family lived in a house without electricity. They used kerosene oil for cooking and lighting and a wood stove for heating. On the family altar, they placed idols or images of different gods and goddesses and an urn containing ashes for holding joss sticks and candle holders. Murals of ancient Chinese paintings were hung on the walls of the living room.

"At night when the flames of the kerosene lamps flickered, different kinds of shadows were cast on the walls and floors that scared the hell out of us," commented Bevan Jangze, one of Cheng's sons. "So we children used to go to bed early. We also had a god in the kitchen and the god of the earth at the main entrance of the house."

Cheng Foo emigrated from Xin Hui (新会) County, Guangdong, to work on the CPR construction, but he was discharged after losing a finger. Undeterred, he started two succcessful businesses in Yale's Chinatown, and later harvested a cherry orchard. He had ten children with his wife, Lena Leong. Courtesy of Cheng Foo's grandson, Kevan Jangze.

Later, Cheng rented an orchard from the Creightons, well-known residents of Yale. It was just over a hectare (about three acres) in size and was located near the railway line. Cheng packed and shipped the fruits to grocery stores in Vancouver, which in turn supplied him with rice and other Chinese goods or specialties for his store. Some Chinese gold miners paid the Fook Woo Store with gold flakes or nuggets instead of cash when they shopped there. Cheng used to take these gold pieces to the goldsmith in Vancouver to make jewellery for his wife and children.

After harvesting all the apples in the fall, Cheng pruned the fruit trees, getting ready for winter. Then he and his older children would go to the bush and gather firewood to heat their home. At times, the winter temperature could plunge down to -20 degrees Celsius in the Fraser Canyon.

"We kids used to play in the snow," recalled Bevan. "We built snowmen during the Christmas season. But sometimes the snowfall was so heavy that the snow could accumulate to four or five feet high on the ground. At times, the snow blocked the door of our house. We kids had to dig a tunnel through before we could get out."

When the older children were ready to attend school, Cheng sent them and his wife to Vancouver. He felt it would be better for his children to attend school in Vancouver because the school in Yale was a one-room institute where children from grades one to eight shared one teacher. He wanted his wife to look after the children in Vancouver. But he would join them after he had harvested all the apples and closed down the store and house in October.

When spring arrived, Cheng would return to Yale and get ready to operate his business and attend to the fruit trees in the orchard. When school closed for the summer, the whole family would return home to Yale and help out in the orchard. At the beginning of summer, Cheng and the older children would harvest cherries. He would pack and ship the cherries to Vancouver. The children would make paper cones using the pages from the Eatons and Sears catalogues, fill each cone with cherries and sell them to train passengers when the train stopped at Yale for water and fuel.

"After we had got the cones filled with cherries, we would put three cones into one of the compartments in a basket, special baskets with dividers woven by the local Indigenous people," recalled Bevan Jangze. "When the train stopped, my siblings and I would each take a basket and go up to the train to sell them to the passengers. We sold each cone for 10 cents or three cones for 25 cents. Our cherries were very sweet and juicy. Many people loved them and bought them from us. Once we were so busy selling cherries that we didn't realize the train had started moving away from Yale. We could not get down. We stayed on the train until it stopped at the next station. Then we walked home!"

The Chengs had very good rapport with the local Indigenous people who commented that the Chengs were friendly and courteous—very good and helpful neighbours in the community.

"In Yale, we lived not too far from the Indian reserve," said Bevan Jangze. "My siblings and I used to have fun with the local Indigenous children. We often played and swam with them in the nearby creeks. They considered us as brothers. Their parents often gave us fish. I remember I had a bad cut on my hand that bled badly. One of the Indigenous Elders gave me some leaves, herbs, I guess, to put on the wound. Immediately the bleeding stopped. And the cut healed quickly too."

Cheng was well respected in the community. He was a member of Yale's Chee Kung Tong. He looked after the aged and the sick, helped unemployed members find work and took care of the Yale joss house, a temple where the Chinese went to pray. Bevan remembered that his father brought an idol for the joss house and organized a big ceremony to venerate the statue in Yale's Chinatown. In Vancouver, he was one of the founders of the Cheng Association on Pender Street and was involved in many projects and activities that helped sustain and preserve the Cheng Association.

During the Great Depression, many people lost their jobs, prices deflated and businesses closed down. Many unemployed people from the east travelled across Canada to find work in BC. Jobless and destitute people simply hopped on the trains and travelled to cities and towns in the province to look for jobs and accommodation. They were referred to as "floaters," "foreigners" or "hobos" who came to BC to get relief subsidies. Yale was one of the stopping places for the unemployed, because many of them would try to find gold in the sandbars along the Fraser River. In the summer of 1930, some of these "floaters" went to the Chengs' orchard, which was situated across the railway track, and helped themselves to the cherries and apples. Cheng did not mind them taking the fruits but resented them for breaking the branches of the fruit trees. When the trees were damaged, they could not produce good crops in the following year.

"My dad pitched a big tent in the orchard, held a shotgun and watched the floaters," said Bevan Jangze. "When he spotted any floaters breaking the branches, he would shoot buckshot at them. I was about eight years old then and I stayed in the tent to keep my dad company."

In September 1930, Cheng's wife and children returned to Vancouver for school. Cheng remained in Yale to harvest the apples. But the fall weather became very cold that year, and Cheng caught a cold and became ill. By the time he went to Vancouver, he had developed pneumonia, and he passed on at the age of seventy-two. After his death, his wife, Lena, was left alone to support the family. She could not manage the business and the orchard and pay the property tax, which was $10.00 for the orchard, a lot of money then. Since she had no other resources, she sold the orchard and closed down the business; it was impossible for her to operate it when the children were still in school. Then the whole family left Yale. During the Depression, she sold the gold and jewellery in her possession to support her family. When her money ran out, she started sewing clothing for other people to put bread and butter on the table.

"My mother only charged 12 cents to sew a pair of denim pants during the Depression," said Bevan Jangze. "Although two loaves of bread only cost 5 cents, not many people could afford to buy them! In summer,

At the Yale railway station, Cheng Foo's children would sell train passengers the cherries that their family grew, charging 10 cents a package. Courtesy of the Royal BC Museum and Archives A-03590.

all of us kids went to work on the farms in Richmond, which was known as the 'small island' [also formerly known as Lulu Island] then. In our teen-age years, I worked in a fish cannery for 15 cents an hour and my youngest brother lived and worked on a farm in Richmond."

In 1944, Bevan and three of his brothers were conscripted into the armed forces to fight against the Japanese in Southeast Asia in World War II. Cheng Foo had a large family and some of his descendants are still living in the Lower Mainland or elsewhere in Canada.

Between 1994 and 1996, archaeological work was carried out by Mr. G. Robin Hooper on the site of the old Yale Chinatown. He found some stone vaults, one of which is believed to have belonged to Kwong Lee & Co. The archaeological work also found a good collection of invaluable artifacts and documents, which are kept in the Yale Historic Site and Museum. Many of them are on display in the museum, which describes the Chinese community as "self-sufficient with its own hospital and doctor, commercial establishments and cultural societies."

The CPR tunnel at Yale. In 1980, the Canadian government finally recognized the Chinese labourers for their integral part in the construction of the CPR. They acknowledged the hardships and mistreatments that the labourers endured. Courtesy of the Royal BC Museum and Archives B-04095.

Recognition by Canada and BC

The contribution of the Chinese labourers to the construction of the Canadian Pacific Railway was officially recognized by the federal government in June 1980. The Historic Sites and Monument Board of Canada designed and installed a bronze plaque at the Yale Historic Site and Museum on September 25, 1982. The text is written in three languages: English, French and Chinese. The English text says:

Chinese Construction Workers on the Pacific Railway

In the early 1880s contractor Andrew Onderdonk brought thousands of labourers from China to help build the Pacific Railway through the mountains of British Columbia. About three-quarters of the men who worked on the section between the Pacific and Craigellachie were Chinese. Although considered excellent workers, they received only a dollar a day, half the pay of a white worker. Hundreds of Chinese died from accidents or illness, for the work was dangerous and living conditions poor. Those who remained in Canada when the railway was completed securely established the basis of British Columbia's Chinese community.

In summer 2009, the board members of the Yale Historic Site and Museum created a tent city at the Yale Historic Site to display Yale's history. The exhibition focused on the Chinese gold miners' housing. Panning for gold was one of the hands-on activities that could be carried out at the site or on the banks of the Fraser River. When fall arrived, the tent city was dismantled and the museum closed down for the season. Since then, the museum has continued to hold tent city exhibitions every summer. Each year, different aspects of the history of Yale and the surrounding region are displayed. These exhibitions enable visitors and tourists to learn about the history of the Fraser Canyon as well as that of the BC Interior.

The Yale Historic Site and Museum has also been making a great effort to restore the On Lee House. In 2016, the house was recognized as a Chinese Canadian Heritage Site, one of seventy-seven sites nominated for this recognition by the public. The sites were selected by Heritage BC, working in cooperation with members of the Legacy Initiatives Advisory Council of the BC Ministry of International Trade and the Heritage Branch of the Ministry of Forests, Lands, and Natural Resource Operations. A commemorative plaque will be installed on the On Lee House site in 2018.

LYTTON: THE SECOND GOLD TOWN

The village of Lytton is the home and centre of the Nlaka'pamux First Nation, located about eighty-five kilometres (fifty-three miles) north of Yale. It is situated at the confluence of the beige-brown Fraser River and the navy-blue Thompson River, a place known as "the Fork" in the early days. Its hot summers have won the village fame as the hottest spot in Canada. In winter, sparkling snowflakes float down from the sky and settle on the branches of the pines and firs and undergrowth shrubs, often turning the village into a winter wonderland.

Lytton is located north of Yale, where the brown Fraser River and the blue Thompson River meet at a confluence known as "the Fork." Courtesy of the Royal BC Museum and Archives I-22434.

51

The Hudson's Bay Company established a trading post near the village site, called Fort Dallas. In 1858, Governor James Douglas named the village Lytton in honour of Sir Edward Bulwer Lytton, the British colonial secretary. It was proposed that Lytton be the capital of British Columbia, but the colonial government selected Fort Victoria instead. During the Fraser gold rush, thousands of gold miners, including the Chinese, flocked to the sandbars in this area and turned Lytton into the second largest gold-mining town and a transportation hub of the Fraser Canyon. In his report to the colonial secretary of British Columbia, Henry M. Ball, the assistant gold commissioner in Lytton, wrote "the mule trains from Lytton have already commenced packing provisions to the Upper Country… via the Chapeau Bonaparte Rivers, making the trip in about twelve to fourteen days, either to Fort Alexandra or to Horsefly Creek."[27] Foot travellers also stopped at Lytton to get supplies before heading to gold-laden sandbars near the confluence of the Fraser and the Thompson rivers. Sternwheelers and canoes carrying goods, gold seekers and other passengers from Boston

When it was discovered that the Fraser and Thompson Rivers were full of sandbars abundant with gold, Lytton became another hub for Chinese immigrants looking to mine. Courtesy of the Royal BC Museum and Archives B-02948.

Bar disembarked at Lytton. Ferries carried miners and prospectors over the Thompson and Fraser rivers to the various goldfields in the area.

Many miners preferred to stay near Lytton to mine or pan for gold. Enterprising individuals established businesses such as livery stables, blacksmith shops and general stores in this gold town. Ball wrote that "the town of Lytton is increasing in size and in importance; many influential storekeepers from Hope and Yale [are] about to locate at Lytton, and establish wholesale stores… The town has now been surveyed and laid off into blocks and town lots."[28]

On April 6, 1860, Ball wrote to the colonial secretary: "Mining season has commenced and those who have been passing the winter [are] are fast returning to their old claims or to the different benches on the rivers… Great numbers of Chinamen are daily arriving in these lower districts, and locating themselves as miners on the different bars, and have shown themselves a peaceful and orderly class of people." The 1860–62 mining records show that numerous Chinese miners had registered their claims. Here is an example of a claim statement:

White Rock Bar

Lytton, May 28th, 1860

This day, seven Chinamen, 1682; 1998; 1699; 1700; 4014; 4012; 4013 have recorded their right to seven claims on White Rock Bar or Flat adjoining the claims of George King surveying downstream. Size of claims 100 feet square, Flat about 2 miles north of the Creek. Possession was taken on May 27, 1860. Numbers [listed] are the same as those appearing on their Free Miners Certicates.

Signed: H. M. Ball

The Chinese names were not written on the certificates; only their licence numbers appear. But they were recorded in the gold commissioner's ledger of 1860 to 1863. The table below illustrates the number of Chinese miners at the different claims in the vicinity of Lytton in 1860.

Names and Number of Chinese Miners, 1860

Names of Claims	Number of Chinese Miners	Possession Date
White Rock Bar	7	May 28
Canyon Flat	3	May 28
Below Rancherie Flat	9	May 28
Rancherie Flat	3	May 28
Rancherie Flat: West Bank	4	May 39
Yankee Flat	2	June 8
12 Mile Flat	3	June 9
Opposite 21 Mile Flat	4	June 10
Flat; west bank of Fraser River	5	June 10
Half-mile below Spring Bar	3	June 11
Two miles north of Kanaka Bar	6	June 30
Lower Yankee Flat	2	July 2
Assim Flat; three miles below Murderer's Bar	4	July 14
China San Flat; three miles south of 4 Mile House	4	July 21
China San Flat	10	July 24
China San Flat	4	July 24
China San Flat	3	July 12
Flat behind Rancherie Flat, west bank	6	July 15
China Eyed Flat	2	July 25
China Eyed Flat	4	July 25
Assim Flat	3	July 26
Assim Flat	9	July 26
Ah Quee Flat	3	July 28
East bank Fraser opposite Last Chance Flat	5	July 30
China Flat	14	July 30
Assim Flat	2	August 5
Scotch Flat	3	August 6
Ah Quee Flat	1	August 7
Ah Fou Flat	10	August 8

China Flat	14	August 8
Task's Bar	2	August 11
China Flat	8	August 11
Assim Flat	1	August 12
North end of Wept Bar	2	August 18
Bank of Thompson River	4	August 21
Last Chance Flat	8	September 3
Half-mile below Spring Flat	3	September 13
South of Cameron's Bar	3	October 29
TOTAL NUMBER	183	

Source: Gold commissioner's ledger, 1860.

The total number indicates those who had registered for their claims in 1860 but does not include those who did not make a specific claim and those who did not apply for their mining licences. Ball complained that "[those who] work with rockers and travel from point to point do not take out their mining licences, as there is no clause in the Act compelling them to do so. A great loss to the revenue is occasioned."[29]

Some Chinese miners purchased claims from white miners. Here is an example of transference of a mining claim:

Transfer: Upper Yankee Flat

This day Houn Chinaman No. 1303 has recorded his right to a claim belonging to Louis Knight P. 281, and transferred by purchase to Houn as per bill of sale

Date: May 10th, 1860

Sometimes more than four Chinese miners formed a mining company to work on a single claim, but the claim was registered under the name of just one member. For example, Ah Chong was the head of the company at China Flat (July 30), and the claim was registered under his name. Places such as China San Flat, China Eyed Flat, Assim Flat and others could have each of their claims covering a large area, since they were recorded more than once within a month by different groups of Chinese miners. Therefore, more than a thousand Chinese miners may have arrived within the four years from 1860 to 1863.

At mining sites, such as the Van Winkle Flat, Chinese miners would scrape rocks clean to get every last bit of gold dust off, and then neatly stack the rocks, creating walls along the rivers. Courtesy of the Lytton Museum and Archives.

According to Ball, the Chinese miners were located on "different flats on both sides of the Fraser, principally between Boston Bar and the Fork [Lytton]… They are yielding $6.00 per head [per day]… most of the best claims are at present worked by Chinamen." This shows that the Chinese miners were doing well in the Lytton area.

Even today, the footprints of the early Chinese miners can still be traced at Van Winkle and Brownings, Chinese mining sites near Lytton. The Chinese miners created numerous stone walls on these sites, as shown in the photograph. Irvine Johnson, a First Nations gentleman, calls these structures "the Chinese condos"! Some local residents say that the Chinese miners removed the stones or boulders from the tailings of their own claims or the claims abandoned by white miners near the bank of the Fraser River, scraped off all the dirt on the boulders and panned the dirt to get the last speck of gold dust. Then they stacked the boulders neatly on the bank. This was how the walls were created.

Today these walls are farther from the river bank than they once were. This indicates that the river has changed its course somewhat over time.

By 1861, gold was almost depleted from the Fraser Valley. Many gold miners, including some of the Chinese, left the mining areas and migrated to the Cariboo (the Upper Country). On July 31, 1861, Ball wrote:

The collections [from mining certificates] of the present year are far below those of the past year in consequence of the migration of many miners to the upper mines... Mr. Oppenheimer, a merchant of Lytton, has just returned from a tour through the mines of the Upper Country, and reports most favourably on all the mines he visited. Already at Antler Creek, a town as large as Lytton has sprung up, and the excitement and business there equals the excitements of the mining town in the early days of California. The claims average from 50 to 150 dollars per day per man, and there is a demand for labourers at 10 dollars per day.

Those Chinese miners who remained in and around Lytton acquired Crown lands to establish farms and market gardens. The following information is gathered from Henry Ball's ledger:

Records of Free Miners and Storekeepers Occupying Crown Land as Gardeners and Residents

Date	Name	Occupation	Locality
1862, May 31	Ah Yung	Storekeeper	Situated on the bench above the corner of the Wagon Road near the town of Lytton, measuring 61 yards from stump mining easterly, thence northerly 66 yards. Plot for garden.
1863, March 10	Ah Song	Free miner	About 2 acres opposite the Court House for gardening purposes.
1863, April 30	Four Chinamen	Free miner	About 5 acres for gardening purposes. Situated behind the Big Bar, right bank of the Fraser River, extending from the ravine and running north alongside the bench to the ravine near a little stream.

1863, May 12	Ah Lchut	Free miner	Garden plot: near China Flat, about 5 acres in the neighbourhood of M. Wha's house.
1863, May 12	A Long and Ah Ching	Free miner	Garden plot near Spring Flat, west bank of the Fraser River, about 3 acres on the mine side of the bench.
1863, October 23	Ah Soup	Free miner	Garden plot about 5 acres south of garden plot of Ah Pow, opposite mouth of the Thompson River.
1864, May 19	Ah Sot	Free miner	5 acres on the bench on the opposite side of the Fraser at the mouth of the Thompson, for making hay.
1864, May 23	Wai Chong	Free miner	5 acres for a garden on Spring Flat north of his claim (mining).
1864, September 7	Chung Lah and Ah Quan	Free miner	10 acres situated on Yankee Flat back from river, under mountain for gardening purposes.
1864, September 19	Kum Sing	Free miner	5 acres situated about 2 miles below the sawmill for a garden above his claim.
1864, October 19	Ah Kum	Free miner	5 acres for a garden plot near New Brunswick Creek, just above their claim near the ditch running from New Brunswick Creek.
1864, October 26	Ah Lok	Free miner	5 acres for a garden plot on Yankee Flat, back from river under mountain. Near the 2 claims of Chung Fat and Ah Quai.
1864, November 2	Kum Sing (different person)	Free miner	5 acres for a garden on a flat west bank of Fraser near Lytton. Opposite the Iunchion claim on the east bank.

1864, November 14	Man Kung	Free miner	5 acres situated on the Fraser between the mouth of Yankee Creek and a ditch running from the said creek on to the claim, a short distance up-stream.
1864, November 14	Ah Lcheng and Ah Fook	Free miner	6 acres on Cameron Flat about 150 yards from their claims between the ditch and the Fraser.
1864, December 19	Ah Pow	Free miner	5 acres for a garden on China Flat where the blacksmith shop is, about 2 miles from Lytton.
1865, January 25	Ah Fook	Free miner	3 acres for a garden above recorded claim.
1865, January 25	Ah Sue	Free miner	1 acre about 300 yards north of above claim.
1865, January 30	Shin Ho	Free miner	5 acres for a garden adjoining his claims on Mooron Bar, this side of the Fraser River.
1865, March 18	Fok Ick	Free miner	5 acres for a garden on a bench in the angle formed by Dallas Creek and the Fraser River, not to interfere with the Indians.
1865, March 22	Ing Tong	Free miner	5 acres for a garden near above record.

Source: *Williams' British Columbia Directory, 1882.*

No records of payments for these lands are found in the ledger. Presumably, most of these miners had staked these places as their mining claims prior to applying them for gardening and residential purposes.

In 1864, Ah Fou, Ah Mow and company were recorded by Henry M. Ball as purchasing a city lot 50 by 100 feet on Block 9, Lot 2, for a sum of £20. On November 20, 1875, Gui Chong, a Chinese man working at the Spatsun Ranch, successfully applied for 160 acres of "unsurveyed, unoccupied, and unreserved Crown Land, within the meaning of the 'Land Act, 1875' for farming."[30] The claim was on the east side of the Thompson River near Spences Bridge.

In addition, some of the Chinese had applied for trading licences to start small businesses. Such licences were only valid for three months, after which they had to renew them. In Lytton, ten Chinese people applied for licences to operate stores, the nature of which was not disclosed, two for blacksmith businesses, one for a butcher shop, two for boat (presumably canoe) transportation and fifteen for packing businesses.[31] The last Chinese name that appeared in the mining record of 1873 is Fook You on China Flat. By then, the village of Lytton had returned to its quiet days.

Arrival of the CPR Construction

Since Lytton is located at a strategic position between two sections of railway construction—Boston Bar to Lytton and Lytton to Junction Flat (about eleven kilometres east of Spences Bridge)—the CPR construction team arrived in the village near the end of 1882. In May of the same year, Onderdonk launched his boat, *Skuzzy*, on the Fraser River near Spuzzum because he needed to transport construction materials from Yale to Lytton. When the boat failed to pass through Hell's Gate, he instructed 125 Chinese labourers to climb the cliffs of Hell's Gate to help the boat sail through; so that construction materials could be brought to Lytton for railway construction. The influx of the construction labourers, engineers, surveyors and administrators brought life to Lytton. In 1882, a journalist who gathered information for the *Williams' British Columbia Directory* wrote:

> "Since the commencement of the railway, which crosses the heights overlooking the town [Lytton], the business of the place has been largely increased... The annual sale of flour and dry goods, owing mainly to the concentration of Indians here, is simply enormous... The European portion has also the look of thriving prosperity."[32]

Businesses included a sawmill, dry goods stores, fruit shops, stables, blacksmith shops, general stores and restaurants. The town had a telegraph and post office, a Railway Medical Assistant office and drug store, a courthouse, a government agency building, a school, railway warehouses, and offices and private residences. This journalist continued describing another section of the town:

> "As we entered we passed the Chinese locality, where numerous Celestials employed on the railway find their peculiar wants

abundantly met within the unique establishments that are being constantly multiplied by enterprising firms… for the sale of goods and for catering [to] the questionable tastes of their acquisitive countrymen."[33]

This description, together with the records of the Chinese applying for trade licences, indicates that there was a Chinese settlement or Chinatown in Lytton, where some Chinese lived and operated their businesses, such as general stores, grocery shops and restaurants. Three Chinese traders—merchants Ah Kee, Hung Wo and Foo Sang, and three Chinese farmers—Ah Chien, Ah Lung and Ah Tye, were listed in the 1882 directory.

The Chinese also established a joss house, a place of worship, at Lot 2, Block 13, on Main Street to honour three deities: Quan Yin, the goddess of compassion and mercy; Shen Nong, the god of agriculture and herbal medicine; and Zhu Rong, the god of fire or the kitchen god. The late Tom Earl, a rancher and one of Lytton's earliest residents, said that the joss house had existed since 1881.[34]

When construction of the CPR moved towards Lytton, the town grew, and Chinese settlers began to open businesses. They also built a place of worship (known as a joss house) on Lytton's Main Street. Pictured here, the joss house is the prominent building on the right side of the street. Courtesy of the Lytton Museum and Archives.

However, the official opening of the joss house took place in April 1883. Chinese visitors from Victoria and New Westminster and a Chinese band came up on the steamboat *Reliance* for the occasion. It was quite a celebration, with balloons, music and firecrackers.[35] As required by traditional Chinese worship rituals, there could have been burning of joss sticks and candles and mock paper money. The offerings could have included roast pig, steamed buns, oranges and rice wine.

Buddhists believe that Quan Yin saves the poor and relieves the suffering of all beings when they call upon her grace with sincerity. She is often depicted carrying a pearl, the symbol of enlightenment, or a small vase of water, the water of life. Devotees will be blessed with physical strength and spiritual peace when this water is sprinkled on them. Quan Yin loves all people and shows compassion and love to those who pray for help, answers their calls and fulfills their needs.

Legend says that Shen Nong (神农), the god of agriculture, invented the wooden plough and taught people how to cultivate soil or land. As a divine patron of traditional Chinese medicine, he taught people how to distinguish edible from poisonous plants as well as to recognize plants for healing fractures, cuts and wounds and relieving pain and discomfort.

Zhu Rong, the son of a tribal leader at Kunlun Mountain (昆仑山), was born with a red face and a hot temper, but he was very smart. His people rubbed two twigs together to produce fire, heat and light. The heat kept them warm and the light enabled them to see in the dark—but they didn't know how to control fire. Zhu then experimented with fire and used it for cooking food and driving wild beasts and insects away. He also realized the destructive power of fire and developed ways of controlling it, and thus people honoured him as the god of fire. Today, many traditional Chinese people honour him as a kitchen god (灶君神), a deity who watches fire in the household. His statue or his name written in Chinese characters on a piece of red paper is placed on an altar in the kitchen.

These three deities reflect not only the beliefs and values of the early Chinese, especially the labourers, but also their physical, emotional and spiritual needs. They were poor and lonely, living in a foreign land, not knowing what their future would be. And a good number of Chinese labourers had already lost their lives during the construction of the CPR in the Fraser Canyon area at Alexandra Bluff, Hell's Gate and other places, and some had died of diseases.[36] Certainly believing in the healing power and mercifulness of Quan Yin would have given them hope and peace.

Since the causes of diseases such as jaundice, beriberi or scurvy were unknown to the Chinese labourers, and the CPR company did not provide
them with medical care when they became sick, they could only turn to the
divine power of Shen Nong for blessing and guidance, especially in taking
food and using herbs that they gathered from plants in the wilderness.
Many Chinese believed these deities could help them ward off diseases
and epidemics.

The Railway Riot

In May 1883, a riot occurred at Hautier's Station, a railway construction
site near Lytton. J. Gray, the railway foreman, was in charge of a gang
of twenty-eight Chinese labourers at the site. He found the performance
of two Chinese workers unsatisfactory. He told the Chinese bookman of
the gang to inform the two members that they were fired. In the evening,
the bookman asked Gray to give these two labourers a second chance.
Whether Gray agreed to the request or not is unclear. Next morning, the
bookman gave his list of twenty-eight members to the timekeeper who
took roll call. The timekeeper checked with the list from Gray that showed
only twenty-six members. He told the bookman about the discrepancy, but
the bookman said that Gray had agreed to allow the two Chinese labourers to continue working. They went to Gray to sort out their differences.
Gray refused to take back the two Chinese labourers. Then the bookman
argued with Gray that these two labourers should be given a quarter-day's
pay for their early dismissal. Gray did not agree. At that point, the timekeeper happened to pick up a stone. The Chinese labourers standing nearby thought that the timekeeper was going to hit the bookman with the
stone. They became angry and agitated, and started shouting and yelling.
Perry, a teamster, heard the uproar and thought that the white men were in
danger. He took a pick handle, waded in and struck the group of Chinese
labourers. His violent interference scattered the crowd, but a few Chinese
labourers were injured. The offence was immediately reported to Officer
Hussey in Lytton. He went to investigate, and he found one Chinese badly
wounded and heard conflicting accounts of the incident. The confronta-
tion seemed to have resolved itself, as some of the Chinese had returned
to work.

That night, a white man pounded on the door of a Chinese camp.
The bookman appeared. The white man told him that he would be the
foreman of the gang in future and the bookman had to smarten up and

do his job according to instructions. He left the place. A few minutes later the bookman saw a group of about twenty white men, each carrying a pole, running into the Chinese camps. The Chinese labourers inside these camps immediately got out of bed and tried to escape. Some were knocked down, and many were hurt, and then the camps caught fire. The white men then departed from the scene. It is unclear whether the fire was deliberately set by the rioters or was an accident. Some of the Chinese labourers whose camps had not been disturbed came out and helped extinguish the fire, while others took care of their wounded co-workers. One Chinese man, Yee Fook, died of a head injury. Another Chinese man, Ah Fook, was badly injured.[37] The deceased and the injured were taken to the joss house in Chinatown.

The next day, Officer Hussey came to the Chinese site and transported Ah Fook and the other wounded Chinese labourers to downtown Lytton. Seven days later, Ah Fook died. A coroner's inquest into Yee Fook's death was held. It was confirmed that Yee Fook had died as the result of violence. But the culprit was not found, and the cause of the fire remained unknown. Also, no one could identify those white men who had rampaged through the Chinese camps. Many law-abiding citizens in Lytton felt that the incident was most unfortunate and feared that the bitter feelings of the Chinese towards the white men might not subside easily, since the attack on the Chinese at night was simply an act of oppressive brutality.

By 1884, anti-Chinese sentiment was simmering. Many anti-Chinese organizations, such as the Workingmen's Protection League in Victoria, had succeeded in convincing industries and businesses not to employ Chinese workers.[38] The same year, almost all the Chinese labourers working on the CPR construction were laid off. They were stranded, since they could not find jobs and did not have the resources to return home to Guangdong. On January 10, 1884, the *Colonist* reported that at least two thousand Chinese in the Spences Bridge area could not find the means to support themselves. Many moved south hoping to find jobs in the Vancouver, Victoria, and New Westminster Chinatowns. The 1891 census recorded only twelve Chinese names in Lytton, illustrating that the Chinese community there was diminishing, and probably the joss house was being neglected.

The Destiny of the Joss House

Guiseppe Taverna, an Italian Canadian who worked for the CPR as a track patrolman, lived next door to the joss house. He had no regard for the deities inside the building but looked upon it as an eyesore, because it was unkempt and decaying, about ready to fall apart. He wanted to acquire the property so that he could build a chicken hut on the lot. He noticed that some Chinese people had been visiting the joss house and occasionally offering sacrifices to the deities. These visitors often brought steamed chickens and fruits as offerings, lit joss sticks or incense and candles, and burnt paper money when they paid homage and respect to the deities. After the ritual, they left the food behind. Vagabonds who travelled on the CPR railway came to know about the food being left behind in the unoccupied joss house. They often crept into the building at night and ate the food. This annoyed Taverna and made him more determined to purchase the property. In 1901, he applied to the Crown to buy the property and pointed out to the land office in Kamloops that the Chinese building was sitting on Crown land without a deed. In the same year, five Chinese men—Hong Wo, Wo Pin, Foo Sang, Lee Seen and Lou Alaak—also filed applications to purchase the property. No party succeeded in acquiring the land, though, because the Dominion government did not want to sell it.

Taverna, however, was very persistent and continued sending letters to the land office in Kamloops to demonstrate his eagerness to purchase the lot. In 1917, with the assistance of James Murphy, a lawyer in Ashcroft, Taverna sent in his request to purchase the property with an offer of $50.00, which he assumed was the worth of the property.[39] The land office then sent a representative to assess the property, but did not follow up or inform Taverna whether his offer was accepted or rejected. In 1918, Murphy sent off another letter on behalf of Taverna to Ottawa, stating that "the building has been more or less forsaken by the Chinese. [It] is now a fire hazard to the Lytton residents."[40] The Dominion government did not respond. But in 1919, the government asked the Kamloops land office for a report on the property. The Kamloops office reported that "the Chinese residents in Lytton believed that although the joss house was not being used or occupied, they might get sick if it was damaged or destroyed as had happened to the Chinese people in 1881." At the time of this communication between government offices, World War I was taking place. In that period, the Dominion government had to focus on international matters and did not have time to deal with the issue of the joss house. So the building remained standing.

In 1927, Taverna resumed his quest to purchase the joss house property, this time offering $35.00 to the government. Eventually, the joss house

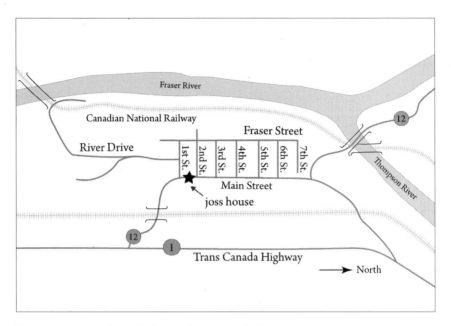

This map of Lytton shows the former location of the joss house.

was put up for sale, and Taverna bought it for $42.00. While the sale transaction was taking place, many Chinese people from the Lower Mainland came with sacrifices to pay homage to the deities in this place of worship. The sale also caught the attention of Chen How Pao, the consul general of the Chinese Republic (Guomintang), who wrote to Ottawa emphasizing that "the joss house and its contents were valued at $3,000 and they belonged to the Chinese Benevolent Association."[41] Apparently, Chen reported the dispute to the Chinese government in Nanking. Claims for the ownership of the property went on for some time. Finally, Taverna won his case and became its owner. He tore down the joss house and put the statues of the deities in a woodshed! In this way, the Chinese joss house disappeared from Lytton. Senior residents noticed when the building was torn down, but did not pay attention when the woodshed vanished. Did anyone take or remove the Chinese statues from the woodshed? Many residents in Lytton still wonder what had happened to the statues of the Chinese deities.

The Chong Family: Long-Time Residents in Lytton

Although the Chinese community had faded away somewhat in Lytton, the Chong family remained there until 2000. In 1885, the grandfather,

Low Gow (刘九), from Dong Mee village (东尾村) in Tsang Cheng County (增城县), Guangdong, arrived in New Westminster by boat and then went to Lytton, probably to meet his friends. In the early days, Chinese immigrants usually went to places where their relatives and friends lived so that they could get support and assistance, especially in finding work. In Lytton, Low Gow went to work on a farm as a labourer and then panned for gold on the banks of the Fraser River. When he came to Canada, he did not bring his wife and children—three sons and a daughter—with him. His eldest son and daughter died soon after he left home. His second son left the village and was killed when he got involved in some illegal activities. Only his wife and their youngest son, Low Bing Chong (刘炳祥), remained at home in the village. In 1903, Low Bing Chong paid the $50.00 head tax to immigrate and join his father in Lytton. Because the immigration officer could not figure out which was the first or last name in the Chinese naming system, Low Bing Chong ended up being addressed as Mr. Chong; hence, his children used "Chong" as their last name.

In Lytton, Low Gow and his son Bing Chong lived in a small building on Main Street. They sold groceries and other necessities to local people and to the few Chinese people in the area.[42] Their business flourished. Eventually, they established a grocery store in Lytton.

Low Bing Chong loved his mother dearly. "As soon as my father had earned some money, he sent money to his mother, because my grandfather did not send money to his wife regularly," said his son, David Chong. "Unfortunately, the postal system in China was not properly organized at that time. My father sent letters and money to my grandmother through a store in the village, trusting that the store owner would forward the letter and remittance to his mother. Quite often, the store owner didn't inform my grandmother about having received a letter and money from my father in Canada. The store owner either forwarded the letter and remittance to her late or never sent them to her. Gradually she became so discouraged, frustrated and despondent. Receiving no support and having heard no news from her son, she eventually committed suicide."

In 1920, Low Bing Chong married Lily Chow Lai Kuan, the daughter of Kai Chow, in Victoria where she was born. In Lytton, she was known as Lily Chong. Together they had one daughter and three sons; all of them were born in Lytton. Peter, the eldest, was born in 1921; Beatrice in 1926 (she passed away in 1994); David in 1933; and Ron, the youngest son, in 1935.

In 1922, Low Bing Chong bought some properties and built a hotel in Williams Lake. He paid for the construction and the setting up of the hotel. Two of his friends became partners in the establishment and operated the business. When he and his partners began operating the hotel business, they walked from Lytton to Lillooet, where they took the Pacific Great Eastern Railway to Williams Lake. At that time, this railway ran from Squamish to Quesnel but it stopped at Williams Lake.

In 1927, senior Low Gow returned home to China. People in the village felt that he needed a wife to take care of him in his old age. A female matchmaker in the village found a young woman and arranged the marriage for him. Together they had a son, Low Bing Kow, who remained in China.

"I had no idea what my father did between the time when he arrived and 1933, the year when I was born," said David Chong.

"I was told dad did some farming when he first arrived," added Peter. "Later, he worked at the Earl's Court Ranch."

Both Peter and David found their parents very disciplined in bringing up their children, but they made sure their children got a good education. "My father was a really serious person," commented Peter.

Low Bing Chong and his wife, Lily, ran the succesful Chong Wah grocery store (pictured here in the 1950s). In the late 1940s, the Chong children began to help run the store, and later they renamed it Lytton Supplies Ltd. Image courtesy of David Chong.

"Yes, I found my father cautious and rather defensive at times," added David. "When he walked in Lytton, he never walked on the sidewalk but in the middle of the street." He paused and then commented about his mother, Lily Chong. "My mother was a very self-disciplined and capable woman," said David. "She operated the original Chong Wah grocery store until it was torn down. In 1935, she built the new Chong Wah Store (祥华商店) at the southwest corner of Third and Main Street and operated it as a general store that sold a wide variety of products including groceries, dry goods, hardware, harness, saddlery and myriad other things. The original Chong Wah building was torn

The tombstones of Lily and Low Bing Chong. Low Bing Chong was born in China, but emigrated to Lytton in 1903 where he joined his father. Lily Lai Kuan was born in Victoria, BC. She married Low Bing in 1920. They had one daughter and three sons, all born in Lytton. Images courtesy of the author.

down in 1940. But the business in the new Chong Wah flourished under her management. In 1946, Peter returned from UBC and helped our mother manage the store. He took over a big load from my mother since then. Later, Peter became the principal manager of the business although my mother remained active in the enterprise."

In the 1960s, the business was taken over by the family and the name of the store was changed to Lytton Supplies Ltd., referred to as Store 1. Low Bing Chong died in 1964 and was buried in the Lytton cemetery.

Lily Chong was a highly esteemed and well respected woman in Lytton. She was a very good friend of Mary Williams, the mother of Rita Haugen, a First Nations woman. She often invited Williams and her sister Lena Charlie to dinner. When fall arrived, Chong and Williams used to go

out together to pick berries in the bush, said the late Rita Haugen.[43] Many
First Nations people in Lytton had shared berries or fresh salmon with the
Chong family and went to Lytton Supplies Ltd. Store 1 to purchase goods.
In 1976, Lily Chong passed on and was buried in the Lytton cemetery, a
few plots away from gravesite of her husband.

Peter Chong attended elementary school in Lytton and continued
his secondary school education at Williams Lake High School, because
there was no secondary school in Lytton then. After graduating from high
school, he went to the University of British Columbia (UBC) to study
and obtained his bachelor's degree in 1944. Then he returned home and
helped his parents operate the grocery store in Lytton. While he was at
UBC, he met Alice, a pretty young girl from Victoria, and fell in love with
her. In 1950, Peter and Alice got married and continued living in Lytton.
They integrated very well into the village community. Peter had developed
a good understanding of the Nlaka'pamux language, which enabled him
to communicate with the First Nations people when they shopped in the
store. Actually, the First Nations people loved to visit the store and socialize
with Peter, besides purchasing goods from the store. Under Peter's leadership and management, the family business flourished. In the 1970s, Lytton
Supplies Ltd. purchased another store in the 400 block of Main Street.
This store was known as Store 2. Peter Chong passed away peacefully at
the age of ninety-six in Vancouver on September 21, 2017.

Kenny Glasgow was a young lad who worked in the Lytton Supplies
stores for six years while he was still in high school. He commented that the
Chongs were great people, easy to get along with. "It was fun to work with
Peter Chong," he said. "He often made baloney sandwiches and hot tea
for lunch when we worked together, especially on Sunday. When we were
having lunch together, Peter joked and said that we were living high on the
hog! And we laughed."

Glasgow also shared his memories of the busy days working at Lytton
Supplies:

> Natives from across the [Fraser] river would come to town once
> a month to purchase groceries from the stores. They usually or-
> dered their purchases ahead of time and bought the goods in
> bulk, such as 100 pounds of flour, 100 pounds of sugar, 100
> pounds of potatoes and 100 pounds of rice, etc. The flour and
> potatoes were stored in the new basement [Store 2] and the rice
> and sugar in the old basement [Store 1]. When the customers

arrived to pick up their purchases, Peter gave me a choice, asking me out of which basement I wanted to pack the goods for the customers. Once I made my choice, he would say out loud, "Let's go! We're in a race." Then he and I would run down the stairs of the two different basements, grab the 100-pound sacks and bring the goods upstairs, panting and laughing… I tell you no man used time so well as Peter [did].[44]

In 1979, the Chong family sold Store 1 to John and Marian Chan, but they continued to operate Store 2. Peter managed Store 2 until 1986, when the family sold the business to the Lytton Indian Band. However, Peter assisted the First Nations people in operating Store 2 for a year or so. He retired in the following year.

Some years later, in 1996, Peter and Alice Chong moved to Vancouver. Before they left Lytton, the community gave them a big farewell party. In 2011, the Lytton Chamber of Commerce and the Lytton community invited Peter, Alice, David and Ron, and their families and many guests, including prominent local citizens, to Lytton to celebrate Peter's ninetieth birthday. More than a hundred people attended the birthday celebration, which was organized and hosted by Bernie Fandrich, president of the Lytton Chamber of Commerce at the Kumsheen Rafting Resort. Indeed, the

Growing up as the only Chinese children in Lyttton, David (left) and Peter (right, with wife Alice) often felt very out of place. However, as their family's store became an integral part of the community, so did they. Courtesy of the author.

First Nations people and the residents of Lytton have many fond memories of Peter and Alice. Today, the Chongs still own a few building lots and some properties in the village.

David Chong also attended elementary school in Lytton and was among the first class of students to graduate from Lytton High School in 1949. "Patricia Williams, one of my classmates, and I always say that we are the first class students in Lytton," chuckled Chong. Like his older brother, he attended UBC, obtained a bachelor of arts and continued studying law. In 1955, he was called to the BC bar. Currently he is an associate at Chen & Leung, Barristers & Solicitors at Oakridge Centre in Vancouver. His younger brother Ron also went to university and studied medical science. He became a professional pharmacist.

The Chong siblings are very friendly and helpful, willing to share what they know about Chinese-Canadian history in Lytton. When they recalled their childhood days, both Peter and David still remembered days when they did not feel they belonged. They were the only Chinese family in town and didn't have many young Canadian friends. They were often looked down on and kept apart from the mainstream. "We were a minority group, and nobody wanted to have very much to do with us," said Peter. "We were poor and almost living like the Natives. There were no social activities for us to participate in." He paused and then continued. "Another reason was the presence of polio and tuberculosis, which were incurable in those days. Measles, chicken pox, scarlet fever and other contagious diseases were quite common. We were kept apart probably from the health point of view too."

The brothers didn't have opportunities to play with the First Nations children either when they were young. "The First Nations children didn't attend the same elementary school as we and other Canadian children did," said David. "They were sent to St. George's Residential School in Lytton to learn farming, carpentry and other skills. Students in grades one to four went to the residential school all day, and those in grades five to eight attended school half a day. After school hours, they had to work in the residential school for the rest of the day. In other words, the First Nations children had to spend two years to finish a school year once they reached grade five. Therefore, it would take the First Nations children twelve years in total to finish elementary school. It was in 1948 that the First Nations children were allowed to attend the Lytton High School at grade nine, after they had completed their education in the residential school. By then they were seventeen or eighteen years old. It was a terrible system for them. Thus, there was hardly any chance for us to get connected or associated with the First Nations kids."

A Challenging Task

During his interview, David Chong commented, "It is not an easy task to track down the Chinese-Canadian history in Lytton. We know there were Chinese people here before us, but we have no recollection of what they did and who they were. The early Chinese didn't leave any children or grandchildren behind, so no one knows what happened to them. Many of them were sojourners. When they had made some money, they would go back to China! We are not as fortunate as the First Nations children, who had grandparents to tell them their history."

In truth, many of the early Chinese immigrants who went to Lytton were in transit. A number of them went there to work on farms or ranches or as cooks in restaurants. But they didn't stay long. Some attempted to run a restaurant but didn't do well. After some time, they packed up and left. Even when the Canadian National Railway began construction in 1910 in the vicinity of Lytton, there were no jobs for Chinese people because the CNR was not allowed to hire Chinese labourers; the company could only employ Chinese people when they not find Canadian workers.

However, David Chong provided the names of a few Chinese men who lived in Lytton between the 1950s and 1960s. They were:

- Cho Weng (曹荣), a man from Poon Yu (Panyu 番禺县) District, who worked at Mckay's Ranch. He returned to China in the late 1950s.
- Leung Shu (梁叔), who worked on Earl's Court Ranch. It is unknown what happened to him later on.
- Cheung Shu (张叔), who ran a grocery store known as Dong Kee (东记) on the west side of the Fraser River.
- Harry Lowe or Lowe Thiem (刘添), who worked as a casual labourer and cook at times in Lytton. He lived with Lucy Williams, who preferred to be identified as Lucy Black, a First Nations woman. Black was the last name of her legal husband, who had left her, but her own surname was Williams.

Lucy Black and son John Lowe in the 1930s. Though cultural tensions often ran high in the early twentieth century, Harry Lowe, a Chinese resident of Lytton, fell in love with Lucy, an Indigenous member of the community. Image courtesy of the late Rita Haugen.

Relationship between the Chinese and the First Nations People

In Lytton, the friendship between the early Chinese immigrants as well as between Chinese Canadians and First Nations people was very commendable. As shown by the friendship between the late Lily Chong and the late Mary Williams, as well as in the business dealings between Peter Chong and his First Nations customers, the friendship among them was tremendous and quite remarkable. Peter Chong even acquired the ability to communicate with the First Nations people in the Nlaka'pamux language, a tool that enhanced understanding and developed friendships.

When Harry Lowe or Lowe Thiem (刘添) worked in Lytton, he met and fell in love with Lucy Black, a First Nations woman. Lowe and Black lived together as husband and wife, and they had five children: Alice, Amelia, James, Leslie and John. Alice Lowe died in 1937 when she was only five months old. Harry signed the death certificate as her father and informant, and he registered her as Chinese instead of as a First Nations child with Chinese ancestry. Leslie was born on November 6, 1933, but he was found dead on the Canadian National Railway main line on June 30, 1956. Apparently he had been hit by an oncoming train that injured his skull. Leslie was then a patrolman for the railway. Again, his father Harry Lowe signed the death certificate as an informant. Lowe and Black lived together until Lucy passed on. After Lucy's death, Harry left Lytton and moved to Vancouver.

Harry Lowe in the 1930s. The First Nations community in Lytton respected the union of Harry and Lucy, and they accepted Harry as a part of their family. Image courtesy of the late Rita Haugen.

The union of this couple proved that loving sentiment had developed between the two people, regardless of differences in their cultural backgrounds and nationalities. It is wonderful to realize that the community in Lytton accepted their union and that the First Nation welcomed Lowe as a member of their family.

Low Bing Chong, however, could not accept Lowe taking a First Nations wife, because Lowe also had a wife and children in China. Low (or rather Chong) interpreted the union as Lowe being irresponsible to his family, and disloyal to his wife at home. The purpose of the Chinese people who came to the Gold Mountain was to find fortune so that they could take care of their families back home and improve their living circumstances. To Chong, taking an Indigenous wife in a foreign country meant abandoning his Chinese family at home in China.

However, the First Nations people in Lytton have been very kind and friendly to the Chinese people in the past and present. For example, John Haugen, a councillor of the Lytton First Nation, generously shared with me the records of deceased Chinese individuals in Lytton from the death registrations in the Royal BC Museum and the BC Archives. Some of the records include the following individuals:

- Yick Lin, fifty-eight years old, a Chinese miner who had been in Canada for twenty years but committed suicide in 1916. He lived on the west side of the Fraser River just north of Lytton where the ferry terminal is located. He was buried in the Lytton Chinese Cemetery. Councillor Haugen suspected many Chinese were buried in the same cemetery, although the records have yet to be found. Ah Chung was also buried in this Chinese cemetery on the west side of the Fraser facing the confluence of the Fraser and Thompson rivers. The Chinese cemetery is not the same cemetery as the one where Low Bing Chong and Lily Chong were buried. Recently, Haugen found an old map produced by Peter O'Reilly on June 24, 1887, indicating that a Chinese cemetery was located at the north end of the Indian reserve Klick-kumcheen No. XVIII IR RS. This area was turned over to construct Highway 95 in the 1950s.
- Tong Kee, eighty-one years old, male, storekeeper of a grocery store who died in June 1928. He had lived in Lytton for fifty years. The informant of his death was Lily Wah or Lily Chong. Low Yip Cheen was the undertaker who buried Tong in Lytton.

- Lim See Man, aged fifty-five, a labourer and miner who died on July 23, 1932. He was born in Canton (Guangzhou). At the time of his death he was residing at Earls Court Ranch. He could have been working as an irrigator or vegetable grower.
- In November 1932, Lee Man Bing, aged forty-seven, died from a gunshot wound, a homicide. He was listed as a merchant in Lytton. The informant was Lee Gung Gow, the cousin of the deceased.
- On April 30, 1948, Gow Joe, a shoemaker in Lytton, passed away at the age of sixty. The date of his arrival in Canada is unknown, but he had lived in Lytton for six years prior to his death.

In addition, Councillor Haugen shared the later history of Lytton Supplies Ltd. after the Chongs had sold the business. He said, "Store 1 still exists as a grocery store. When the next group of people bought the business from John and Marian Chan, they expanded it, and they bought the old community hall too. They constructed the AG Foods that still exists today. AG Foods is the principal grocery, butcher shop and bakery. The last three sets of owners are of Korean ancestry." Apparently, Haugen had worked with Peter in the Lytton Supplies store when he was a high school student.

The Spirit of the Past Remains!

The Chinese community in Lytton had its most glorious days during the Fraser gold rush and the construction of the CPR. These events not only attracted people from many countries, including China, to Lytton but also stimulated economic growth in the Fraser Canyon. Unfortunately, as alternative transportation routes were developed in the province, Lytton lost its role as a transportation hub. The Trans-Canada Highway (1957) reduced traffic and the Coquihalla Highway, built in 1986, bypasses Lytton. Eventually, businesses in the village became sluggish and people moved away. As David Chong said, "When I was a boy, I saw people stopping in Lytton overnight, but not today. Now you can reach Vancouver from Lytton within a few hours." The shorter route also prevents travellers from stopping at Lytton. Although both the CPR and CNR pass through Lytton daily, they are freight trains and seldom stop there. The new infrastructure has shortened travelling time but has also caused some businesses to close down, including stables, blacksmiths and others related to wagons and pack trains. Although the general population in Lytton resurged in 1910 during the construction of the Canadian National Railway, Chinese workers were not employed.

History has shown that thousands of Chinese reached the area during the two historical events—the Fraser gold rush and the construction of the CPR—and a thriving Chinese community was present in Lytton. It is sad that these Chinese people could not continue living in Lytton and their legacy was lost. But the Chinese-Canadian heritage sites, such as the rock pilings at the Chinese mining sites, remain and have attracted visitors and tourists and caught the attention of people in many walks of life. And Councillor Haugen contributed his time and effort to lead visitors to these mining sites so that the present generation of Canadians would be able to visit these areas and gain some understanding of the lives of Chinese miners and their ventures.

Although the joss house was torn down, people remember its existence. An article by George M. Murray, entitled "Gods in a Lytton Woodshed," published in the *Province* in 1933, has stimulated scholars and researchers to unearth its history and find out more about its functions. Between 1940 and 1980, the lot on which the joss house was built changed hands many times. It is very fortunate that in 1980 the site was bought by Bernie and Lorna Fandrich, the founders and operators of Lytton's Kumsheen Rafting Resort. The Fandriches were committed to reconstructing and reviving the spirit of the joss house, once the Chinese communal building in Lytton. In 2012, they bought the lot adjacent to site of the joss house with the intention of constructing a Lytton Chinese History Museum on both lots to commemorate the joss house. It is wonderful to have Canadians like the Fandrichs who appreciate and help preserve Chinese-Canadian heritage and history in Lytton as well as in the Nicola Valley. As well, Rev. Koten, a Buddhist abbot at the Lions Gate Buddhist Priory in Lytton, is very interested in the Chinese-Canadian history in the area and has carried out extensive research on it.

In 2012, the New Pathways to Gold Society (NPTG) invited Senator Lillian Dyck Quan, a Gordon First Nations woman with Chinese ancestry, and the former Senator Vivienne Poy to visit the Fraser Canyon and tour the Chinese mining sites at Brownings and Van Winkle. The NPTG also sponsored a Fraser River raft trip for the Chinese Canadian Historical Society of British Columbia (CCHSBC) so members could visit various sites where the early Chinese left their footprints along the Fraser River. About twenty CCHSBC members went on the trip, after which scholars and students of UBC visited the mining sites in the following years. Archaeological studies have been carried out on these sites in the past few years.

In 2015, the Honourable Minister Teresa Wat of the Ministry of International Trade and Multiculturalism (MIT) visited the mining sites with a few members of the Legacy Initiatives Advisory Council (LIAC). All the tours to the Chinese mining sites were led and guided by Councillor Haugen.

In 2016, the mining sites and the joss house in Lytton were recognized by the MIT and the Ministry of Forests, Lands, and Natural Resources Operations as Chinese-Canadian heritage sites. In addition, the Lytton First Nation was offered resources by LIAC of MIT for the production and installation of a commemorative plaque in the village. So the Chinese-Canadian history and heritage in Lytton will remain for remembrance and commemoration and for further research purposes.

On May 13, 2017, Bernie and Lorna Fandrich held a ribbon cutting ceremony for the grand opening of the Lytton Chinese History Museum. More then two hundred people were in attendance, including local dignitairies: Mayor Jessoa Lightfoot, Chief Janet Webster of the Lytton First Nations Band, David Chong and author Lily Chow. The Lion Dance was performed in celebration by the Vancouver Shaolin Lion Dance troupe.

KAMLOOPS: THE RAILWAY TOWN

The City of Kamloops is located at the confluence of the North and South Thompson rivers in the territory of the Secwepemc (Shuswap) people of British Columbia. It is about 355 kilometres (220 miles) from Vancouver. The name Kamloops originated in the Indigenous word Tk'emlups, meaning the place where two rivers meet—an appropriate description of its location.

During the fur trade era, the Thompson River was a major artery for transporting furs from the Interior to Fort Victoria. Around 1812, the Northwest Company and the Pacific Fur Company both established fur trading posts on the shores of the North Thompson. The Husdson's Bay Company built the first Fort Kamloops in 1842 on the west bank of the North Thompson, but the site was abandoned in 1862 for the new fort built on the Thompson River at the confluence of the North and South Thompson. Besides trading fur with the Indigenous people, the staff of the HBC cultivated

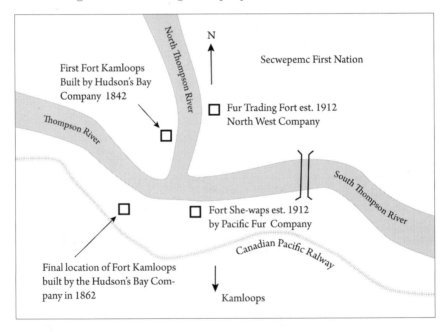

The Thompson River was an important transportation route during the fur trade era. The Pacific Fur Company, the North West Company and the Hudson's Bay Company all built forts in the area between 1812 and 1862.

crops and raised cattle to supply meat and vegetables for themselves as well as for members of other trading posts in southern BC. The agricultural and cattle industries expanded and became one of the food supplies for miners in the Fraser Canyon and the Cariboo during the gold rushes.

By 1884, the construction of the Canadian Pacific Railway (CPR) had reached Fort Kamloops. From there, the construction continued towards the east and was completed in the Kootenay. Construction of the CPR brought a new era to the BC Interior. For many years, its track ran down Main Street in Kamloops. For this reason, many old-timers, including the late Peter Wing, referred to the city as the Railway Town.[45] After the completion of the CPR in 1885, mining and forestry, including logging and the production of lumber, became the main industries in the neighbourhood of Fort Kamloops. The lumber provided building supplies for construction in the area and on the booming Prairies. Houses, hotels, stores and other buildings, such as churches, schools and a hospital, mushroomed in the village where the trading post was established. In 1914, the village was incorporated as the City of South Kamloops.

The city grew rapidly. Settlements spread out and extended to the north shore across the Thompson. In 1946, the north shore settlement was incorporated as the City of North Kamloops. Today, Kamloops comprises both South Kamloops and North Kamloops; the amalgamation of these two cities took place on November 4, 1967.

Arrival of Chinese Immigrants

At the beginning of the Fraser gold rush, about three hundred of the Chinese miners migrated to Tranquille Creek, a stream on the north shore of Kamloops Lake, to pan for gold. They were soon joined by their countrymen directly from Guangdong and Hong Kong. Some Chinese miners who found gold mining to be unprofitable settled in the west end of Kamloops on Main Street, the oldest part of town. This street was known then as Victoria Street West, and Chinese settlement began to take root. Main Street was a commercial centre with hotels, shops, warehouses and residences on both sides of the CPR main line. In the Chinese settlement, some settlers operated laundry shops, restaurants and grocery stores, while others cultivated vegetable gardens and sold produce in the neighbourhood or worked as labourers at ranches, as cooks in local sawmills or as domestic servants in private homes. A few worked at odd jobs such as chopping wood or carrying water for local residents.

In 1884, construction of the CPR brought hundreds of Chinese labourers to perform grading work in Fort Kamloops. G. B. Martin, a member of the provincial government, wrote to Prime Minister MacDonald stating that "celestials as thick as mosquitoes and twice as nasty"[46] had arrived to commence railway construction in Kamloops. The Chinese labourers set up tents along the railway construction sites to serve as their living quarters. Some camped on an Indian reserve at Salmon River, east of Kamloops. The Indian agent asked Andrew Onderdonk to pay rent for the Chinese camps on the reserve land. Onderdonk notified the Chinese gangs that they would be charged for use of the camp grounds. "John refused to submit and struck at the work... interfering with other work," stated the *Inland Sentinel.* On June 11, 1885, Officer Todd took a force of Specials to the scene, prepared for any eventuality. The news reporter expected "a good deal of interest... in the look-out." But no exciting follow-up has been found.

After the railway in the Kamloops area was completed, the Chinese labourers left and moved farther east to other construction sites. By October 1885, CPR construction had reached Craigellachie in the Kootenay. Almost all the Chinese workers had been laid off by then except a few kept on to carry out maintenance in winter. Many unemployed Chinese workers migrated to and settled down in Kamloops. Some ventured into gold panning. On April 29, 1886, the *Kamloops Sentinel* reported "A 'Spec of war' was recently hovering around Scotch Creek. Some white miners had difficulty in some diggings and sold their claims to Mr. Mackay." But Mackay instructed the white miners to destroy sluices on the Chinese claims nearby when he took over the claims from them. The Chinese miners retaliated and took Mackay to court. The case was dismissed with Mackay paying the penalty.

Chinatown: Merchants and Businesses

Several Chinese merchants, like Ah Hoy and Chan Ah Mee, were noted in the Chinese settlement, known as Chinatown by the mainstream community. Hop Lee and Yee Chong in Chinatown appeared in the *Williams' BC Directory.* The famous Kwong Lee company also opened a store in Kamloops. In May 1886, a Chinese doctor advertised in the *Kamloops Sentinel* that "Jang Ding Tong [the doctor] has 15 years' experience in San Francisco and Victoria, as Physician and Surgeon; and is now located at Kamloops."

By 1887, Chinatown had expanded from Main Street to Lorne Street and was bounded by First and Second avenues. The table below shows the Chinese businesses recorded in the *Williams' BC Directory* in 1887–90.

Names of Chinese Shops

Williams' BC Directory	Names	Business
1887–88	Ah Lee	General merchant
	Kwong On Wo	General merchant
	Kwong Fat	General merchant
	Kwong Tai	General merchant
	Kwong Joy	General merchant
	Yee Chong	General merchant
1889–90	Ah Loy	General merchant
	Chan Dang Tong	Physician and surgeon
	Chong Lee & Company	Grocery and dry goods
	Joy Lun	Physician and surgeon
	Hop Lee	General merchant
	Jang Ding Tong	Physician and surgeon
	Kee Sam	Laundry
	Kwong Ching	Laundry
	Kwong Joy Shing	General merchant
	Kwong Lung	General merchant
	Kwong On Wo & Company	General merchant
	Kwong Tai	Employment office
	Voo Lee	Laundry
	Wing Fong	Laundry
	Wah Lee	Merchant

Source: *Williams' British Columbia Directory, 1887–88, 1889–90.*

On November 26, 1887, the *Inland Sentinel* reported that the unemployed Chinese labourers "set up tents upon the river bank and near the [railway] station… [And] they moved into quarters in Chinatown [for the winter]. A number also migrated to the coast."

However, it is interesting to note that the 1888–89 *Williams' BC Directory* stated that there were 754 white people in Kamloops with "about the same number of Chinese." In its heyday, the Chinese population was estimated at about 500. Some Chinese shops and houses were found scattered along the east side of Main Street and a few were on Lorne Street. This area consisted of several general stores, restaurants, laundry shops, herb stores and a couple of rooming houses for bachelors or single men who were married but who did not bring their wives and children with them when they immigrated to this country.

On February 11, 1888, the *Kamloops Sentinel* reported that the Chinese celebrated Chinese New Year with "splendour, innumerable fire crackers being exploded from 12 o'clock until daylight. All the residences of Chinatown were open for the reception of visitors and a cordial welcome was given to partake of a variety of refreshments."

Chinatown, however, had suffered a series of fires. In June 1892, a fire broke out in Chung Lee's house on the north side of Main Street. The blaze jumped across the street and the railway track and engulfed some Chinese properties, including a laundry, some other businesses and several homes. On the night of September 17 the same year, another fire destroyed the Wing Fong Laundry, the Kwong On Wo and Chong Lee general stores, several small Chinese shacks and some white homes and businesses in the vicinity. In this fire, Chan Ah Mee, a Chinese laundryman who had joined the fire brigade, was hailed as a hero. "He [Chan] bravely perched himself on the roof [of a building on fire] and directed the stream of water at the flames. He used an axe to cut down charred debris in an attempt to save lives and properties," stated a couple of local newspapers. Chan saved the house of John Mara, MP, in this fire. In 1893, another fire occurred in the same area. After the fire, the white merchants sold their businesses and moved farther east in town, and the Chinese then took over these businesses. In 1912, yet another fire occurred, again destroying some buildings in Chinatown.

By the late 1910s, forty-one Chinese residents had obtained licences for their businesses: eight to operate laundries, three to run general stores, six to operate groceries, three cafés, twelve fruit and vegetable peddlers, one tailor, two shoemakers and two barbershops, all in Chinatown.[47]

Despite Ah Mee and other Chinese settlers' attempts to become integrated into the mainstream community, anti-Chinese sentiment existed in Kamloops. In 1917, the *Standard Sentinel* editorial said that "Kamloops

Ah Tom and Yee Lee from Lorne Street. Information courtesy of Kay Sinclair, who is the baby girl sitting on Yee Lee's lap. Photograph by Mary Spencer. Photo courtesy of the Kamloops Museum and Archives, photo collection #1053.

has no need of a commercial Chinese quarter… [We should] confine this detrimental movement to one part of the city. The salvation of prosperity in Kamloops is the prosperity of a white Kamloops…" Similarly, in 1919, the city council passed a resolution restricting all laundries to Main Street west of Nicola Road, effectively confining the Chinese to the west end of town. But life went on with the Chinese settlers.

Meanwhile, in the vicinity of Kamloops, agricultural products like tomatoes, beans and other vegetables grew in abundance. Before the age of refrigeration, perishable vegetables such as tomatoes and beans were canned and shipped out to grocery stores and markets in other provinces and in the United States. In 1915, the North Kamloops Cannery was the first cannery to be established. Three other tomato canneries followed— the Kamloops Cannery (1926–28), the Carlin Canning Company (1929) and the Columbia Cannery (1930)—and a few more canneries were in operation. Chinese workers were hired by these tomato and vegetable canneries to cultivate tomatoes and pick these vegetables on leased land on the Indian reserve. Women of many races—Chinese, Indigenous, East Indian and white—and girls as young as thirteen years old were hired to peel and cut the tomatoes and fill cans. White males performed skilled work in the canning process. Chinese men put labels on the cans and packed them into cases for shipment.[48]

The producers in the United States were strong competitors for the Kamloops canneries. As time went by, it became difficult for the Kamloops canneries to find local or national markets for their products. Consequently, many of them closed down and many Chinese workers lost their jobs. Compounded by the poor economy during the Great Depression and the discrimination against the Chinese, a few small Chinese businesses closed down in Chinatown and many Chinese workers moved to the coast or other larger cities. Gradually the Chinese population in Chinatown decreased. By then, several Chinese organizations, such as the Chinese Mission Hall (the Chinese Methodist Church), the Kamloops Chinese Freemasons society and the Kamloops Chinese Nationalist League (Guomindang) had been established, and they remained in Chinatown. Their functions and activities had been reported on by local newspapers since their inception.

The Chinese Mission Hall

In 1877, the Methodist Church mission arrived in Kamloops. When the mission first arrived, Rev. Dowsley was appointed to assist volunteers in establishing the denomination. Rev. Dowsley understood the Chinese language and culture well and spoke fluent Cantonese, because he had spent seven years in missionary work in China before taking up pastoral work in Kamloops. Wing and Chew Quan volunteered to act as interpreters for the missionary work.[49]

The Chinese Mission Hall, a property of the Methodist Church, would not have existed without the generosity of Mah Mow, the original owner of the building. Mah, also known as James Eberts, suffered from tuberculosis while he was living in Vancouver. He moved to Kamloops hoping to get better medical care. After living in Kamloops for about a year, he seemed to be getting better and thought he would recover completely. So he built a house at 190 Main Street with the intention of opening a store there. In late 1890, he had a relapse and became very ill. His friends, some fellow Chinese Christians, took care of him until he died. To show his gratitude and appreciation for his fellow Christians, he left the building in his will to the Missionary Society of the Methodist Church. When he died, the Methodist Church held a solemn funeral service for him and looked after his burial.[50]

The Chinese Mission Hall became an integral part of the Kamloops Chinese community, acting as a meeting place, a place of worship and a place of celebration. Courtesy of the Kamloops Museum and Archives, photo collection #1853.

In the fall of 1896, Rev. Gardner, the superintendent of the Methodist Chinese Mission in Vancouver, went to Kamloops to hold a ceremony for transferring ownership of the building. Rev. Gardner delivered his sermon fluently in Cantonese. Many Chinese residents who were in the congregation were touched by his preaching and donated a generous sum of money to the church.[51] A night school was then established to teach the Chinese people the English language. Rev. Laidley was appointed pastor of the church and teacher in the school. Over the years, the Methodist Church held Sunday services, bible study classes and choir practices, and celebrated Christmas and Good Friday and other festivities in the Chinese Mission Hall.

The first Chinese wedding, the marriage of Chan Ah Mee and Cherry Jip Ti He, a young woman from Victoria, was held in the Kamloops Chinese Mission Hall. It was a colourful ceremony that attracted many people in Kamloops. The wedding took place on January 22, 1891. Before the ceremony began, the church was packed, and many of the guests and spectators had only standing room. Inside the hall, a dozen chairs were set up on a platform for the bridal party, which consisted of the bride and the groom, the best man and the bridesmaid, and eight other

Chinese men. The bridesmaid, Annie Leake, who had known the bride for many years, was the matron of the Methodist Mission Home in Victoria. The best man, Ah Sing, was the brother of the groom.

"At 2 o'clock sharp, the music of the Wedding March announced the arrival of the wedding party," stated the *Inland Sentinel*. "The bride, smiling bewitchingly and leaning on the arm of her bridesmaid, walked in at the head of the procession, followed by Ah Mee, the bridegroom, and Ah Sing and the eight cheerful men." After the party had arrived at the altar, Rev. T. Hall performed the wedding ceremony according to the Methodist rites.

At the conclusion of the ceremony, the wedding party and guests were showered with tiny pieces of red paper as they marched out of the church. Wedding bells rang and firecrackers exploded. Cherry, now Mrs. Chan, was introduced to several female guests. Soon, a horse and buggy arrived to carry the bride and the bridesmaid to the Oriental Hotel where a reception was held for the wedding party and guests. Since the carriage had room for only three persons, the bride and bridesmaid had to sit on either side of the driver. The groom and best man walked beside the carriage to the hotel. In the evening, a big feast was held at the groom's residence. This first Chinese wedding in Kamloops has become a legend.

Unfortunately, Chan Ah Mee, a well-respected Chinese old-timer, would only spend forty-nine years of his life in Kamloops. On July 2, 1926, at around 10:00 pm, Chan was struck by a car driven by Clair Dalgleish. Chan was riding on his bicycle without a light along the sidewalk on Lansdowne Street, and was crossing onto Third Avenue. Dalgleish and two members of the Vancouver baseball team were on their way to the Vendome. As soon as Dalgleish realized that he had hit the cyclist, he slammed on the brakes and swerved to the left. His actions landed his car in a nearby ditch. Another car driven by F. LaRoeque, manager of the city baseball team, was following behind. LaRoeque stopped and immediately took Chan to the Royal Inland Hospital while Mr. Dalgleish proceeded to the police station to report the accident. Besides various cuts and bruises on his head and face, Chan had suffered a broken left collar bone, his right thigh bone was smashed, and three left ribs were cracked. After remaining in the hospital for five days, he passed away, survived by his wife, Cherry, his son, Jim Mee, and a granddaughter, Annie May. He was sixty-nine years old. On July 11, the Kamloops Chinese Freemasons society conducted the funeral rites for Ah Mee. The coffin and the family mourners left the family residence at 234 Lansdowne Street and proceeded to the

Freemasons lodge for the funeral rites. After the ceremony, a procession of men scattering paper money led the coffin from the lodge to the Chinese cemetery in Powers Addition for the burial. Incense, candles and brown papers with gold and silver leaves were burned, and steamed rice, small cups of white wine and fruits were left at the graveside for his spirit.

In court, Dalgleish was found not guilty so no fine was imposed. The jury declared that "in our opinion, no blame whatsoever should be attached to the driver. According to the evidence produced, Ah Mee was riding on his bicycle without light of any description."[52]

Besides preaching and attempting to convert the Chinese residents to Christianity, the Methodist Church helped many unemployed fellow Christians find work, taught them and other Chinese residents the English language and provided interpretation services for those who could not speak English but needed assistance in their daily lives, such as applying for work and business licences, paying utility bills in government offices and communicating with people in the mainstream community.

In July 1951, the Mission Hall building burned down. The *Kamloops Sentinel* reported that "the minister's home at 190 and 194 Victoria West was a total loss… The blaze started on Sunday at 8:00 pm between the two [buildings and] swept up the walls to the roof… The Kamloops Fire Department was summoned and they fought the stubborn fire for two

The Kamloops Chinese Cemetery, pictured here in 2012, was officially designated in 1892. In the 1920s, several of the deceased were exhumed, and their remains were returned to China. Image courtesy of the author.

hours. Although they were unable to save the buildings [they] prevented the flames from [spreading] further... The only article of any value in the Mission Hall was an organ and some chairs and other pieces of furniture."

The Chinese Cemetery

In Kamloops, deceased Chinese were not permitted to be buried in the Pioneer Cemetery but had to be interred in the Chinese Cemetery located in the current Powers Addition subdivision. In June 1887, a journalist from the *Inland Sentinel* stumbled upon a solitary grave "on rambling over the heights overlooking Kamloops." On taking a closer look, he found a headboard with Chinese inscriptions that affirmed "a body of a Celestial was buried underneath." This open grassland, located north of Fernie Road or Lombard Avenue of today and east of the Hudson's Bay Trail, was the burial ground for the deceased Chinese, and many Chinese labourers who died during the construction of the Canadian Pacific Railway in the area were buried there.

Research indicates that the land was pre-empted from a Crown grant to Mr. Fernie, who sold it to Mr. George Bower, a rancher. In 1885, Bower donated the small land parcel, two by two chains, at the Hudson's Bay Trail to the Chinese community, held in trust by Kwon Lung, so that when his Chinese ranch helpers passed on, they would have a resting place. This donation was much appreciated by the Chinese community, since they would now have a place to bury their departed friends and relatives. In 1892, the cemetery was officially designated for the Chinese community of Kamloops.[53]

Hundreds of dead Chinese were buried in this cemetery. In the early 1920s, many of the graves were exhumed and the remains sent back to various villages in Guangdong through the Benevolent Consolidated Association in Victoria. The exhumation of Chinese graves was stopped in 1936 by the government due to health regulations. A few of the remaining graves had brick markers, while many others were marked by wooden boards. Some graves did not have any marker. As time went by, many of the wood markers rotted away and the inscriptions faded. Although the Chinese Cemetery was maintained alternatively by two associations—the Kamloops Chinese Freemasons society and the Kamloops Chinese Nationalist League or Guomingdang—in the early days, yet the site appeared rundown, unattended and overgrown with sage.

The Kamloops Chinese Freemasons Society

According to the publication of the thirty-first national convention of the Chinese Freemasons in Canada, the Kamloops chapter of the Chinese Freemasons society was established in 1888. In August 1894, the Kamloops Sentinel reported that "the last few days of last week saw the inauguration of a secret order among Chinamen... The ceremonies opened with the unusual volley of firecrackers after which, among other things, there was sumptuous feasting, conspicuous on the table on which was a pig roasted whole. A number of the brethren from Victoria, Westminster and Vancouver were present."

In the early days, the Freemasons society helped its members find employment and provided them with services such as reading and writing letters and helping them to send money home to China. The society became the main contact and mailing address for many of its members, especially for the single men. It subscribed to Chinese newspapers from Vancouver and California for the directors, caretaker and the members who resided in its rooming house to read and to learn about the situation in China as well as in their home villages. When the Freemasons society received news from the headquarters in Vancouver or from China, particularly about events and incidents that had occurred in Guangdong, the board members would often share the news with the members. The society also offered recreational activities like gambling, checkers playing and so on, to members and the Chinese who resided in Chinatown. The society also looked after funeral arrangements and burials for its deceased local members.

On January 15, 1911, the Kamloops Chinese Freemasons society held a grand opening for its lodge on 39 Main Street West and invited many very important people to the celebration. They also invited Dr. Sun Yat-sen (孙中山), who had just arrived in Vancouver, to the event. Sun could not attend the event due to previous commitments but he sent a telegram congratulating the society and stating that he would visit the chapter at a later date.

On February 15 of the same year, Sun Yat-sen, accompanied by Li Bing Chen (李丙辰), took a CPR train to Kamloops. Key members of the Kamloops Chinese Freemasons society waited with a band on the platform of the Kamloops railway station to receive them. As soon as Sun and Li emerged from the train, the band blared out with trumpets and trombones accompanied by clashing cymbals and a banging drum to welcome them. Then the welcoming party took the guests in a car to the lodge, where a lunch reception was held for them. Sun was very pleased to see the Chinese flag fastened on the wall of the assembly hall. After lunch, Sun and Li were taken to the Dominion Hotel to rest. In the evening, the society held a banquet of ten tables for Sun and Li as well as its members and other guests. After the banquet, Sun addressed society members and others who had come to the banquet. It is estimated that more than 150 people were present. Sun promoted his fundraising campaign by saying that funds were very much needed for the Chinese revolution that aimed to overthrow the Qing regime and establish a Chinese republic. He further explained why he was selected by the Chinese Alliance Party, or Tong Meng Hui (同盟会), to spearhead the fundraising campaign in North America. He said that Hu Han Min (胡汉民) was first appointed to the mission in North America. Hu rejected the appointment because he had never visited North America before. Then the party selected Huang Ke Qiang (黄克强) or Huang Xing (黄兴), the leader of Xing Zhong Hui (兴中会), to represent the Chinese Alliance Party in its fundraising campaigns. But Huang, a native of Hunan, could not speak Cantonese or the Siyi dialect, a language very much needed for communication with the overseas Chinese in North America because almost all the overseas Chinese had emigrated from the Siyi counties in Guangdong Province. Therefore, Huang was not the best candidate for the mission. Finally, the Chinese Alliance Party delegated Sun, a native of the Zhong Shan County in Guangdong who could speak Cantonese fluently, to carry out fundraising in North America. Sun told the assembly that $30,000.00 CAD would be needed to support the revolutionary movement, and urged everyone to donate generously to support the revolution. He emphasized that anyone who donated $5.00 or more would be reimbursed twice the amount if the Chinese Alliance Party succeeded in overthrowing the Qing regime. Sun's appeals motivated the audience to debate and discuss various issues and actions needed to carry out the revolution. Finally, they decided to donate money to support the revolution. Some members suggested selling the building as a mean of supporting the revolution. But, they were reminded, the building could not be sold because it had been mortgaged to F. J. Falton for the sum of $2,500.00. In the end, the Kamloops Chinese Freemasons society managed to collect $500.00 from the assembly. The meeting ended at midnight.[54]

By the end of 1911, Sun had succeeded in forming Chinese Alliance Party chapters in Vancouver, Victoria and some other cities in North America that he had visited. He encouraged all the members of the Chinese

Freemasons society in North America to join these chapters and vice versa. After he left the continent, his comrade, Feng Zi You (冯自由), continued to recruit members from among the Freemasons to join the Chinese Alliance Party chapters and encouraged party members to join the Freemasons. The entry of these new members to the Freemasons society created factions within it, as old and young members each had different ideologies. After the formation of the Chinese republic in 1912, the Tong Meng Hui or Chinese Alliance Party in China changed its name to China Guomindang (中国国民党) or Chinese Nationalist League or Party; so did all the party chapters around the world!

In 1912, the Chinese Freemasons of Canada passed a resolution requesting that all Chinese men cut off their queues, in deference to Sun Yat-sen and the ideology of the Chinese republican government. Unfortunately, the relationship between Sun and the Chinese Freemasons society soon turned sour. Apparently, Sun had another agenda in addition to raising funds; he wanted the Chinese Alliance Party to absorb the membership of the Freemasons society so that the Freemasons would gradually disappear in Canada. The old-timers of the Chinese Freemasons society realized that Sun had betrayed them, and that their society was on the

The Chinese Freemasons society was revered for their traditional funeral rites, such as this procession held for Yuen Lee in downtown Kamloops in 1908. Courtesy of the Kamloops Museum and Archives, photo collection #1052.

verge of being displaced by the Chinese Nationalist League. Some of the wise and faithful Freemasons created the Dart Coon Club within the society to protect their interests. In 1915, the Dart Coon Club was established in Kamloops. The birth of the Dart Coon Club breathed new life into the Freemasons society and rejuvenated the sense of brotherhood among its members.

On December 28, 1928, the Chinese Freemasons society chapter in Kamloops held the fifth national conference of the society. It was a grand event showcasing lion and dragon dances, songs and music, and a parade in town. In the evening, a banquet was held with entertainment for representatives from Vancouver headquarters and other chapters in Canada as well as from the United States. Many prominent local citizens were invited to join in the celebration.

In 1932, the Kamloops Chinese Freemasons society lost its English-language secretary, Sam Jang Hung, who was a court interpreter by profession. Hung had come from Revelstoke and had worked in the Kamloops court for several years. When he passed on, he was only thirty-four years old. His funeral was held at the lodge on 39 Main Street. Wey Suey, the lodge master, conducted the funeral and Charlie Lim presented a eulogy. The coffin was placed and opened outside the lodge. Incense sticks were lit and inserted in an urn on a large table where flowers and food were placed at one end of the coffin. Hundreds of Chinese people in the vicinity of Kamloops attended the funeral. After the ceremony, the coffin was closed and gold and silver paper money was burned. Then the funeral procession began, with a Chinese orchestra leading and mourners dressed in white and friends of the deceased following behind the coffin to the Chinese Cemetery. The mourners called out his name on the way from the Freemasons lodge on Main via Third Avenue and St. Paul Street to the cemetery. When they reached the gravesite, the mourners again burned gold and silver paper money, and left behind rice, buns, oranges and cigarettes beside the grave. This was one of the spectacular funerals that the Kamloops Chinese Freemasons society performed.

The Kamloops Freemasons lodge burned down in 1953, but it was soon rebuilt at 39 West Main Street, the same location. In 1976, George and Elsie Cheung and their two-year-old daughter immigrated to Canada from Hong Kong. When they arrived in Kamloops, George engaged in the restaurant business and Elsie went to work at the Inland Royal Hospital as a qualified nurse in the female wards. Although Elsie was a graduate of the

Hong Kong Nursing School, she was still required to take an examination to obtain a nursing certificate before she could work in the hospital.

Since Elsie's parents were staunch members of the Chinese Freemasons society, they joined the Kamloops chapter, and later George was elected as an executive member. Elsie could not become a board member because the society would not elect female members as directors then. But she participated in many of its functions. In 1979, when the city widened West Victoria Street, the society building had to be torn down. The society then set up its offices at 576 Battle Street.

In 1986, the society bought a duplex at 815–817 Battle Street while George was on the board, but city bylaws did not permit them to operate the society in that location. So they rented it out as an investment property. In the same year, the constitution of the Chinese Freemasons society was modified to allow women to sit on the board; this enabled Elsie to become a board member of the Kamloops chapter. In 1993, the society participated in the Kamloops Centennial Parade and won second place. The following year, the Kamloops Chinese Freemasons society received the Centennial Award from the City of Kamloops honouring the society's hundred years of service.

In 1994, when George was elected president of the Kamloops chapter, he undertook the task of acquiring a building for the society. Elsie assisted and supported her husband's efforts; she lobbied for funds from the Vancouver headquarters and Chinese Freemasons society chapters in other cities to support the endeavour. In 1995, the property on Battle Street was sold and the society bought the building at 474 Tranquille, where both the Freemasons society and the Dart Coon Club served their members and carried out their functions.

The same year, Elsie was elected president of the Kamloops Chinese Freemasons society—the first female president in the history of the Chinese Freemasons society throughout Canada! George, however, remained committed to his project and became president of the Dart Coon Club. Both husband and wife succeeded in purchasing a building for the society and held a grand opening for the new lodge in 1996. Under the leadership of the Cheungs, many new people joined the society. Two years later, they invited Chen Pak, a kung fu master in Vancouver, to Kamloops three days a month to teach members of the martial arts group the skills and discipline of the lion dance. The membership of the martial arts group consisted of both men and women, ranging in age from five to sixty-five years. Elsie took over coaching in the absence of Chen. Both husband and wife also operated a Chinese school to teach young Chinese Canadians and other Canadians the Chinese language in Mandarin and in Cantonese twice a week. To-day, the Kamloops Chinese Freemasons society remains active and vibrant under the leadership of the Cheungs.

Besides carrying out its mandate, the Freemasons society made a great effort throughout its history to perpetuate the Chinese culture by celebrating Chinese New Year and other festivities, and to reach out to the mainstream community. During Chinese New Year celebrations and its anniversaries, the society always invited guests from local government, and leaders of other organizations and friends in the mainstream to join them to celebrate. The society was also involved in many of the city's functions. In the past four decades, George and Elsie Cheung have contributed a great deal to the success and achievements of the society. Today, they still lead the organization.

The Chinese Nationalist League—Guomindang

After his visits to North America, Sun Yat-sen's ambitions materialized. Many chapters of the Chinese Nationalist League or Guomindang were established in North America. Thus, it should not be surprising to find a chapter in Kamloops. On March 10, 1925, the *Kamloops Sentinel* reported that the local Chinese Nationalist League celebrated its fifth anniversary at 45 Main Street. On that day, the assembly hall of the building was decorated with ribbons and paper flowers. A large picture of Sun Yat-sen was hung on the wall of the far end of the assembly hall, flanked by a Chinese Nationalist League flag (青天白日) on the left and a Chinese republic flag (青天白日满地红) on the right. A large crowd of people, including local members, delegates from the Chinese Nationalist League branch in Ashcroft, and representatives of the Methodist school and the Methodist church minister attended the celebration. At the beginning of the cele-bration, Chan You, the English secretary of the branch, welcomed the guests and nationalist league members, and expounded the "Three Princi-ples of the People"[55] (三民主义) of the Chinese Nationalist League. Then Wong D. Dong, the president, addressed and informed the assembly about the "remarkable improvements politically, socially and financially in the league" in China and thanked the members for their support. Following this, Lee Wing, the Chinese secretary, read out congratulatory telegrams and letters from other party branches and friends of the Guomindang in

Canada. A few key members took turns speaking at the meeting, emphasizing the importance of friendship and business connections between Canadians and Chinese people. The celebration ended with Chow Ling leading the singing of the Chinese national anthem, after which a group photograph was taken. Then tea was served to all who were present.

On October 10, 1925, the Kamloops branch of the Chinese Nationalist League held a banquet to commemorate the fourteenth year since the Republic of China had been founded. In his address, President Wong D. Dong said, "We need not be discouraged by the failure of Chinese militarism. The cause of constitutional changes in government is stronger than ever... What is happening now amounts to a demonstration of the impossibility of solving China's problem by substituting one group of militarists for another..." His speech reflected the power struggles among the warlords in various provinces and the breakdown of the republican government at the national level. He encouraged the Chinese Nationalist League members to strive for "true Chinese republicanism."

The situation in China in that period had, indeed, caused great concern and anxiety among many Chinese immigrants. They had left their families in the country and could not bring them over to Canada for many reasons, chiefly those caused by the Canadian immigration acts. They felt lost and disturbed by their own financial inability to send for their loved ones, because many of them were living from hand to mouth. The infamous Chinese Exclusion Act, enacted in 1923, prohibited them from bringing their family members over. And they also had no desire to return home because of the uprisings of warlords, political turmoil and social disorder in China. They felt helpless having left their families in a homeland of endless insurrections. For this reason, they always wanted to obtain news about the situation in China.

From 1927 to 1942, the *Kamloops Sentinel* reported on the anniversary celebrations of the Chinese Nationalist League branch every year. On the eighth anniversary, a play was performed by a dramatic club from Vancouver to entertain guests and members.

The play began by introducing Jen Wai Kou, a very wealthy Chinese merchant in North America and his son, Jen Hong Ho, who decided to return to China with the intention of assisting the country to attain peace in whatever ways they could. After they arrived in Canton (Guangzhou), Ho enrolled in the Whampo Military Academy (黄埔军校) for military training. Meanwhile, he met and fell in love with Lee

The Chinese Nationalist League held an anniversary celebration every year. In 1928, they celebrated their eighth anniversary by putting on a play for their members, in association with a drama club from Vancouver. Courtesy of the Kamloops Museum and Archives #6985.

Get Yu, a female student at the Normal School in Guangzhou. But they promised each other they wouldn't get married until they had completed their training.

While Ho was at the military academy, Sue Shew Ching, a Chinese Communist leader in Guangzhou, and his party members looted and burned houses, killing and murdering people. Ho's family was slaughtered! Lee detested the Chinese Communist Party and enlisted in the nationalist army in Guangdong. Soon she was sent to Chungchow as a member of the military reserve, ready to fight the warlords in the north.

After completing his military training in the Whampo Military Academy, Ho returned home and found that his father and family members had been killed by the Communists and his sweetheart Lee had disappeared. He vowed to take revenge. In the meantime, the national revolutionary army recruited and sent him to Zhangzhou, the very place where Lee was stationed. He and Lee were then reunited in Zhangzhou.

In the finale, both Ho and Lee went to the front with the national revolutionary army in the Northern Expedition under the command of Chiang Kai Shek (蔣介石) and defeated the warlords, thus uniting north and south China.

The Chinese Nationalist Leaue, also known as Guomindang, at their eighth anniversary celebration in 1928. The celebrations were decorated with a large photograph of Sun Yat-Sen, the
president of the Republic of China. Courtesy of the Kamloops Museum and Archives #6986.

The scriptwriter, Gaw Han Kin, had skilfully woven a romance into
a political drama that informed the audience about the turbulent situation
in China. The little fantasy was certainly entertaining, and the revolutionary story played upon the feelings and empathy of the Chinese immigrants
for China. The play was propaganda against the Communist Party.

On March 10, 1929, the Chinese Nationalist League in Kamloops
celebrated its ninth anniversary in a similar fashion. However, a large
photograph of Chiang Kai Shek was hung beside that of Sun Yat-sen.
At the assembly, one of the executive members declared that "this is the
first year the Nationalist Party in China has achieved triumph over the
warlords... The new nationalist government established in Nanking is
recognized by foreign powers as the central government of the Chinese
republic."[56] He believed that the new government would transform China
into a modern civilization and a prosperous country. He also informed the
audience that the Nanking nationalist government had issued $40,000,000
worth of bonds to which many Chinese people had eagerly subscribed.

As time went by, the Chinese Nationalist League established two
prominent sub-groups: the Morning Bell Dramatic Club (晨钟剧社) and

the Chinese Ladies Patriotic Committee. The dramatic club produced plays on anniversaries and at other important occasions such as the celebration of "Double Ten," a date on which the Chinese Nationalist League commemorated the success of the October 1911 Chinese revolution. The dramatic club also had an orchestra to accompany plays and other performances. Their productions reflected their patriotism towards China and advocacy for the Literary Revolution (文学革命), which escalated after the May 4th Movement (五四运动) of 1919.[57]

On November 18, 1930, the *Kamloops Sentinel* reported that the Chinese Nationalist League branch had held an event to raise funds for the local hospital. The play, "The Three Barons," produced by the dramatic club, had raised $400.00 for the hospital. Similarly, they raised another $270.00 for the Royal Inland Hospital in 1935. The newspaper reported that "the play 'Love Finds a Way' presented by the Morning Bell Dramatic Club under the auspices of the Chinese Nationalist League was excellent... Those who witnessed the play were lavish in their praise of the talent and of the beautiful Chinese costumes." These two plays denounced arranged marriages and other traditions that repressed the freedom and individual rights of their contemporaries.

In 1936, the local party branch donated a railway car full of produce to drought-stricken areas in Saskatchewan and delivered ten tons of produce annually to the Royal Inland Hospital. When Japan dropped a bomb on the Marco Polo Bridge in Beijing on July 7, 1937, triggering the Second Sino-Japanese War, Chinese Nationalist League branches throughout the world called upon their members to denounce the Japanese and to boycott Japanese goods. That kind of patriotism towards China influenced the Chinese vegetable growers and pickers in the Kamloops area; they threatened to quit work if their employers hired Japanese people at the farms and orchards.

On December 3, 1942, the *Kamloops Sentinel* reported that the Chinese Ladies Patriotic Committee held a tea reception to raise funds for the Red Cross Relief Fund in China. At the reception, Dr. Margaret Forster of the Tranquille Hospital, who had spent twelve years in China, was invited to speak about the changes and situation in China in recent years. Tea was served by a number of Chinese ladies, including Leung Lin, the mother of Peter Wing. At the end of this tea party, a vote of thanks was given by Peter Wing to Miss Queenie Chow, the chairperson of the ladies' committee.

After the formation of the People's Republic of China (中华人民共和国), this local Chinese Nationalist League branch gradually disappeared.

But it was a surprise to find in March 1990 a plaque installed by the local branch commemorating its comrades in the Chinese Heritage Cemetery.

The Wing or Eng Family

In 1901, Eng Wing Him (吴荣添) immigrated to Canada at the age of sixteen, sponsored by his uncle, a member of the Methodist parish. When he arrived, the immigration officer registered his name as Wing Him, leaving out his surname Eng. Henceforth, he was known as Wing Him and Wing became his surname and the last name of his descendants.

The Methodist Chinese Mission in Kamloops taught Wing to read and write the Chinese language and to speak English, and found him a job as a houseboy and gardener in the Beattie family. Once he mastered enough spoken English, he went to work in a restaurant at the CPR station. In 1906, he partnered with a couple of friends to open the American Café and the Good Eats Café in the 200 and 300 blocks of Main Street respectively. The restaurant businesses flourished. When he had saved up enough money, he went home in 1911 to marry Leung Lin (梁莲), a bride chosen by his parents. In 1913, the couple returned to Kamloops. Wing paid the $500.00 head tax for Leung to gain entry to Canada. In Kamloops, they lived in a small house with a living room, a kitchen and two bedrooms in the 300 block of Lansdowne Street. On May 4, 1914, Peter, their first son, was born. As time went by, Wing and Leung had seven children: Peter, May (1915), Lily (1920), John (1923), James (1925), Jean (1927) and David (1936). After the birth of May, Leung began to suffer from chronic asthma.

"My father was a very resourceful person, a man with a good business sense," said Peter Wing. "In 1916, he and his partners bought the property at 258 Main (Victoria) Street, where they opened a general store, the City Cash Grocery, the first 'cash and carry' store in Kamloops. They also bought a 1913 Model T van to deliver goods to their clients." He paused to recollect his childhood days for a few seconds and continued, "When May and I were young, my parents did not buy us toys. Dad took the toys from the general store, let us play with them for a little while and then returned them to the shop for retailing. My father always said to us 'don't keep anything unless you have paid for it!' "

His father believed that his children—especially the first son—should help out in the family business. When Peter was old enough, he was assigned to work in the cafés. His tasks included breaking up lumps of coal to feed the kitchen ranges, washing dishes and peeling potatoes. His father taught his children to address all the chefs in the restaurants and the Chinese men of his generation as uncles and the women as aunties, a very traditional Chinese way of greeting the older generations.

Peter attended elementary school at the Stuart Wood School. The white students often scorned him with racist slurs such as "chingee, chingee, Chinaman, earn a dollar, spend two cents!" or teasing like "Peter, Peter, pumpkin eater." "As a child I felt offended and disturbed and told my parents about it," said Peter. "But my father advised me, 'No fight back, just walk away…! Remember, we are Chinese, peace-loving and tolerant people. Also, as Christians we should forgive.' This is the way my father taught me to handle racist situations."

Once Peter became competent in reading and writing English, he became his father's interpreter, especially when both father and son went to Vancouver to purchase supplies for their businesses. Peter read the names of goods and prices in English and checked invoices and bills of their purchases for his father.

The members of the Wing or Eng family were devoted Methodists. They always went to church on Sunday, rain or shine. When Peter turned eight, he took piano lessons and played the organ for Sunday services at the Methodist Mission Hall. He was an active member of the music ministry, and accompanied May Cheong at the organ by playing the violin. When the Methodist Mission Hall closed down in the late 1940s, he joined the choir in the Kamloops United Church.

After completing elementary school, Peter went to Kamloops High School. When he reached grade nine, he suffered from rheumatic fever and was hospitalized for some time. The doctors advised him to take long-term rest at home after he was discharged from the hospital, so he had to quit school. To him, the long period of rest was a blessing, because it offered him time to read many classics, such as *Tom Sawyer*, *David Copperfield*, *Lord of the Rings* and so on, books that were loaned to him by A. C. Taylor, the superintendent of the Methodist Sunday school. Taylor also sent him *World Travels* magazines and publications by Margaret Meade, the well-known anthropologist. These readings shaped his views and understanding of people, cultures and government, which motivated and guided him in public service later on.

When he wasn't reading, Peter watched cars passing by from the windows of his room and listened to the sound of their engines. Gradually he became able to identify many models of automobiles by their engine sound without looking at them as they went by. During his period of recuperation, his father bought the first family radio, which required him to scan the airwaves in order to tune into distant broadcasting stations. After his father traded the family car, a Model T roadster, for a Chevrolet sedan, Peter became the family's chauffeur, driving the family around and occasionally taking his father to Paul Lake to fish. He did not go back to school full-time after he had recovered. Instead, he took a special commercial course in the high school that helped him develop business strategies.

In a wedding arranged by their parents, Peter Wing (top left) and Kim Kwong (top right) were married at the Chinese Mission Hall in 1932. They remained important members of the Kamloops community for decades, as Peter became the first Chinese-Canadian mayor in Canada. Courtesy of the Kamloops Museum and Archives, photo collection #6877.

The family business expanded and became a grocery dealer for other stores, not only in Kamloops, but also in other places, such as Kelowna, Vernon and Revelstoke. In 1930, Peter left school and worked with his father in a new grocery store, the Cut Rate Self-Serve Grocery. The same year, the Wings purchased a lot at the corner of Victoria Street and Third Avenue, contemplating erecting a building on the property. The idea of building a house motivated Peter to study plumbing and electrical wiring.

In 1931, Peter met the Kwong girls—Jean, Kim and Doris—from Revelstoke. They are the daughters of Wong Kwong (黄光), one of the Wings' business associates. Like the Wings, Wong Kwong had his family name and first name mixed up by an immigration officer when he first arrived in Canada. So Kwong became the family name. The Kwong girls went to Kamloops to visit their brother, Sam Kwong, who was hospitalized in the King Edward Sanitarium at Tranquille. Peter was asked to pick the girls up when they arrived in Kamloops. This mission offered Peter the opportunity to meet and get acquainted with the girls, a rare occasion for young Chinese males at that time. Later, Kim Kwong married Peter. One wonders if there was romantic rendezvous between the couple prior to their wedding.

"No romance," said Peter. "Actually, we hardly went out by ourselves. Whenever we went out, some of my siblings or hers always tagged along! After the girls came visiting a few times, both families recognized that Kim and I were compatible, so they arranged an engagement for Kim and me. A few months later, Kim's father passed on. Since we were already engaged, Mr. Yee, the gentleman who looked after the Kwong family, suggested to my parents that they organize the wedding." He paused, turned around to look at his loving wife who sat nearby, smiled and continued, "It is my greatest blessing to have married her. She has been my pillar, supporting me in all my endeavours! Our lives together are truly destined by God."

On November 6, 1932, the wedding of Peter and Kim took place at the Chinese Mission Hall in Kamloops. Peter's parents then held a reception in the hall for relatives and friends. After the wedding, the newlywed couple lived with Peter's parents and his siblings. Kim managed the household and took care of her mother-in-law, who was suffering from asthma. A few months later, Wing went with a few family members to Hong Kong, leaving Peter and May, the second daughter, to look after the family business. In 1934, Wing returned from Hong Kong so that Peter and Kim could go visit relatives in Hong Kong for a couple of months. When they returned to Kamloops, Kim was pregnant. Unfortunately, her pregnancy ended with a miscarriage.

Besides operating the grocery business and participating in the Methodist church activities, Peter often helped interpret English for Chinese merchants in town as well as in court proceedings. He was invited to join the Kamloops Board of Trade and became the youngest member on the board. In 1953, he was elected as its president. He continued serving the organization for many years. In 1942, he joined the Kamloops chapter of the International Rotary Club and served on many committees of the club. Among the its many activities, Peter felt the student exchange program was most invaluable, since it promoted goodwill and understanding among different nations. He was elected president of the Rotary Chapter in 1967–77 and as governor of District 506 in 1981–82. His involvement with the Rotary Club offered him and his wife opportunities to meet people from many nations as well as travel to different countries, such as Brazil and the United States, to attend conferences. These activities widened their social contacts.

In 1943, Peter bought an orchard of thirty-five acres (fourteen hectares) with a building and equipment for fruit cultivation from George Oishi, a Japanese immigrant. Oishi was forced to leave Kamloops for an internment camp, so he had no choice but to sell his property. Prior to going to the internment camp, Oishi taught Peter the skills required to manage the orchard. Peter also gave him a fair deal for the property and vowed to assist him in whatever way possible while he was in the camp and after the internment. Certainly, a good friendship had developed between these young men, even though Chinese then were not supposed to associate with Japanese people.

The building at the orchard was the first house bought and owned by Peter and Kim, but it became a family gathering place for the Wings. Peter's parents and siblings often visited the couple to see if they could help out in any way. Their visits kept Kim busy preparing tea, snacks and meals for her in-laws.

To cultivate an orchard, Peter had to learn how to operate and maintain the equipment as well as how to manage the irrigation system, leading him to acquire another manual skill. The fruit-growing business prompted Peter to associate with the BC Fruit Growers' Association (BCFGA). In 1944, he was appointed as a director of the BCFGA in the Kamloops area and held that position for thirteen years. Although he was busy operating the orchard and getting involved with community work, he did not neglect helping out with the Wings' family businesses. In 1947, his father constructed the Wing Building at the corner of Third Avenue and Victoria Street. Peter was responsible for overseeing the construction and undertaking half of the electrical wiring in the building. The same year, Wing became a Canadian citizen.

While working on the farm, Peter was often required to lift heavy equipment that strained the muscles of his back, giving him great pain. In 1954, he went for major back surgery. Meanwhile, the BC fruit industry was facing fierce competition from growers in California and Oregon, causing fruit growing in the Okanagan to become less profitable. His back problems plus the poor economy in the fruit-growing industries made Peter decide to sell the orchard in 1957. Then he joined Hall and Pruden Real Estate and became a real estate and insurance agent. Within two years, he had bought the business and renamed it Peter Wing Real Estate.

Peter also engaged in civic politics. In the fall of 1959, he ran in the municipal election and was elected as an alderman. He served on the Kamloops city council for three consecutive terms. As an alderman, he attended the meeting of the Okanagan Valley Municipal Association and was elected as a director. When he became president of the association, he proposed that it change its name to the Okanagan-Mainline Municipal Association (OMMA). In 1963, he was appointed to represent the OMMA at the twenty-sixth annual conference of the Federation of Mayors and Municipalities.

The First Chinese-Canadian Mayor

In the fall of 1965, Peter ran for the position of mayor in the Kamloops municipal election and defeated his opponents, C. H. Day, the former mayor, and alderman J. G. Boultbee, who were both in the race. He captured 880 votes and became the very first Chinese-Canadian mayor, not only in BC but also in the country.[58] Soon after he took office as the mayor of Kamloops, he participated in a series of national and international events such as the conference in Arnprior, Ontario, that explored the roles of local government in the outbreak of disease epidemics and the International Union of Local Authorities in Bangkok, among other events. In 1968, he was invited by W. A. C. Bennett, BC's premier, to be one of BC's delegates at the Constitutional Conference in Ottawa. Peter was very impressed by the statement on a constitutional charter of human rights that was presented by the late Hon. P. E. Trudeau, then the minister of justice and the attorney general. "This is the most significant conference I ever attended," Peter said.

As time went by, Peter's eyesight became very poor and his back problem recurred. In 1971, he retired from the mayor's office, but he remained active in the community. The same year, his father, Wing, passed away. But his mother, Leong Lin, lived on until she reached the age of ninety-nine. In 1990, Peter went for another surgery on his back. A few years later, he and Kim moved down to Vancouver, where many of his siblings, nieces and nephews were living. On December 27, 2007, Peter died at the age of eighty-three from a stroke. His deeds and contributions to Kamloops and Canada are enormous—very commendable and admirable. In his lifetime, he received many awards including the Freeman, City of Kamloops (1972), the Order of Canada (1976), the Queen's Jubilee medal (1977), the Order of British Columbia (1990), the 125th Confederation Anniversary

Medal (1992) and many others.[59] The history of his family, the Wing or Eng family, provides a good memoir of the Chinese community in Kamloops at the dawn of the twentieth century.

Maintenance of the Chinese Cemetery Continued

During the 1920s, improvements on the cemetery took place. A fence was built around it with cement corner posts, and incense burners and an altar were erected. The burials of the deceased there occurred between 1930 and 1960. After the People's Republic of China was founded on October 1, 1949, the Chinese Nationalist League in Kamloops gradually declined, so the Kamloops Chinese Freemasons society became the only group that looked after the cemetery. In 1956, the City of Kamloops initiated a meeting with the society and representatives of the Chinese community to form the Kamloops Chinese Cemetery Association, and entrusted the association with the responsibility of looking after the cemetery for the city, which held the land title to the site. The Chinese community recognized the need to expand the site. Through the efforts of the association, the Chinese community raised sufficient funds to purchase the adjacent land.

Joe Leung, the former president of the Kamloops Chinese Cultural Association, standing in front of the pavilion in the Chinese [heritage] Cemetary. Photo courtesy of the author.

The site of the Chinese Cemetery was then extended to cover an area of about 3,035 square metres (0.75 acres).[60]

In March 1971, the Chinese Cemetery was registered under the Crown. The last burial occurred in 1976. In April 1979, the Chinese Cemetery was officially closed to future burials, but those who were buried there were not forgotten. Friends and members of the Chinese Cemetery Association took responsibility for getting new wooden markers on which they wrote "Rest in Peace" in Chinese characters (入土为安) for many of the unknown deceased Chinese, especially the CPR workers, who were buried there.

Over the years, the City of Kamloops together with the association attempted to upgrade and improve the site of the Chinese Cemetery. In 1979, the city and the Chinese community invited Donald Luxton and Associates and Dr. David Chuenyan Lai to study the site and offer suggestions to improve its appearance. After the study, these experts produced and delivered a proposal including architectural blueprints for upgrading the site. The city and the Chinese community accepted the proposal and executed the plan. In 1982, the Chinese Cemetery was declared a Kamloops heritage site. Subsequently, a gate in authentic Chinese architectural style was erected, with two stone lions installed on each side of the gate. These stone lions, donated by the Chinese Consulate General in Vancouver, were shipped from Guangdong. On March 31, 1996, the Chinese consul general, Mr. Zhou Xinpei, and other consuls from the Vancouver General Consulate of the People's Republic of China visited the cemetery and painted the eyes of the stone lions at the entrance to the cemetery with red paint.

In March 1998, a new committee for maintaining the Kamloops Chinese Cemetery was struck. Subsequently, the Kamloops Chinese Heritage Cemetery Society was established with the city's endorsement. On April 6 the same year, the society approached the Kamloops Chinese Freemasons society to contribute to the restoration and preservation of the Chinese Cemetery.

In both past and present years, relatives and friends have brought flowers, fruits and foods, such as roast pork, boiled chickens, steamed buns and so on, to pay homage to the deceased in the cemetery during the Qing Ming Festival, a season in which the departed ones are honoured. In the Qing Ming season, many Chinese organizations visit the cemetery collectively to pay respect to those who are buried there and to help clean up the graves. In front of the markers, they place offerings including white wine and black tea. They also burn artificial paper money and silver and gold leaves printed on brown papers on the gravesites to symbolize sending money to the spirits of the deceased. After the ritual, the participants usually consume the food in the cemetery before returning home, a practice commonly referred to by the younger generations of Chinese Canadians as a picnic in the cemetery. Actually, Qing Ming Day is referring to the day of clarity and brightness of the year and is known as a cold food day in many villages in China.

Today, this cemetery is looked after by Kamloops Chinese Heritage Cemetery Society, which comprises the City of Kamloops, the Kamloops Chinese Freemasons society and the Kamloops Chinese Cultural Association. They are responsible for upgrading and preserving this Kamloops Chinese-Canadian heritage site and plan to create an authentic Chinese garden within the cemetery. Today, the Chinese Cemetery is the only historic landmark of the Chinese community that remains in Kamloops.

The Kamloops Chinese Cultural Association

The Kamloops Chinese Cultural Association, a non-profit social and cultural organization, aims to promote Chinese culture, encourage cultural exchange and support charitable activities and community goodwill programs. It was incorporated in 1977. Over the years, the cultural association has hosted Asian Heritage Month in May, participated in Canada Day by setting up a food booth, and observed and celebrated the Dragon Boat Festival in summer and the Mid-Autumn Moon Festival. It also supports the University of the Cariboo, now Thompson Rivers University, through scholarship and bursary programs, and engages in many cultural and social activities with the Chinese students and teachers who come from overseas. In the past, the cultural association has raised funds for the Royal Inland Hospital to purchase medical equipment. As mentioned above, the Kamloops Chinese Cultural Association has been a key member of the Kamloops Chinese Heritage Cemetery Society and has played a vital role in preserving and maintaining the Kamloops Chinese Cemetery. When Qing Ming Day arrived, Joe Leong, the former president of the Kamloops Chinese Cultural Association, and his wife would lead some members to the cemetery to clean up the graves and offer sacrifices to the deceased who were buried there. In the last two decades, Leong and his wife, as well as a few dedicated cultural association members, have taken responsibility for replacing the old and rotten markers with new ones. And they wrote

"Rest in Peace" in Chinese characters (入土为安) on new wooden markers for many of the unknown deceased.

Joe Leong immigrated to Canada with his mother in 1954 but his father and uncle arrived in 1937. The senior Leongs ran the Lin On Farm on the Musqueam Indian reserve, now known as the Chinese Market Gardens. They felt safe and found peace on the farm. Yet after Leong joined his father, he often heard his father crying at midnight and telling his mother that he could not make enough money or could not get a loan to raise his family and to send money to his own mother at home. "In the early days, they [his father and uncle] could only sell their produce to Chinatown merchants [in Vancouver]," said Leong. "There was too much competition from other Chinese farmers."

Gone are the hard times for Leong. Today, he is a well-known and respected Chinese Canadian in Kamloops. It is not known when he came to Kamloops, but he was a founding member of the Kamloops Chinese Cultural Association and held the position of president for many years. He was instrumental in organizing the Folkfest, the celebration of Canada Day on July 1, together with the Kamloops Multicultural Society for a number of years and building bridges between the Chinese community and other ethnic groups in Kamloops. The many initiatives and projects of the Kamloops Chinese Cultural Association mentioned above were implemented and achieved under his leadership.

In 1990, Leong entered civic politics and was elected as a councillor to the Kamloops city council; he held the position of councillor for five consecutive terms and was the second-longest sitting councillor in Kamloops city hall. He was also the treasurer of the Kamloops Heritage Railway Society and a board member of the Kamloops Multicultural Society.

In August 2004, Leong initiated the "Heroes of Confederation," a project of the Kamloops Chinese Cultural Association. The main objective of the project is to celebrate and recognize the Chinese labourers who worked on constructing the Canadian Pacific Railway as nation-builders who contributed to the Confederation of Canada. He has also contemplated establishing a Kamloops Heritage Railway Museum in the future. The project of the Heroes of Confederation motivated the Canadian Pacific Railway company to designate the interchange of the Canadian National Railway and the Canadian Pacific Railway at the Kamloops Railway Station as the Cheng Interchange in honour of Cheng Ging Butt, one of the Chinese labourers who built the CPR in BC.

Today, Leong has stepped down as president of the Kamloops Chinese Cultural Association but as past president continues giving advice to the new board. He is still very active in the association and plays a vital role in the Kamloops Chinese Heritage Cemetery Society on its behalf. Currently, the president of the Kamloops Chinese Cultural Association is Dr. Dali Li (李达立牙医), a Kamloops dentist who is also an energetic and enthusiastic community activist.

A Well-Known First Nations Man with Chinese Ancestry

Besides the late Peter Wing and Joe Leong, Gordon Chow, a First Nations man with Chinese ancestry, also attempted to engage in civic politics. Chow has resided in Kamloops for more than forty years. His mother, Annie Helen, a member of the North Bend-Boston Bar First Nation, married Quai On Chow, who immigrated to Canada from Guangdong in the 1920s. Gordon Chow was educated in Kamloops and attended high school at NorKam Secondary School. He was soft-spoken and good-natured, a hard-working and likable person who never gossiped about other people. He worked for Stan Brevik as a painter for more than thirty years. When he went to paint the house for Brevik, who rented it out to Councillor Pat Wallace, he and Wallace often talked about politics. Wallace was amazed by how much Chow knew about federal, provincial and local politics. "He was not an uneducated man," commented Wallace.

Chow's grade twelve English teacher, Pierce Graham, remarked that his "clarity of thought, intensity of effort, and sincerity of purpose in his writing were, quite obviously, memorable." Indeed, Chow was a knowledgeable person who spent his leisure time reading different kinds of magazines and books. His favourite movies were the Harry Potter series.

"Some people misjudged him [Chow]. He was a labourer by trade but he knew about math and economics, very smart. And he knew what made a community and a country tick," added Mel Rothenburger.[61]

Chow entered the mayoral race in the Kamloops municipal election in 1988 and 2011 but was defeated in both elections. He came third in the 2011 election, with 441 votes. On March 7, 2014, he died of heart failure at the age of sixty-four, predeceased by his mother, who had passed away in 1980, and his brother, Charlie, who died in 2013. Chow was buried in Hillside Cemetery in Kamloops.

Kamloops Chinese Heritage Recognized

In January 2016, the Kamloops Chinese Heritage Cemetery was recognized as a Chinese Canadian Heritage Site by the Legacy Initiatives Advisory Council of the Ministry of International Trade and Responsible for Asia Pacific Strategy and Multiculturalism and the Ministry of Forests, Lands and Natural Resource Operations. In March 2017, a commemorative plaque for the site was installed by the Kamloops Chinese Canadian Heritage Society on the site. Minister Teresa Wat of the international trade ministry, Minister Todd Stone of the Ministry of Transport and Infrastructure and Minister Terry Lake of the Ministry of Health, some members of the Legacy Initiatives Advisory Council, and more than a hundred people from the community attended the event when the plaque was unveiled at the cemetery.

VERNON: THE PAST COW TOWN

The City of Vernon is located between Swan Lake and Kalamalka Lake in the Okanagan Valley, territory of the Interior Salish First Nations—the Okanagan people (now Syilx). In the early days, this area was a rolling plain covered by luxuriant grassland dotted with deciduous trees. The landscape and mild weather attracted many pioneers to settle there and they created the townsite known as Priest Valley. In 1863, Forbes George Vernon and his older brother, Charles Albert Vernon, together with Colonel Charles F. Houghton, a Crimean veteran, immigrated to British Columbia and went north to the Okanagan Valley. The Vernon brothers mined at Cherry Creek and pre-empted the land between Priest Valley and Okanagan Landing.[62]

In 1864, Charles F. Houghton pre-empted the land along the banks of a stream in this area and established the Coldstream Ranch. Two years later, he exchanged the Coldstream Ranch for the property of the Vernon brothers at Okanagan Landing. The Vernon brothers worked hard on the ranch and soon expanded it to 5,261 hectares (13,000 acres), which helped develop the Priest Valley. In 1894, the Coldstream Ranch was sold to Lord Aberdeen.

The city of Vernon. Courtesy of the Royal BC Museum and Archives B-03298.

At the same time, Frank J. Barnard, a pioneer of transportation in British Columbia, also established a ranch, the BX, north of Priest Valley, to raise horses for his trains of stagecoaches that transported miners and goods from Ashcroft to the Cariboo goldfields.[63] In 1892, when the construction of the Shuswap and Okanagan Railway from Sicamous to Okanagan Lake was completed, the railway (a CPR subsidiary) became the main mode of transportation, and this transformed the townsite of Priest Valley into a busy city. In December of that year, the town was incorporated as a city named Vernon, in honour of the Vernon brothers. Soon the City of Vernon, the oldest city in the Okanagan, became the centre of all federal and provincial government services in the region. Today, Vernon is a tourist centre, famous for its outdoor recreational activities, such as horse riding, boating, canoeing and swimming, in addition to its production of dairy products, fruits and wines.

Chinese Migration

After the Fraser gold rush, around 1862, many miners, including the Chinese, either moved north to the Cariboo or east to the Big Bend and Wild Horse in the Kootenay to continue making their fortune in mining. Some Chinese miners, however, migrated to the Okanagan. In 1867, May Long Gue and twenty other Chinese miners were noted panning for gold in Mission Creek and in Cherry Creek.[64] The gushing streams from these creeks provided plenty of water for sluicing. Besides mining, a few of the Chinese miners cultivated garden patches along the banks of these creeks.[65] As more Chinese miners migrated to the area, some of them lived in Vernon and walked about sixty kilometres to their claims for placer mining. Ng Shu Kwong and Chang Yee were two of these. After he stopped mining, Ng went to work for S. C. Smith Lumber in Vernon. In later years, Ng opened Kwong Hing Lung, a grocery store at the corner of Coldstream Avenue and Thirty-fourth Street. But the *Vernon News* reported on May 19, 1892, that Chang had died a pauper. The local government looked after his burial and the government agent buried his body in the garden patch behind the government office.

In 1885, Cayopye Hwang, a Chinese labourer on the Canadian Pacific Railway, was laid off. He went to Cherry Creek to pan for gold. Luck wasn't with him, so he abandoned mining and went to Kamloops to work as a houseboy for Mr. Cotton. Five years later, he came to Priest Valley and worked at odd jobs. Later, he opened a general store in town.

Formal portrait of the Kwong family of Vernon. Left to right: Mrs. Kwong, Harry Kwong and Mr. Kwong holding Bertha Kwong. Courtesy of the Greater Vernon Museum and Archives 1362.

Like Hwang, many unemployed Chinese labourers came to the area and took odd jobs as cooks and kitchen helpers in restaurants, as domestic servants in private homes and as casual workers on ranches, in orchards and in vegetable gardening.[66]

Chinese Workers on Ranches

Indeed, a good number of ranchers hired Chinese labourers to work on their ranches. The late Walter Joe, a long-time Vernon resident, said that Chow You and Lum Lit were two of the Chinese employees of the O'Keefe Ranch in the early days.

In 1896, Frank Barnard hired Harold Parke to manage the BX Ranch. His wife, Alice Barrett, kept a diary recording the work of Lou-ee, her Chinese cook, and Ah Chung, the gardener at the BX Ranch. In her diary, Alice wrote, "He [Lou-ee] was a very good cook and often prepared some delicious desserts or snacks such as ice cream, plum pudding and

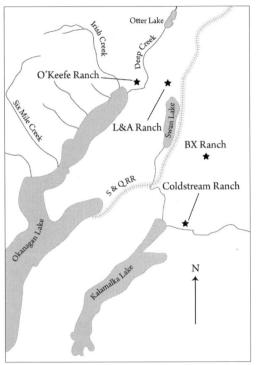

The land in and around Vernon made for fruitful farmland, so several ranches were established. These ranches provided a variety of jobs for Vernon's Chinese residents, like farmhands or housekeepers.

others for the family... Hal says I have certainly won Lou-ee's heart, for he always has some extra little dainty ready for our table."[67]

Parke commented that Lou-ee was a conscientious worker and would perform any tasks required of him. He helped mend the store-room, washed the walls of the house, and pickled green tomatoes for the family. Once, Alice accidentally cut the knuckle of her first finger with a piece of broken glass. The wound was deep and a chunk of skin had peeled off at the knuckle. Immediately, Lou-ee volunteered to do all of the washing and other household chores for her and continued to do so until her wound was healed. His good heart and kind spirit touched her. "He is not supposed to do all the work [for me]," wrote Alice in her diary.

Alice admitted she was prejudiced against Chinese people before meeting Lou-ee. Many of her acquaintances had advised her to be very strict and exacting with Chinamen. They told her, "You can't give them any privileges or they will take advantage of you." But in her diary she remarked, "I think it is a mistake... I am beginning to think that perhaps Chinamen are not as bad as they were painted, and they act differently... because they are treated unlike them [whites]."

She also reflected on the news about a great many people wanting to raise the head tax on the Chinese from $50.00 to $500.00. On February 7, 1897, she wrote:

I don't think it is right to tax them at all. One cannot help seeing that it is a "curse come home to roost" on the Chinese themselves.

For so many years they closed their ports to foreigners and now the boomerang has returned to their own head a blow... We despised and blamed the Chinese for being so narrow and selfish and now we turn around and follow their example... If we have awakened their hatred and antagonism, it isn't going to make matters any better for us... I don't see any sense in shutting them out. I suppose I have not enough knowledge to be a judge in these national problems.

It is fortunate that Alice expressed her sensible outlook on the Chinese issues. Like many, she could see the misconceptions and misunderstandings of the white community about the Chinese people. During the anti-Chinese movements motivated by the Workingmen's Protective Association in 1878, any arguments that favoured the Chinese would have been considered a betrayal. However, Alice was correct in her comments about China closing its ports to foreigners, because over the past thousand years China had been very conservative in its foreign policy. The decline of the Qing dynasty was partly due to its closed-door policy, which triggered the intrusion of western powers into China, and partly because of the Qing government's incompetence in dealing with the foreign aggressors.

In her diary, Alice recorded one interesting episode about Lou-ee bargaining with an Indigenous woman:

The other day a Native woman brought a string of fish to the Ranch and attempted to sell them to Lou-ee. Neither of them could understand the language of the other. I peeped through the window and watched the amusing bargaining. "Haf a dolla," Lou-ee said and pointed at all the salmon. "Good salmon, good salmon..." chanted the Native woman. Apparently, she could not make out Lou-ee's offering. After some haggling back and forth, Lou-ee decided that the fish were no good, and the Native woman did not make a sale."[68]

Communication between Alice and Lou-ee was a challenge. "I wish he could speak English," wrote Alice in her diary. "I believe he understands me better than I understand him... Nearly everyone talks a kind of broken English to the Chinamen. I don't wonder they never learn to speak well."

Lou-ee, too, felt frustrated when he could not make his employers and the white workers understand him. Alice came to his aid and took the initiative to teach him English, half an hour in each session in the evening. In the beginning, Lou-ee could not recognize or pronounce the alphabet, but he wrote some Chinese characters beside each letter to help him remember. He loved to learn reading and writing English. Since he was keen to learn, Alice often extended her instruction time for him. After six lessons, he was able to spell his name in English. Alice then bought him some books with both Chinese and English words so that he could speed up his learning. When he received the books, he grinned from ear to ear and bowed to Alice many times to express his gratitude. Alice once asked him how long it took him to learn the Chinese language. He said seven years and he had attended school for eleven years in China. He told Alice that students in China went to school at 5:00 am and returned home for breakfast at 7:00 am. By 7:30 am, they would be back at school to continue their lessons until noon. They went home for lunch and returned to school for lessons until 7:00 pm.[69]

In reality, Alice treated Lou-ee more like a friend than an employee. At one time, Lou-ee was sick to his stomach and looked very miserable. He tied a piece of a white cloth around his head and told Alice that "all the same knives [are] sticking in my head." She offered to help him with his cooking and other chores, but he refused because he felt he could handle the work. But she washed the dishes after meals that day.

Lou-ee was not only a dedicated servant but also a grateful person who often made efforts to show his appreciation to his employers. Besides his day off on Sunday, he seldom took leave on working days except two occasions—Chinese New Year and the day when his cousin, Ah Jim in Vernon, left for China. Usually he went to town and bought some gifts on one of his Sunday trips before the Chinese New Year. In 1897, he gave Hal a box of cigars and a beautiful big white silk handkerchief and Alice two embroidered silk handkerchiefs, a pot of preserved ginger and some oranges as Chinese New Year's gifts. Again, the day before he went off for the Chinese New Year celebrations, he gave them one bottle of whisky and one bottle of Chinese wine. He always finished whatever jobs he had to get done before going to Vernon for the festive celebration and promptly returned to work the next evening.

On May 25, 1897, Lou-ee's cousin, Ah Jim, returned from China. Lou-ee cancelled the English lesson that night and went to Vernon to visit his cousin. A few months later, Ah Jim came to the ranch to visit him, and they spent nearly the whole afternoon talking. After this visit, Lou-ee asked for a few days off to go with Ah Jim to Penticton, but he arranged for Ah Sing, another cousin, to replace him. Although Ah Sing was pretty clean and did his job well, Alice still preferred Lou-ee. She hoped that Ah Jim would not persuade Lou-ee to stay in Penticton, because a cook could earn $40.00 a month at a hotel in Penticton, whereas he was paid only $25.00 working at the ranch. She was very happy when Lou-ee returned to the ranch after five days.

Alice also recorded her observations of Ah Chung, the Chinese gardener. She mentioned that Ah Chung was rather bold and comical, read English quite well and liked to use long words. He was a good gardener, and watered and weeded the flower garden well and trimmed the paths in the garden beautifully. On one occasion, he told her that girls in China usually get married at the age of seventeen. He said his sister, who was nineteen years old, had already given birth to two sons after two years of marriage. After December 10, 1897, the record of these two Chinese men faded from Alice's diary; what happened to them remains unknown.

Chinese Farmlands

Many Chinese settlers turned to farming in the Okanagan Valley. They leased land from the white ranchers and farmers as well as from the local Indigenous people to cultivate vegetable gardens. Among them were Mar Que, Lee Kar Shong, Lee Kee, Oh He Fong and Walter Joe.[70] "Leong Bai Choy had a vegetable farm on the Indian reserve," stated Joe. "He was the first Chinese to rent the land from Okanagan Band No. 1. In 1929, Leong passed away and Lee Kee went there to continue farming." In later years, Joe himself also leased three or more acres (1.2 hectares) of land from the O'Keefe Ranch to grow produce for his Joe Market at 3203 Twenty-eighth Street (Ellison).

The Chinese farmlands covered a large area along the shores of Coldstream Creek as far as Lavington on the east, on the Bella Vista Road northeast of Okanagan Lake, and to the north as far as the O'Keefe Ranch. On their cultivated land, they grew potatoes, tomatoes, carrots and Chinese vegetables such as bai choy, winter melons and other produce. One of the biggest crops was onions. The farmers supplied restaurants and grocery stores with their produce, and some peddled the vegetables from door to door downtown.

The success of Chinese vegetable gardening created fear and resentment among the white farmers. On January 10, 1917, Thomas Richmond addressed the members of the Farmers' Institute at a meeting. He pointed out the "undesirable" elements of renting cultivated lands to Chinese farmers. He claimed that Chinese farmers did not practise crop rotation, thereby depleting nutrients from the soil. He accused them of paying more in rent, thereby giving white men no chance to bid for the land. The Chinese could stand the heat from the sun and worked longer hours in the fields each day. They made good profits on their produce but they sent the greater part of their earnings to China, thus making a constant drain on the wealth of the country. Richmond emphasized that the money should remain in this land for the betterment and prosperity of the country. He was annoyed that the Chinese farmers sold and shipped their produce directly to Chinese companies instead of through a white company. He feared that within a short time the Chinese farmers would take control of the shipping industry. The system of management in the Chinese farming industry also disturbed him. When a Chinese farmer rented land, he secured the necessary labour by forming a company with two or three of his countrymen. He provided his partners only with food and lodging and paid them no wages. His partners were only paid from the profits after they sold the produce. And the Chinese company purchased its farming equipment, other supplies and provisions from Chinese merchants on credit. The Chinese management system imposed some problems on the labour market, said Richmond. The enterprising Chinese men preferred to form their own farming companies, thus only the "lazy and worthless among them are left" for hiring by the white men's ranches and farms. However, he recognized that the white farmers could not get rid of the Chinese entirely, because their labour was very much needed on the ranches. "In plain words, we cannot get along without him [Chinese labour] today." And he urged the landowners not to rent out land for cultivation to the Chinese farmers. Instead, he recommended the landowners enter into partnerships with the Chinese farmers, making the Chinese raise the crops on a shared basis with the white farm owners. The white farmers would do all the selling, and then pay the Chinese their share in cash after the crops were sold.[71]

At least one Chinese-First Nations relationship resulted from the custom of Chinese farmers renting plots of land from local Indigenous people to cultivate vegetable gardens, and from hiring Indigenous people to help them in the fields. The Indigenous people and the early Chinese in Vernon not only worked together in agriculture, such as gardening and ranching, but also developed friendships, some of which led to intermarriage or common-law relationships. "My family worked in many fields that belonged to the Chinese, because Chinese farms… would hire Native people," said Dorothy Christian, an Okanagan-Shuswap woman with Chinese ancestry.[72] "I am the total sum of my Native mother and my Chinese father."

It was unclear when Dorothy's mother, Delphine Christian, entered into a common-law relationship with Dong Park, a Chinese farmer who worked in the area surrounding Vernon. Dorothy only knows that she is the first child the couple had. When she was born, her mother had just turned seventeen. She has only a very faint memory of her father, because she was raised by her grandparents after the relationship of her parents broke down. At the age of four, she was returned to her mother to live with her stepfather and other siblings. However, she had one sweet memory of her natural father.

"I don't know how old I was, perhaps two or three years old," wrote Dorothy. "He [Dong Park] came to the fields my family was working in. I had been sleeping in the back of a truck. Though I have tried, I cannot remember his face… as he pulls back the truck's tarp, calling for me to come out. He holds something out and encourages me to take it. It is candy… I eagerly grab and stuff it in my mouth. It is spicy, and I spit it out as quickly as I put it in my mouth, ginger candy."

The late Walter Joe met Dong Park at a few Chinese gathering places, such as the rooming houses of the few clan associations and the Chinese Freemasons building. Joe said that Dong came from Panyu County, Guangdong, but he did not know when Dong immigrated to Canada. "We [Joe and Dong's friends] do not know if he has a family in China. But we all know that Dong used to work as market gardener either in Vernon or Enderby. At times, he worked for other farmers but there were occasions when he rented out plots from other people for farming. Judging from the age of his death, it is most likely he came to Canada prior to 1923," stated Joe.

"Dong Park was quite a tall and handsome guy, and very closely resembled Thelma, his second daughter," said Mrs. Hughie Jong in Armstrong. "At the time when we met him he was a market gardener in Coldstream. His wife, Delphine, and children used to dine in our restaurant and talk to us. We closed down the restaurant business about ten years ago and we lost touch with them." Dong Park passed away at the age of sixty on July 20, 1964, and was buried in the Vernon Cemetery on Pleasant Valley Road.

Vernon's Chinatown

At the turn of the nineteenth century, the Chinese population in Vernon was about a thousand people,[73] but the numbers fluctuated with harvest seasons, said Walter Joe. The Chinese settlers were mainly retirees from mining, ranches and farms. Many Chinese farmers did not want to continue gardening when the leases to their land expired, added Joe. Meanwhile, Chinese people from nearby regions and the Lower Mainland migrated to Vernon to start small businesses. Most of the Chinese homes and businesses were located in the downtown area between Twenty-eighth Avenue (Ellison) and Thirty-third Street (Vance). This area of the Chinese settlement was commonly referred to as Chinatown. The Chinese houses were "unpainted, boxlike, two-storey buildings. They were dimly lit. In the background, the unfamiliar tones of a stringed instrument were heard... Noise coming from one building [indicated] a gambling game was underway. Everything was serene."[74]

A few old-timers remembered some well-known Chinese settlers in the Chinese community. For example, Guang Chong, a retired miner, had established Kwong Sing Long, a general store at the corner between Twenty-

Kwong Lung Chan was one of the Chinese general stores in Vernon's flourishing Chinatown in the early twentieth century. Courtesy of the Greater Vernon Museum and Archives 2725.

ninth Avenue and Thirty-third Street (Vance). Later, he opened another Chinese general store, Kwong Lung Chan, at the corner of Twenty-eighth Avenue and Thirty-third Street.[75] On the second floor of this store was the Hua Yin Restaurant, the first Chinese restaurant in Vernon.

Loo Jim, an Elder in the Chinese community, migrated to Vernon after the completion of the CPR in 1885. He owned and operated Kong Wing Tai, a grocery store near the present-day Canton Restaurant.

Lee Siong Bing opened a laundry shop on Thirty-fifth Street near the present Safeway store. Later, he left his laundry shop and opened a general store known as Sung Lee Lung at the corner of Twenty-eighth Avenue and Thirty-third Street. He was also a labour contractor who recruited workers from the Lower Mainland and the surrounding districts to pick fruit in harvest season at ranches and orchards. In 1931, he returned to China and left his business, property and personal effects to his two sons, Lee Wing Sing and Lee Mon Cow.[76]

Hop Sing, a laundry shop, was located at the corner of Thirty-second Street and Coldstream Street (28A Avenue); and Hong Kee, another laundry, was located at 2810 Thirty-third Street, the current address of the Hong Kong Village Restaurant.[77] The Chinese restaurants consisted of

View of Vernon's Chinatown businesses, located on twenty-eighth Avenue looking east. Some of the businesses shown include: Kwong Hing Chong Co., Kwong Yuen Chong Co. and Wing Wah Lung. Courtesy of the Greater Vernon Museum and Archives 2766.

the BC Café, operated by the Lee brothers; the Devin Point Café, operated by Wong Foo and his sons; and the Wong Ming Fat Café, owned by Wong Ming. There were also a number of Chinese residences on Ellison.[78]

Next to the Kong Wing Tai Grocery was Gong Yik (公益), a Chinese communal house that provided accommodation for single Chinese men who worked either in Chinese businesses or on vegetable farms in the surrounding area. This communal house was operated by Chinese people from Jang Sang (Zeng Cheng 增城) county in Guangdong.

Law Kum Onn, the secretary of the Chinese Freemasons society in Vernon, said:

> There were at least two more similar communal houses in town. They were Why Wah Yuen (维华园) at 2804 Thirty-third Street and Sing Lee Lung (胜利隆) at 3208 Twenty-eighth Avenue (Ellison).[79] Even in the 1940s, all these buildings were fully occupied by single men. During weekends, many Chinese workers from farms in the surrounding area came to town to visit friends and to collect mail from these communal houses or send letters home through these establishments. They came to these houses to gather news about the situation in China as well as to share information about the people from their home villages. They usually spent a night in these communal houses, relaxed, read newspapers, and played a few fan tan games.

Another rooming house was located at 2812 Thirty-second Street and was managed by Quan Lee.

Since most of the early Chinese immigrants were single men who did not or could not bring their families with them when they immigrated to Canada, they formed clan associations to maintain kinship and to provide one another with support and assistance. Clan associations like the Jang Sang Fangkou (增城房口) or Club in Chinatown indicate that their members came from the same villages. These organizations often offered temporary accommodations to members who came to the area as seasonal workers. Although these rooming houses collected rent from their tenants, the income was not enough to cover maintenance of the building, payments for utilities and property taxes, wages for a housekeeper to look after the place, and other costs. For this reason, these clan associations often leased out their premises to some Chinese people in town or from the Lower Mainland to operate gambling dens so that they would make enough money to cover the expenses as well as to provide some recreation and excitement for the tenants and other people—Chinese, whites, Indigenous people—who went there for fun.

Unfortunately, one of the gambling dens in Vernon suffered consequences for operating a gaming venture. On February 26, 1913, Police Chief Constable Fraser, Constable McDonald, Constable Clerk, and others surrounded Hop Yik Long in Chinatown where gambling was underway. They prevented the doorkeeper from entering the house to alert the gamblers. The police rushed in and went to the back room on the upper floor where twenty-seven Chinese men were gambling. The raid was so sudden and unexpected that the gamblers had no time to escape but hid under the tables and other furniture in the room. One of them jumped from the verandah to escape. In the midst of the confusion, the dealer of the game did not even have time to cover the money, the fan tan beads, and other items related to the game. All of the gamblers were sent to the police station that night, and bail was arranged by their friends and relatives to get them released. The court case was held the next day, and the courtroom was packed with curious white people and sympathetic Chinese men. In the end, Hop Yik Long was fined $50.00; nine defendants were found guilty and fined $20.00 to $25.00 each.[80]

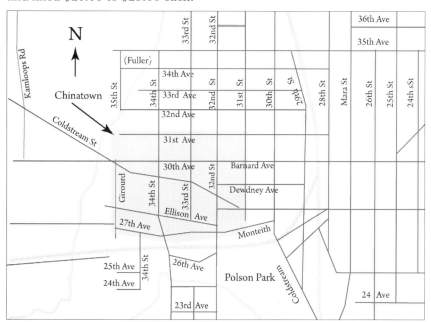

Vernon's Chinatown was located on 28th and 29th avenues and from 32nd to 35th Street. It was bordered by the train tracks and Polson Park.

The Elders of the Chinese organizations played an important role in maintaining unity and harmony in the Chinese community. If a dispute occurred among two or three individuals or groups, the parties involved always reported the case to Sing Lee Lung,[81] Li Kwong or Loo Jim, three well-known and respected Elders in the Chinese community. When an argument or disagreement was reported to these Elders, they listened to the complaints and investigated the causes before resolving the problem. The resolution always ended with one party offering a cup of Chinese tea to the other as a gesture of apology. Then the case was resolved or settled. The parties usually honoured the decisions made by the Elders and refrained from further antagonizing each other. The "right" party usually accepted and appreciated the apology from the "wrong" party.

Besides the various Chinese clan associations, a few fraternal organizations, such as the Chinese Freemasons society, the Dart Coon Club, the Chinese Nationalist League, and the Good Angel Mission Chinese Church, also existed in Chinatown. Each of these fraternal organizations had its own objectives, but many of their activities were related to communication and connections with families in Guangdong. These organizations obtained news and information by mail, telegrams and newspapers, and shared them with their members as well as other Chinese residents in the community. During the second Sino-Japanese War (1937–45), these organizations made great efforts to raise funds and send money to China for the war effort.

The victory of China over Japan at the end of World War II in 1945 called for celebration in the Chinese community. On August 23, 1945, the *Vernon News* reported:

> When Vernon's fire siren sounded the end of World War II…
> the business section of the town came alive… In the impromptu
> parade… the Chinese theme took possession of the throngs, as
> the fascinating dragon, drums and cymbals led a parade… The
> Chinese ritual led a parade of gaiety, laughter, honking horns
> and jubilance as flags fluttered and bunting spilled across the
> streets… Then the dragon dance paid its traditional respect to
> each of the Oriental business establishments in town… Fire-
> crackers popped wildly as the dragon [attempted to] reach for
> the "lucky money" [hanging out] before each business prem-
> ise… It was the Chinese parade [that] created a wave of en-
> thusiasm that started Vernon's all night celebration heralding
> the coming of peace to the world once again.

As time went by, Chinatown gradually faded away. Many of the old-timers had passed on and their descendants left town. In 1947, Chinatown began to show signs of neglect and deterioration. The *Vernon News* stated, "A Chinese puzzle of no mean proportion will be tackled... that oldest part of Vernon... has more kinks than in fabled Topsy's mop. A barber shop stands several feet out in the street where a lane should be. A lean-to shed projects nine and a half feet onto a neighbour's lot; a garden, a chicken house, and a telephone pole obstruct what once was a lane. Buildings and fences show utter disregard of orderly, parallel thoroughfares."[82] This report prompted the city council to investigate the situation, and plans for developing new subdivisions took off. Many Chinese families moved away from Chinatown to the subdivisions.

The Chinese Freemasons Society

Some of the Chinese fraternal organizations deserve recognition for their importance to the history of Vernon's Chinatown. The national headquarters of the Chinese Freemasons of Canada in Vancouver recorded that the lodge of Vernon's Chinese Freemasons society was founded between 1886 and 1912.[83] The 1948 *BC Directory* indicates that the society's building was located at 3300 Twenty-eighth Avenue and that its important branch, the Dart Coon Club, was located in the building next door at 3301 Twenty-eighth Avenue. It is possible that the Chinese Freemasons society had more than one building in town, as the headquarters of the Chinese Freemasons society, a powerful organization in Canada, always supports and encourages its branches to grow and develop. Like the headquarters and other branches, the Vernon chapter looked after the welfare of its members, assisted members to find jobs and connected them with their families in Guangdong. It also provided interpretation services for members to reach out and interact with the mainstream community and helped its members and other Chinese residents to pay utility bills, apply for business licences, and make necessary inquiries at government offices.

"In the early days, there was no Chinese doctor in town," said Walter Joe, a dedicated member of the society. "Whenever a Chinese person became ill, I was called upon to make a doctor's appointment, to accompany the sick person to the doctor's office and to tell the doctor the reasons for visiting. After the doctor had examined the patient, I related the doctor's diagnosis and instructions for taking medication to the patient."

When a member passed on, the Chinese Freemasons society looked after the funeral and burial, and sent messages to the home of the deceased in China about the person's illness and death; and it settled the estate, if there was any. The society would also provide members from out of town with temporary accommodation in the rooming house when they

Members of the Chinese Freemasons stand in front of the one of their Vernon branches during a national convention in 1926. Courtesy of the Greater Vernon Museum and Archives 1679.

visited the city or came in to look for work. Quite often, those who came to seek work were not required to pay rent until they had found employment.

The formation of the Dart Coon Club within the Chinese Freemasons society is related to Dr. Sun Yat-sen's ambitions after he became a Freemason. When Sun was in North America on a fundraising campaign to support an insurrection against the Qing government, he persuaded some overseas Chinese to join the Chinese Alliance Party, of which he was a leader. His influence led to the formation of party branches across North America and he encouraged party members to join the Chinese Freemasons society. The entry of the party members to the Freemasons society created factions among the CFS members, as both old and new members had ideological differences. Gradually, the old-timers in the Chinese Freemasons society realized that their society was on the verge of being displaced by Chinese Alliance Party members. Some of the wise and faithful Freemasons thus created the Dart Coon Club within the society to protect their own interests.

In Vernon, the Dart Coon Club was established in 1919. Its mandate was similar to that of the Chinese Freemasons society, but it played an important role in teaching its members martial arts or kung fu for self-defence and dragon and lion dances to preserve Chinese heritage. Collectively, both the society and the club observed Qing Ming (清明), Yue Lan XV (孟兰) and Zhong Yang (重阳), the occasions on which deceased members were commemorated.

In 1930, the Sixth National Convention of the Chinese Freemasons of Canada was held in Vernon. It was quite an event, for more than a hundred members representing all the chapters across Canada attended the convention. A banquet was held and a lion dance performed to entertain the participants as well as the invited guests and prominent members of the local and provincial governments.

Throughout the years, the local Chinese Freemasons society and the Dart Coon Club made efforts to reach out to the mainstream community. In 1948, the local newspaper reported that they celebrated Chinese New Year with lion dances and explosions of firecrackers. When they celebrated the Chinese New Year in 1956, they held a dinner for members at a building on Thirty-third Street, and Mr. J. Wong, president of the Freemasons society, sent out special invitations to the dinner to prominent local citizens. In the following year, the society and the club hosted the Seventh National Convention of the Chinese Freemasons of Canada in Vernon again.[84]

The prize-winning Chinese float in Vernon's centennial-year parade. Courtesy of Harry Low.

In 1967, the City of Vernon celebrated Canada's centennial year. The Dart Coon Club, chaired by Walter Joe, wrote a letter to Mr. L. H. Mercier, the mayor of Vernon, saying that the club would donate a tea house (茶亭) to the city to commemorate Canada's centennial. The tea house still exists in Polson Park. It offers residents and visitors a place to relax and hold picnics, since there are tables and chairs in the tea house and picnic tables are placed next to the building. After the completion of the tea house, both the Chinese Freemasons society and the Dart Coon Club invited the mayor and aldermen in the city council to attend the grand opening on June 24, 1967.

In the same year, Vernon's Centennial Year Organizing Committee approached the Freemasons and Dart Coon Club, asking them to participate in the centennial celebration. "So Harry Low and I spearheaded the project and built a float for the parade," said Walter Joe. "I asked some friends in the CPR to supply a few pieces of ties for us to build a short railway track on a sixteen-foot trailer, a vehicle that belonged to George Lee. We decorated the float appropriately and some of us dressed up like the old-timers who had worked in the CPR construction, sitting on the float during the parade in town. I am very proud to tell you, we won the first prize!"

Frequently, these two organizations donated large sums of money to the regional hospital. In 1950 and 1998, they collected donations from the

The Chinese Freemasons society and the Dart Coon Club donated a tea house to the city to celebrate Canada's centennial year in 1967. It still stands in Polson Park. Image courtesy of the author.

Chinese community to relieve flood victims in China. "We collected the money and sent it to the Freemasons' headquarters in Vancouver, which dispatched the money to China through the Red Cross," said Law Kum Onn, secretary of the Vernon Freemasons.

Unfortunately, in 1978, the Dart Coon Club building at 3301 Twenty-eighth Avenue (Ellison) burned down. The destruction of the building did not dampen the spirit of brotherhood and benevolence shared by the leaders. They remained active and continued to administer the affairs of the organization and reach out to the mainstream community.

The Chinese National League or Guomindang

After the Chinese revolution, the Chinese Alliance Party (同盟会) became the governing party and formed the Chinese republic. The party changed its name to Guomindang (国民党), also known as the Chinese Nationalist League. Many Chinese immigrants in Vernon were members of the party. Its building was located at the corner of Vance and Ellison streets. The chairman of the Vernon branch was Lee Chung Hing, the secretary was Wong Chow Lai and the board members consisted of Chung Chow, Wong

Ming, Mee Chung and Chung Yet Shong. On August 19, 1919, the branch held a grand opening and invited Mayor Shatford, the fire chief and other prominent local citizens to the event. Sixty local members were present. The ceremony began with singing the Chinese anthem, followed by a recitation of the principles of the Chinese Nationalist League, namely: (1) to maintain political unity; (2) to expand local self-government; (3) to enforce the assimilation of race; (4) to adopt the best policies of socialism; and (5) to maintain international peace, all of which were related to the politics in China. Then the assembly saluted the picture of Dr. Sun Yat-sen on the wall behind the rostrum. Chairman Lee addressed the assembly, followed by speeches from some of the dignitaries. The ceremony ended with the singing of "God Save the King." The attendees were invited to a reception.[85]

The Vernon branch received telegraphs from the Chinese Nationalist Party headquarters in Canton (Guangdong) regularly via the Canadian Pacific Railway telegram office. For instance, on July 11, 1922, a message was received from the Chinese republican government about aggression by the warlords in the Tianjing region. The situation triggered the government of the Republic of China to issue liberty bonds with a face value of $100.00 each and to urge the Chinese nationals to purchase the bonds.[86] On March 12, 1923, the Vernon branch received an alarming telegraph saying that Dr. Sun Yat-sen had passed away. All the branches of the Chinese Nationalist League throughout the world were asked to display a Chinese national flag at half-mast to pay tribute to Sun, the father of the Chinese republic. The following day, the Vernon branch called an emergency meeting to raise donations for Sun's funeral expenses. A total of $2,100.00 was collected and sent to China through the headquarters in Vancouver. On March 20, the Vernon branch received a message from the Vancouver headquarters saying that a memorial service would be held for Sun in Vancouver.

In the summer of 1928, the warlords were defeated and the Guomindang succeeded in unifying the country, but when they purged the Chinese Communist Party members, civil war broke out. On September 18, 1931, the Mukden (Shenyang) Incident took place, which formed the pretext for the Japanese invasion of Manchuria.[87] The civil war stopped after Japan bombed the Marco Polo Bridge in Beijing in July 7, 1931, triggering the second Sino-Japanese War.

On September 18, 1931, the *Vernon News* reported that "the central executives of the CNL [Chinese Nationalist League] in Vancouver had raised and dispatched $15,000.00 to Shanghai... A drive for funds to assist China in current military operations against Japan is to be commenced in this city...The drive is to be conducted thoroughly over Vernon and all the outlying environs..." But the newspaper did not report the amount of money raised in Vernon in a follow-up article.

One year after World War II ended, the civil war between the Chinese Nationalist League and the Chinese Communist Party resumed in China. In 1949, the Communists won the war and established the People's Republic of China. Many branches of the Chinese Nationalist League in Canada gradually closed down. The building of the Vernon branch was demolished in 1965.

The Good Angel Mission Church

Although a great majority of the Chinese immigrants registered themselves as Buddhists or Confucians when they first entered Canada, some were Christians. As early as the eighteenth century, missionaries from different Christian churches went to different provinces in China to evangelize the Chinese. So some of the Chinese immigrants were Christians. In Vernon, a Chinese church, the Good Angel Mission Church, was founded in 1920 at 3307 Twenty-eighth Avenue in Chinatown.[88] This Anglican church, a two-storey wood house, was built around 1924 by the Anglican Forward Movement. On the top floor was a suite for the resident priest. On the ground floor was a hall furnished with tables and stools for church services, meetings, and classes to teach the English and Chinese languages.

On November 4, 1924, the formal opening of the Good Angel Mission Church took place. At the beginning of the ceremony, the bishop of the diocese offered an opening prayer, introduced his fellow priests, and welcomed the congregation. Representatives from the Chinese Freemasons society, the Vernon Chinese Nationalist League, and other Chinese clan associations in Vernon and from Kamloops attended the event. The Salvation Army band contributed music and led the hymn singing. A contribution of $65.00 was collected for the church.[89] At the end of the service, refreshments were served.

The resident priest was Rev. G. Lim Yuen, who had spent eighteen years in China evangelizing the Chinese. He opened a school in the church to teach the Canadian-born Chinese children the Chinese language and held classes in the afternoon and evening. On Sundays, he taught Bible classes and celebrated the Sabbath. He also preached the gospel in the streets on Sunday afternoons after the Bible class.[90] Rev. Yuen had three sons and two daughters, all successful Chinese-Canadians; one of his sons, Paul Lim, was a well-known scholar and diplomat.

As time went by, attendance at the church gradually diminished. The church authorities claimed that immigration from China virtually stopped between1924 and 1948 due to the Chinese Exclusion Act that was enacted in 1923, and that Canadian-born Chinese children usually attended churches that gave sermons in English. By 1948, the church was rented out as a private home. In early 1953, the building was sold to Wah Fong Gunn for $1,600.00. It was finally torn down at the end of 1976 to make way for city redevelopment.

The Late Walter Joe and His Family

The Joe family is well-known in Vernon; two generations of this family, at least, have settled in the city. Stanley Joe came to Canada in 1878 on a sailing ship at the age of sixteen and landed in Victoria. Later, he worked on the CPR construction (1880–85) in New Westminster. After the construction was completed, he went to Yale, where he did some mining and helped out in the On Lee Store. There he met Constance Chang (Tsang), the first daughter of Chang Woon Cheung, the owner of On Lee. In 1908, Stanley and Constance were married in Yale. After the wedding, they moved to Vernon and spent their entire lives there. When they first arrived in Vernon, Stanley worked for Peter Dickson, a well-known Vernon resident and owner of a ranch in the district. At the same time, they opened a coffee shop behind the Kwong Hing Lung Store. In 1930, Stanley retired from the ranch due to ill health. On April 18, 1945, Stanley passed on at the age of eighty-three, survived by his widow, Constance, and their children. They had four sons, Henry, Frank, Cpl. Walter Joe, RCAF, and Edward, and seven daughters, Mrs. Arthur Lee, Mrs. Jack Leong, Mrs. Harry Cumyou, Pearl, Laura, Hazel and Margaret.[91] Among the children, Walter Joe was well known in Vernon, a caring and compassionate man and an active member of the Chinese community.

Walter Joe was born on November 6, 1916, and lived his entire life in Vernon except for the period when he served in the military during World War II. He went to school in Vernon and attended the Chinese school operated by the Rev. Lim Yuen.

"Rev. Lim is a very good Chinese scholar," said Joe. "He used the old classical Chinese textbook, *Tian Di Yuen Wong* (天地玄黄) or *Sam Zi Ging* (三字经) to teach the Chinese kids to read and write in Cantonese. It was quite laborious for us kids, especially in writing Chinese characters, and quite boring too; we just sat in class and followed the teacher reading. There was no phonetics to guide the pronunciation. Everything had to be learned by heart."

In his childhood, Joe encountered much teasing and name-calling. Being young and intolerant, he often got into fights with the white kids.

"When I came home with a bleeding nose, my mother knew right away that I had been involved in a fight," recalled Joe. "And she always assumed that whenever I got into a fight, it was my fault and I had not followed her advice. First, she would scold. Her usual line was 'You, bad boy! You got into a fight with the white kids again! It must be your fault, otherwise people would not hit you.' Then she would clean my face and wipe away the blood from my nose. In the process of tidying me up, she would repeat what she always had said: 'Don't fight with the whites. No matter what they call you, just ignore them. If you do not listen to me next time, I will give you a good thrashing.' It was easy for her to say. But when the white kids called me 'Chinky, chinky, Chinaman' my anger simply flared up."

There were a couple of incidents that Joe could not forget. In the spring of 1924, all the Chinese residents—men, women and children—lined up on the pavement at Kwong Lung Chan and registered themselves as immigrants. It was clearly stated on the registration card that immigrants had no status or the privileges of a citizen. "I used to show the registration card to my buddies in the air force and say to them, 'Look, I was born here and yet I was treated as an alien.' I said that just for the kick of it, to let steam out! Thank goodness, it was history. We Chinese-Canadians have come a long way. Despite all the prejudice and discrimination I have encountered, I have no regrets living in this country," said Joe.

When World War II broke out in 1939, the Royal Canadian Air Force set up a recruiting office on the top floor of Vernon's city hall. The air force advertised in the newspapers: "Gentlemen out there. We Want You." Joe went to the office to enlist. But he was told "no Chinamen are wanted in the air force."

"I was upset," said Joe. "I took a few steps away from the recruitment desk. Then I went back and asked the officer, 'Hypothetically sir, if I shoot down an enemy, does he know that he is being shot by a Chinaman?' Then I stomped out of the office."

Later, Joe joined the militia and had his training near Mission Hill, Kelowna. His unit volunteered to join the air force twice but was turned down each time. In 1942, he wrote to the air force superintendent and asked the air force to give him a button or some piece of evidence to show that he had twice volunteered his service to the air force and had twice been rejected. A few months later, he received a reply saying that the regulations had been changed and Chinese immigrants were now allowed to enlist in the service. He sent in his application, passed his medical examination and was accepted into the air force. He was sent to Vancouver for a few weeks' training and then to Montreal to take some courses in wireless communication and aviation. After graduating, he was stationed at the No. 1 Central Navigation School at Red River in Manitoba. There he learned and practised flying until World War II ended.

"If the air force had taken me in at the beginning, probably I would not be able to talk to you today," remarked Joe. "If I had had my training earlier, most likely I would have been sent to the battle front and killed. Perhaps I was destined to live a long life."

After World War II, Joe returned to Vernon and operated the grocery store that he had started prior to going for military training. Later, he went into the taxi business. He also purchased a gas station and was doing very well in business. In 1954, he married Yasuko Chiba, a Japanese woman. Over the years, three children—one son and two daughters—were added to the family. His son and one of the daughters moved to Vancouver, while the youngest daughter lived in Honolulu.

Both husband and wife were very civic-minded. Chiba volunteered at All Saints Anglican Church, whereas Joe was always called upon to interpret for sick Chinese people, especially the seniors who could not speak English. "I was so happy when Dr. King, the first Chinese doctor, arrived in town," said Joe. "Finally, the Chinese patients could speak and relate to the doctor directly about the symptoms of their illnesses."

Joe was a staunch member of the Chinese Freemasons chapter in Vernon. He was elected as the chairman of the Dart Coon Club for a good number of years consecutively. He was a member of the Royal Canadian Legion beginning in 1942, a member of the Rotary Club after 1946, and belonged to the Caucasian Masonic Lodge and the Shriners. In 1993, he was honoured by the City of Vernon as the "Good Citizen of the Year."

He also received the Paul Harris Award from the Rotary Club for his perfect attendance for thirty-eight years.

In early 1990, Joe's wife had a stroke. He then resigned from the Rotary Club and cut down on his community involvement so that he would have more time to be with his wife. In 1997, his wife passed away, but Joe remained in Vernon. "I would feel lost if I moved to Vancouver," said Joe. "I have many friends here. Life has been very good to me after the war. Although my children are not with me, they are great people and visit me very often. I still attend the Rotary Club meetings every now and then."

Walter Joe, indeed, was an honourable and admirable senior. Although he experienced discrimination in his younger days, he harboured no ill feeling towards the white community. Instead, he volunteered his time and services to the mainstream community whenever needed. He witnessed the change of attitude among the whites towards Chinese Canadians, happy to see the ways that Chinese Canadians and new immigrants were being accepted in Canadian society. He shared his experiences as a Canadian-born Chinese and felt that it was important to acknowledge the past. However, he mentioned several times that the systems of both the federal and provincial governments were flawed, and people were caught in systems that precipitated prejudice and discrimination against the Chinese immigrants in the early days.

On September 22, 2005, Joe passed away at the age of eighty-eight years, survived by his children: Brian and his wife, June; Donna and her husband, Dieter; Vicky; his granddaughter, Samantha Joe; and his sisters: Hazel, Edith, Ruth, Laura and Margaret.

Other Notable Chinese Canadians

Besides the late Walter Joe, Harry Low and other leaders in various Chinese organizations, many notable Chinese-Canadians have left their legacies in Vernon. It is impossible to document all of them, and only four of them are included here.

When Mission Hill became one of the leading training centres in western Canada, the late Dick Low, a Chinese tailor, sewed military uniforms for soldiers and officers. In 1943, a newspaper reporter wrote that "the bespectacled and gray tinged Dick Low is starting to feel the pressure. He locks his front door and ignores all [customers] at the door while he and his female staff try to catch up with the orders [from the training centre]. The glass counter in his shop is full of badges of all descriptions used by the troops."[92] Low had lived in Vernon for more than forty years at the time this news was reported.

Larry Kwong, the first Chinese Canadian and the first person of Asian ancestry to play in the National Hockey League, was born in Vernon on June 17, 1923. When he was young, he loved hockey and developed his skills in the sport and became a right-winger. In the hockey seasons of 1939–40 and 1940–41, he played with the Vernon Hydrophones. Following that, he played with the Trail Smoke Eaters, the Nanaimo Clippers and the Red Deer Wheelers. In the 1947–48 season, he made his way to the New York Rangers. Despite playing only a single game in the NHL, his hockey career was remarkable, very impressive. Kwong is a true hockey star, a Canadian hockey hero.[93]

Gillian Hwang, the wife of Dr. Samuel Huang Xinxin, devoted her time and energy towards preserving Chinese culture in Vernon. In 1949, Dr. Xinxin and his family migrated to Hong Kong from Guangdong. Unfortunately, Dr. Huang could not practise medicine in Hong Kong, so he immigrated to Canada and studied medicine at the University of Alberta. In 1957, he graduated from medical school and sent for Gillian and his children to join him in Alberta, where he practised medicine. One year, they toured various cities in BC and felt that Vernon would be the place for their retirement. In 1969, Dr. Huang and his wife, Gillian, migrated to Vernon, where their children attended high school. After they graduated from high school, their children attended university in Alberta.

Gillian participated in many activities in the Chinese community as well as those that were hosted by the Chinese Freemasons society and the Vernon Multicultural Society. In 1972, she and other Chinese Canadians founded the Vernon Chinese Cultural Association, and she was elected to be its president. The association aims to promote Chinese culture and to provide opportunities for the younger generation to learn and retain the Chinese language.

"After we formed the association, the Multicultural Society approached us to participate in the Folkfest. They also asked me find out from the Chinese community if they would join the celebration and set up a booth in the event to celebrate Canada Day," said Gillian. "The community responded with enthusiasm. With the help of a few restaurants, the Chinese community set up a food booth and some young Chinese girls performed a Chinese folk dance on Canada Day. We, a couple of Chinese ladies and I, taught the dancers the Chinese folk dance."[94]

After Folkfest, the Vernon Multicultural Society helped the Chinese cultural association apply for a grant from Heritage Canada to establish a Chinese school. "We succeeded in getting the grant," said Gillian. "We used the funds to buy textbooks and other teaching materials such as flash cards, exercise books, and to provide juices and snacks for the students during breaks. When the Chinese school started, Mrs. Gong and Mrs. Chow Bing Yit volunteered to teach thirty students. The classes were held in the Chinese Freemasons society building every Sunday morning for two hours. Unfortunately, the school only lasted two years."

"In class, we made efforts to keep Chinese culture alive by telling stories and legends about the origins of many Chinese festivals, customs and traditions," added Mrs. Chow Bing Yit, also known as Chan Yue Juan (陈月娟). "We also taught the students Chinese songs and poetry and helped them to read and write Chinese characters." She paused and then continued, "But, you know, Chinese is not an easy language to learn. And writing Chinese characters was a challenge for the students, especially those who were born and raised here. Because the class time was short, just two hours, we gave students homework, writing Chinese characters and memorizing Chinese poetry at home. As they had already cultivated the habit of not doing much homework in public schools, imposing homework discouraged them from attending the Chinese school. Gradually they lost their interest in Chinese school and enrollment went down. Besides, many of the students had to help out in their parents' businesses, especially those whose owned restaurants. So we had no choice but to close down the Chinese school."

"Another reason for dropping out of Chinese school was due to the fact that students were not able to use the language taught in Chinese lessons with their parents and grandparents," echoed Gillian. "The students spoke different Chinese dialects at home and many children communicated with their parents and family members in English." After heaving a soft sigh, Gillian brightened up and said, "But many of the Chinese girls loved the folk dances, so we formed the dancing club for them. The association then invited Mimi Ho, a professional dance instructor in the Chinese community in the Strathcona neighbourhood of Vancouver, to come up and teach them folk dances. Mimi Ho volunteered her time teaching the girls dancing, which was very kind and generous of her. The Vernon Chinese Cultural Association and the Chinese community paid for her travelling expenses. When she came up, she stayed in my house and a few Chinese restaurants provided meals for her."

Dancers required costumes. So Chow, Low Chui Ha (Harry Low's wife), and a few Chinese ladies in the Chinese community volunteered to sew costumes for the girls.

"Our folk dance club was very popular," said Gillian. "During the six years when the club was active, we were often invited by the Chinese communities in the nearby regions to perform during Chinese festivals. In 1977, the local television station filmed and telecast our folk dances on television. As time passed by, these teenagers left town to attend universities in the Lower Mainland after they had graduated from high school. Somehow, it became harder to recruit young girls of the same age group to join the dance club."

Chan Yue Juan, a Chinese-Canadian woman with limited education, believed that success could be achieved through determination and

The Vernon Chinese Cultural Association began a dance club to teach young Chinese girls in the community traditional folk dances. Image courtesy of Gillian Hwang.

hard work. In 1972, she and her husband immigrated to Canada from Hong Kong and started a family in Vernon. After their arrival, her husband worked in a grocery store, and she stayed home to take care of their children. A few years later, she went to work in a Chinese restaurant as a dishwasher and a waitress.

"In the mid-1970s, Vernon was a very busy city," said Chan. "The restaurant where I worked hired about a hundred employees, including cooks, kitchen helpers, dishwashers, cashiers, waiters and waitresses. They worked in shifts. During weekends, the smorgasbord attracted many customers and we worked non-stop. As a waitress, I earned about $1.50 an hour but the tips amounted to more than $50.00 a night, especially on the weekend. On average, my wages for the month were around $300.00 but tips would increase my income to approximately $500.00 per month. With that kind of business going on, you can imagine how busy the city was."[95]

After she stopped working in restaurants, Chan went to work as a seamstress in the Far West Skiwear Company, which manufactured skiwear clothing in Vernon. In the factory, there were 130 sewing machines, many large tables for tailoring, and other equipment. The employees were mainly Chinese and Vietnamese. After fourteen years working in the factory, she was promoted to the position of supervisor, taking charge of more than 140 workers.

"It took me a long way to get there," Chan sighed. "Before I became the supervisor, the company would hire some white person with no experience in the manufacturing business to be my superior. I had to listen and take orders from them—quite frustrating working in that kind of situation.

Regardless, I stayed working in the Far West Skiwear manufacturing factory and got promoted. I only had an elementary education in Hong Kong and attended night school to study English for three years. This shows that willingness to learn and adapt to working situations does pay off.

Working as a supervisor gave me the opportunity to go with my manager to represent the Far West Skiwear Company at the exhibition in one of the Atlantic cities. I truly believe efforts and determination will help us to achieve our goals. But good education is important. This is why I encourage my children to study well in school."

In 1988, the grocery store where her husband had worked as a produce manager closed down. Instead of looking for other employment, both husband and his wife purchased and operated the Appleton Restaurant.

"When we started the restaurant business, I was still working in the skiwear factory," said Chan. "I only helped out in the restaurant after work. It was too much for me to carry on with two jobs and being the mother of three teenagers in those years. So in 1993, I retired from the skiwear factory and managed this restaurant full-time. I am glad my oldest child had graduated from university and he is working in Kelowna now. The two younger ones are attending school at the University of Victoria."

Both Chan and Huang agreed that they had many advantages living in a small Chinese community.

"Truly, the Chinese Freemasons chapter is very helpful and obliging not only to their members but also to the Chinese residents in town" said Huang. "Whenever the Chinese Cultural Association has a function, the Chinese Freemasons chapter always lends its hand. We truly appreciate and respect the Elders of that organization."

"We are seldom left out of any happy occasions like weddings, birthdays or celebration of the full moon for a newborn child," added Chan. "The Chinese community is very united and cooperative. Everyone is friendly and helpful."

Continuing Relationships with the First Nations People

Michael Wong, the former owner of King's Restaurant, admitted he had very good relationships with the First Nations people in the area. "The Native people in this area are very good, trustworthy," commented Wong. "At times, when they came to eat in my restaurant without money, I gave them credit and never asked them to sign an IOU because they always honoured the 'gentleman's agreement.' They always paid me back whenever they had money."[96]

Wong sold his restaurant in 2000 and then worked at a restaurant owned by a retired First Nations chief on the North Okanagan Indian reserve No. 1. "When I operated the King's Restaurant, Chief Ronald Bonor was my regular customer. He used to bring twenty to thirty people, including members of his family and extended family, to eat in my restaurant. When he learned that I was selling my business, he invited me to help him set up a restaurant on his reserve. I helped him but told him I could only work for him as long as I stay healthy. I managed his restaurant for about two years. The restaurant is still there, doing a flourishing business. Now his son is managing it and I've learned that they want to expand it."

This account demonstrates a positive relationship between Chinese Canadians and the First Nations people, very heartening and admirable.

Vernon: A Rich Chinese History

Although situated in an agricultural region in the BC Interior, far away from big cities where many early Chinese settlers were living, Vernon and its surrounding area certainly contains a rich Chinese-Canadian history unknown to many Chinese Canadians and immigrants of today. Research indicates that many early Chinese immigrants in Vernon were competent and skillful farmers who helped orchards produce fruit, the most important industry in the Okanagan in the first half of the twentieth century. Many of them were excellent workers on ranches that helped produce hay to feed cattle, and therefore they contributed to the production of meat and dairy products for the region, if not the whole of BC. The historical evidence refutes the stereotypical perception of many people that the occupations of the early Chinese immigrants were mainly operating small businesses, such as grocery stores and laundry shops, and providing domestic services and manual labour.

Although the Chinatown in Vernon disintegrated, its legacy remains. Today, a large number of Chinese Canadians as well as recent Chinese immigrants have chosen to live in Vernon, a place of great natural beauty where outdoor recreational activities such as fishing, boating and skiing are within a stone's throw. These recent arrivals have helped keep Chinese culture alive. As usual, the Chinese community celebrates Chinese New Year and the Mid-Autumn Moon Festival and often attempts to promote Chinese culture through music and songs, dances and visual arts.

KELOWNA: HOME OF OGOPOGO

The City of Kelowna is located at the midway point on the shoreline of the deep and long Okanagan Lake, the Syilx First Nation territory. Legends say an aquatic monster, Ogopogo, or N'ha-a-tik in the Indigenous language, was sighted in Okanagan Lake near Kelowna. As a result, the annual Ogopogo Festival has become one of the tourist highlights in the city.

In October 1859, the Oblates of Mary Immaculate missionaries, led by Father Charles Pandosy, arrived in the Okanagan and pre-empted the land on the east side of Okanagan Lake near the townsite of Kelowna. The Oblate Fathers called this site the Revere de L'Anse au Sable; it encompassed several miles in radii of fertile soil with luxuriant vegetation. They built a house, a church and a school on the site and called it the Okanagan Mission. The mission became a focal point for the early white immigrants who arrived in the Okanagan. Father Pandosy was instrumental in teaching agriculture to the Indigenous people and Indigenous techniques of survival to the white settlers.[97]

The rich soil and the ideal climate, mild winters and warm summers, attracted people from different countries to immigrate and settle in the area, and to grow vegetables and cultivate food and fruit crops. The fruit products led to the development of agricultural industries with packing houses that exported fruits such as cherries, grapes, peaches and apples to different parts of Canada, as well as to wineries and fruit canneries.

In 1892, the townsite was laid out and given the name Kelowna, a term for grizzly bear in the local Indigenous language. On May 4, 1905, Kelowna was incorporated as a city, but a Chinese community already existed within the townsite near the city park.

The Chinese Immigrants

No one knows the exact year the first Chinese immigrants arrived in the area. After the gold rushes in the Fraser and the Cariboo, some Chinese gold miners migrated to the Okanagan and panned for gold in Mission Creek. In 1868, Lum Lock (林乐), a young Chinese man, was spotted at the Mission Valley panning for gold and working at chores for the ranches nearby.[98] After the completion of the Canadian Pacific Railway (CPR) construction, some unemployed Chinese labourers migrated to Kelowna and its vicinity to work for farmers and orchardists, while a few operated small businesses such as cafés and laundries in town. In 1892, a new hotel, the Lakeview Hotel, was built in the city, and the first sternwheeler, the *Aberdeen*, stopped at Okanagan Landing. One of the hotel cooks was a Chinese person, and so were the two cooks on the sternwheeler. In May 12, 1893, the railway from Sicamous to Vernon was constructed and extended farther west to Okanagan Landing. More than a hundred Chinese labourers were hired in this railway construction. After the completion of this subsidiary railway, the Chinese labourers were dismissed. The unemployed Chinese workers migrated to Kelowna and its vicinity, and rented lands from the Indigenous people to cultivate vegetables and food crops such as corn, barley and potatoes. Some of them worked for local farmers and orchardists.[99]

In 1903, when Charles Clement built his home on (Ellis) Harvey Avenue near the city park, he hired a Chinese gardener. One day after work, the Chinese gardener noticed some weeds near the fence of the garden while he was walking home. Immediately he jumped over the fence and pulled the weeds out. The Clement family was pleased and commented on the good work ethic of the Chinese gardener.

The Okanagan Boat Landing, where the Republic of China's president Sun Yat-Sen would arrive on the *Aberdeen* in 1911. Courtesy of the Royal BC Museum and Archives D-01810.

Early white residents and news journalists noted that the Chinese immigrants in Kelowna were wearing "their hair long and braided in a queue, sometimes hanging down their back but mostly coiled around their heads." This description indicates that many early Chinese immigrants arrived, in Kelowna at least, prior to the formation of the Republic of China in 1911. During the Chinese revolution, Dr. Sun Yat-Sen, the father of the Chinese revolution, encouraged all Chinese men in the world to cut off their queues as a symbol of defiance towards the Qing government. After the formation of the Chinese republic, Chinese people in China as well as overseas began to cut off their queues.

The Chinese Settlement: Chinatown

By 1903, Chinese immigrants had already erected houses on Harvey Avenue across from the Parkview Motel in Kelowna. One of their first houses was at the corner of Ellis Street and Bernard Avenue and another shack on the lakeshore next to the city park.[100] Sam Lee Laundry was noted in 1904. Around 1906, Tape Quong (or Kwan) and his family arrived in Kelowna and established the City Park Café at the corner of Abbott Street and

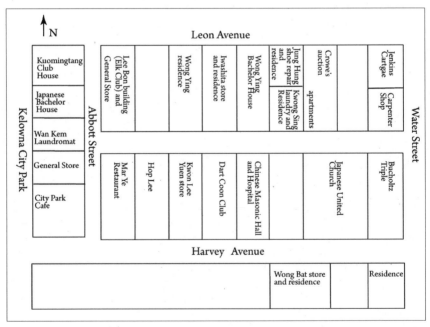

Kelowna's Chinatown was in formation before Kelowna was even incorporated as a city. The area remained, expanded and thrived. Map research courtesy of the Okanagan Chinese Canadian Assocation and the Kelowna Chinese Freemasons society.

Harvey Avenue.[101] The existence of these small businesses and Chinese houses indicates that Chinese settlement had taken place and the birth of Chinatown had begun.

Quong, owner of the City Park Café, was often seen riding his bicycle in town to pick up groceries and meat. Many long-time and senior residents in Kelowna still remember the tender and juicy large steaks, the chunky golden French fries, toasts and bowls of rich clam chowder served at this café. As well, several elderly residents still recall the endless fan tan games that went on continuously in the "Blue Room" at the back of Quong's café. Rumour said that one of the best players was a local policeman.

The majority of the early Chinese settlers in Kelowna were men. But on November 21, 1907, Lum Lock brought his new wife, Lee Quon Ho, the first Chinese bride there, to Kelowna from Victoria. Lee had arrived in Victoria on the *Empress of Japan* on December 27, 1903, at the age of twelve. She was sent away from her home in Shanghai for safety by her father, a general in the Chinese army.[102] After landing in British Columbia, she lived

The City Park Café, owned by Tape Quong, was one of the first businesses in Kelowna's Chinatown. Courtesy of the Kelowna Museums Society 1978.002.001.

with the Lee Tai family, which operated a store in Victoria's Chinatown. In 1907, the Lee family arranged her marriage with Lum Lock, then a successful merchant. Lum owned and operated a store at the corner of Abbott Street and Harvey Avenue and had a house near the present Canadian National Railway station in Kelowna. He also grew tobacco in the Benvoulin area near Mission Creek.[103]

As the years went by, this couple had four children: one girl and three boys. All their children were born in Kelowna. Unfortunately the first child, a girl, died at birth in 1908; the last boy arrived in 1913.[104]

On April 5, 1909, the Hop Lee Laundry, owned and operated by Wong Chung Ark, obtained a contract washing blankets for the city jail; Sam Kee washed blankets for the Kelowna fire hall. As time went by, the Chinese settlement extended north from Ellis Avenue (now Harvey Avenue) to Leon Avenue, and east from Abbot Street to Water Street. North of City Park Café stood the Kwong Sing Laundry, owned and operated by Wong Kim. Farther north on Abbott Street were two stores with hostels on the upper floors of the buildings to provide accommodations for Chinese labourers who worked for farmers and orchardists in the surrounding regions. These Chinese labourers were single men—bachelors or married men who had left their wives and family members in their home villages in Guangdong, China. Many of the Chinese labourers secured their work through employment contractors.[105] Lee Bon was one of the labour contractors or "bosses" who recruited workers for local famers, orchardists, packing houses and canneries. He had a rooming house, a brick building on Leon Avenue, to provide accommodations for Chinese labourers. And he owned and operated a general store on the ground floor of the building.

The buildings in Chinatown were separated by two lanes in the block. One lane ran through three-quarters of the block between Leon and Harvey avenues in the centre. The other lane was perpendicular to the first one; it cut through the block on the west. The lane at the centre of the block between Leon and Harvey avenues was the main access to the buildings. A raised wooden sidewalk covered three-quarters of the lane. Two Chinese organization buildings, the Chinese Freemasons society and the Dart Coon Club, and the Kwong Lee Yuen, a general and grocery store, were found between the perpendicular lane and Harvey Avenue. The front parts of all the buildings faced the lane covered with the raised wooden sidewalk, except the one on 245 Leon, the home of Wong Lee Sue Ping (黃李淑萍). On the west end of Chinatown were the Lee Bon Store, the

KUO MIN TANG

Chinese Nationalist Party.

The Chinese Nationalist Party had a branch in Kelowna, located on the west end of the city's Chinatown. Courtesy of the Kelowna Museums Society 1978.002.003.

Mar Ye restaurant, the Chinese Nationalist Party or Guomindang (中国国民党) building, two rooming houses, the Wong Kem Laundry and the City Park Café.

In 1909, the following Chinese businesses were listed in Chinatown:

Quong's City Park Café
Chung Kee Grocery
Kwong Lee Yuen General and Grocery
Wo Yuen Merchant
Yee Fung Merchant
Hop Lee Laundry
Sam Kee Laundry
Sun Sing Laundry
Ying Kee Laundry

Each house in Chinatown had a vegetable garden and wooden racks in the yard that faced the lanes for drying green vegetables in the sun during summer. These dried vegetables would become their produce in winter when fresh suppies ran short.

In the early days, the Chinese community in Chinatown was vibrant. When the Chinese settlers celebrated Chinese New Year, they hit drums and clapped cymbals to accompany lion dances—spectacular and joyful. A few journalists and writers commented that during Chinese New Year celebrations, "fireworks lit up the entire Chinatown as though it was going up in flames."[106] Chinese merchants and organizations hung strings of firecrackers on the fronts of their buildings and set them off during the Spring Festival. It was said that one local Chinese person set off one million firecrackers in one of the celebrations.

But members in the mainstream community seldom ventured to visit Chinatown except for going to the City Park Café at the edge of the Chinese settlement. The white population felt that Chinatown was a peculiar and immoral place occupied by men and only a few women. They noticed a couple of strange women visited the place occasionally to entertain the single men. And some buildings in Chinatown operated gambling dens and opium parlours.

"Many Caucasians did not realize the difficult time the Chinese had in the early days," said the late Ben Lee. "In a small community like ours, the Chinese had to have their own social clubs where they could play some cards and socialize with one another. Sure, they gambled, but not for big stakes. It was a form of recreation for them."

Tun Wong also stated that white people seldom, possibly never, visited Chinatown during the years when his family was living there. "Neither did the police go there, even when they were called," he said. "We, the residents of Chinatown, were pretty much on our own, helping and protecting one another." He noticed that a white person had described Chinese people as producing a gargling sound when they smoked opium with a pipe. "He is incorrect. The gargling sound came from Chinese smoking tobacco with a water pipe, not from smoking opium," Wong explained. "As the water in the pipe filtered the tobacco smoke, the gargling sound was produced in the process. Obviously, he did not visit Chinatown and see Chinese smoking with water pipes. A Chinese water pipe can be found in the Kelowna Centennial Museum [now the Okanagan Heritage Museum]."

The Chinese Labourers

Many of the Chinese labourers, if not all, were accommodated in rooming houses. In rooming houses, a few labourers—especially those who wanted privacy and could afford to pay higher rent—lived in small cubicles. The majority of the tenants lived in dormitories furnished with bunk beds without springs or mattresses, just bamboo or straw mats and blankets. Each occupant was provided with a small chest to keep their belongings in. On the ground floor of these rooming houses, usually at the back, was a communal kitchen where the tenants could cook their own meals.

In winter when no field work was available, the Chinese labourers either returned to the Lower Mainland or remained in the rooming houses. Labour bosses were happy to have them remain, because they could be insured of supplying labour forces to the farmers and orchardists the next season. Often, these labour bosses would advance their tenant's money against the next working season. The labourers would then be in debt and under the control of these bosses. Yet the labourers also had to pay a commission to the labour contractors for finding them work. The wages of a Chinese labourer did not exceed $1.25 per day.[107]

Every morning they got up at the crack of dawn, cooked congee for breakfast, and prepared lunch that they put in food containers before they went to work. After breakfast, they changed into their work clothes, a loose blouse with a narrow collar and opening in front over a sleeveless top, a pair of baggy pants and a pair of flat shoes made of cloth or straw. They took with them a straw hat with a pointed top and broad rim in one hand or on their head and carried a lunch container in the other hand as they left the rooming houses. They walked with lifted knees in single file to downtown, as though they were walking on narrow ridges in the rice fields at home. Many white people found their clothing different and strange and their manner of walking comical and weird. The Chinese spoken language sounded like gibberish, strange to the ears of the white people and hard to understand.[108]

The tasks the Chinese workers performed in orchards included planting herbs and shrubs, thinning and pruning trees, and picking and packing fruits. In farmlands and vegetable gardens, the Chinese labourers germinated seeds in hotbeds, transplanted seedlings in the fields, and cleared weeds and watered plants during the growing season. Some built and managed water flumes to irrigate hay and vegetable gardens for ranches in the Okanagan Valley.

A good number of Chinese were hired in fruit canneries.[109] Their jobs included removing the hot cans with a retort from the steamer, labelling the cans, packing them in a crate and loading them in boxes for shipment. Only a few Chinese workers were employed in wineries to label and pack bottles of wines or liquor for retail.

In the evening, the labourers returned to their rooming houses and cooked dinner. After their meal, they gathered and talked to one another, read Chinese newspapers or went to gambling dens to try their luck. They usually retired before midnight.

The Visit of Dr. Sun Yat-Sen

On February 19, 1911, Dr. Sun, together with Xie Qiu (谢秋), Li Bing Shen (李丙辰) and others travelled from Vernon to Kelowna on the *Aberdeen* stern-wheeler. They arrived at Okanagan Landing around 4:00 pm. A Chinese welcoming party was waiting for Sun and his delegation at the landing. This welcoming party, led by Lum Lock on a white steed, consisted of more than thirty Chinese Freemasons society members and a Chinese band. When Sun and his delegates landed, the band blasted out loudly to welcome them. A few Chinese guards carried guns and knives, to protect Sun and his comrades. The late Lee Yick Wai (李奕伟), a staunch Freemasons member, was one of those who carried a gun with him to the event.[110]

The welcoming party escorted Sun and his comrades to the Lakeview Hotel for a light meal. At the reception, Sun told his hosts that he had been labelled as a political criminal and was being pursued by the Qing government; therefore, he would prefer a quieter reception. But he thanked the Chinese Freemasons society members for their hospitality and their assistance in raising funds for the revolutionary effort. In the evening, the society held a formal welcoming dinner for Sun and his party at the Kwong Lee Yuen building (广利源宝号), a general store owned and operated by Lee Yee (李义). The society's premises were too small to accommodate the large crowd of people who wanted to attend Sun's presentation, so they rented the Kelowna Movie Theatre (the current Paramount Theatre) for Sun to address the audience. The next morning, Sun spoke to the local Chinese people and members of the mainstream community at the theatre. In his presentation, Sun emphasized that revolution was the only way to overthrow the Qing government. At the end of the meeting, a fundraising committee was formed. Wong Chu (黄柱) was elected as the chair and Leong Kwong (梁广) the vice-chair of this committee. Following the meeting, Lum Lock and Lee Yee accompanied Sun and his comrades on a visit to every house in Chinatown, where they persuaded the residents to donate money for the revolution. Together, they collected $300.00 CAD. On February 21, Sun and his comrades departed Kelowna and went to Victoria. Chen Zhen, a member of the Kelowna branch of the Chinese Freemasons society, was appointed as their guide to return to Vancouver.[111]

After the departure of Sun and his delegates, the Freemasons society members continued collecting and sending funds to China to help the Chinese revolution. Lee Yick Wai donated a large sum of his savings to support Sun in the revolutionary efforts at the beginning of the Guangzhou Huang Hua Gang Uprising (黄花岗起义) in April 1911.

After World War I

In August 1914, World War I began. Many white labourers, especially those who had emigrated from England, felt that they were obliged to go "home" to defend their motherland. Their departure created labour shortages in agriculture that generated more opportunities for Chinese labourers to secure work at farms and orchards in the Okanagan. Actually, farmers and orchardists preferred to hire Chinese and Japanese over the white workers because they were hard-working and reliable.

After World War I, many veterans returned to the Okanagan to continue working in the agricultural industries. By then, farmers and orchardists had forgotten about the efforts and merits of the Chinese workers who had worked in the absence of the white workers during World War I. In 1918, at the convention of the BC Fruit Growers' Association (BCFGA), they forwarded a proposal to the federal government to contract with the Chinese government to import indentured labourers at a set price per head. This brought vigorous opposition from the white population because it was seen as "simply opening the door to the penetration of BC by the 'Yellow Peril' who would take over and subjugate the white population to oriental conditions."[112]

In January 1920, the Great War Veterans Association (GWVA) of Kelowna held a meeting to discuss the "Oriental question" and passed the following resolutions:[113]

> Whereas the ownership of land in BC by Japanese and Chinese is continually increasing and constitutes a peril to our ideal of a white British Columbia, as it is impossible for the Japanese and

the Chinese to become assimilated as Canadian citizens, therefore, be it resolved that we, the Great War Veterans Association
of Kelowna, pledge ourselves by every lawful means to prevent
the further sale of land to these people in this district, and that
any persons selling lands to these people will be publicly con-
demned by GWVA.

And be it further resolved that the Dominion Government
be requested to onset legislation at the next session of Parliament which will effectively prevent Japanese and Chinese from
acquiring any further real estate in the Dominion.

At the end of this meeting, it was decided to call a public meeting the
next Sunday at the Empress Theatre "to arouse public opinions on this
question."

Many white people attended the public meeting called by the GWVA;
the Empress Theatre was packed. The question of Asian immigration and
land ownership by Chinese and Japanese people were the two main topics
on the agenda. Colonel Moody, who presided over the meeting, said that
he had not been aware until very recently of the seriousness of the question. He felt that something should be done, or the [white] people would
soon be wondering who owned Canada.[114]

These few events in the mainstream community—the convention of
the BCFGA and the meetings organized and called by the GWVA—indicate the existence of anti-Chinese sentiments in Kelowna at that time.

The Chinese Freemasons Society

Although members of the Chinese Freemasons society in Kelowna participated in organizing the welcoming party for Dr. Sun and his comrades earlier, the society did not have a lodge. In January 1920, the grand opening
of the Chinese Masonic Hall building took place. At that event, Mah Yen
Yuen, the grand master of the Chinese Freemasons society of Canada from
Nova Scotia, came and attended the event together with large numbers of
delegates from Vancouver, Victoria and Princeton. The function began with
a huge display of fireworks in front of the lodge. The building was decorated with lights and evergreens. Inside the hall, a Chinese band provided
music for the occasion. Election and installation of new officers took place.
The following day, a banquet was held for members, delegates and invited

The fifth national convention of the Chinese Freemasons society, with participants from chapters across Canada. Image courtesy of Lee Shui Dong.

guests. The mayor of Kelowna, a few aldermen and more than fifteen local merchants were invited to the banquet. The membership of the Chinese Freemasons society chapter then was in the neighbourhood of a hundred.[115]

Besides the grand opening, the Chinese Freemasons society held its annual banquet during Chinese New Year for several years. The society's board of directors always invited the mayor, aldermen, fire chief, police chief, health inspector, government agent and other prominent citizens to these occasions. "This demonstrated that the leaders in the Chinese organizations had attempted to reach out, very good networking," remarked Tun Wong. "I regret to say that these occasions might have been the only times that the Caucasians visited Chinatown."

In 1924, the Chinese Freemasons society of Canada held its fifth convention in the building of the Kelowna chapter. Representatives from the society's headquarters and various chapters across Canada gathered in Kelowna for the convention. More than a hundred members attended this convention.

The Chinese Nationalist League

At the corner of Abbot and Leon streets stood a small building, the local headquarters of the Chinese Nationalist League or Party (中国国民党), or Guomindang, a Chinese political body established around 1924 in Kelowna. Very little information about the functions and activities of this organization have been found except that it issued a public notice forbidding the Chinese to have any dealings with the Japanese in the area during the Sino-Japanese War that began in 1937. The notice, written in Chinese, said that "Owing to the conditions of the present situation in the homeland, the Chinese community in Kelowna, including the Chinese merchants and restaurant proprietors, are forbidden to sell goods to members of the Japanese race as of this date—July 1937." Meanwhile, this organization encouraged Chinese settlers to purchase Chinese bonds to support the war effort. Some of the Chinese labourers who were members of this organization refused to work at farms, orchards and ranches where their employers also hired Japanese workers.

Incidents and Encounters

A couple of incidents related to raids on gambling and opium smoking dens occurred in Chinatown. On January 22, 1914, police went to Lee Bon's premises and arrested twenty-three Chinese people for gambling. Lee was fined $25.00 and charges against the gamblers were dismissed.[116] In February of the same year, the chief constable reported that the police department had raided one opium parlour and three gambling dens; the fines levied amounted to $191.00.[117]

In July that same year, another raid was carried out at a gambling den hosted by the proprietor of Kwong (Quong) Lee Yuen on Harvey Avenue. The raid took place on a Saturday night. The police force, led by Constable Thomas, placed guards at the front and the back of the building before entering the house, where a large crowd of Chinese men were gambling. Some were sitting around a table playing dominos, known as "pie cow" in Cantonese. The banker of the game noticed the police coming in, quickly grabbed a tin can containing money and took flight. He spilled some out on the floor but managed to duck out. Forty-six Chinese men including the proprietor were arrested and kept in jail for the weekend. The police also took away the tables and the gambling apparatus. The following Monday, the gamblers were released on bail except, for four of them.

Later, a court case was held with J. F. Burns appearing as prosecutor for the city and R. B. Kerr for the defence. Mee Wah Ling served as an interpreter for the Chinese. The story of the raid was presented at the trial, presided over by Magistrate Edwin Weddell. During the trial, "lawyer Kerr contended that as there was no 'bank' produced in evidence, the game could have been just a friendly one." He also conducted a rigorous cross-examination of Chief Thomas. At the end of the trial, Magistrate Weddell found Quong Tape guilty and sentenced him to a fine of $50.00 or two months in jail; another eighteen men were sentenced to a fine of $20.00 each or one month in jail, and the remaining ones were released. The total fines amounted to $410.00.[118]

On December 17, 1914, Lum Lock, who had led the welcoming party to welcome Sun, passed away at the age of fifty-four. [119] Lum had resided in Kelowna for twenty-one years and owned no less than thirty-four lots in Chinatown, including the one where he and his family lived. His business was closed down, because his widow, Lee Quon Ho, did not know how to manage it. Lee also did not realize that she had to pay taxes on Lum's assets. Eventually, the properties were taken away from her. After the death of her husband, she remained in the city for a few years working at casual jobs in fruit canneries and at odd jobs to raise her children and send them to school. In 1917, she and her children moved to Victoria.

In 1918, when the Spanish influenza epidemic broke out, the little brick house between the buildings of the Chinese Freemasons society and the Dart Coon Club was used as a hospital for the Chinese people. The epidemic was contained by November 19 of that year and the Emergency Chinese Hospital was closed.

Legal restrictions were applied to Chinese merchants. In the 1920s, the Kelowna city council refused applications from Mah Wee and Wing Fung of the Vancouver Café, and from Charlie Sing, Mah Joe and Mah Jack of the St. Jude Café, for licences to sell "near beer" beverages.[120] In June 1920, Quong Tape, the proprietor of the City Park Café was charged for "supplying liquor to Indians" and fined $200.00 in court.[121]

In March 1924, a "deputation of eight Chinamen presented a petition signed by approximately 100 of their countrymen asking for an investigation into the conviction of C. H. Cong by Magistrate Weddell on a charge laid by the RCMP of having in his possession a narcotic drug without lawful authority. Several members of the council voted to refer the matter to the Board of the Commissioners of Police" for further investigation.[122]

On August 17, 1931, the committee of the Kelowna Executive Council on Unemployment issued instructions for registering the unemployed but stated in the instructions not to include the unemployed Orientals. But the Chinese helped one another. For instance, many Chinese merchants and individuals, such as the Kon Wo Company, Kwong Sing Lung, G. H. Lee, the Lee Sang Lung Company, Kwong Lee Yuen, Yick Lee and Got

Chung Lung, donated and distributed groceries to destitute families and unemployed single Chinese men. Kwong Sing Lung, a Chinese store, also supplied food and shelter to some needy Chinese.[123]

The anti-Chinese sentiments created fear and anxiety, pessimism and insecurity for many Chinese, especially the labourers. Many single men became depressed and a few committed suicide. On November 25, 1931, the body of Lee Ping, aged fifty-three, was found suspended from a rafter in the garage next to the Royal Bank downtown. It was believed that he had hanged himself and was not a murder victim. The box on which he had stepped on and kicked off was found nearby. He had no wife or children but was survived by his aged mother in China.[124]

A gruesome murder took place in Chinatown. On November 1, 1932, a Tuesday, Wong Bat Hong Suam (黄鸿心), a prominent merchant and the manager of the Kon Wo Store (共和号), was murdered at the entrance to his house on Harvey Avenue. His body was found lying face down in the yard by his wife, Wong Lee Sue Ping (黄李淑萍), early the next morning. She immediately contacted Wong Chung Ark, the cousin of Wong Bat, who owned and operated the Hop Lee Laundry, and her neighbours, who in turn informed the police. When Wong Chung Ark arrived at the scene he saw the deceased on the ground and found Sue Ping crying nearby. As it was about to rain, he covered the deceased with a straw mat and waited for the police to arrive. When the police arrived, they started an investigation at once; a piece of lumber was found near the body of the deceased. An autopsy performed by Dr. B. F. Boyce revealed that Wong had been hit on his skull from the back by a two-by-two piece of lumber. The blow was so hard that his skull was fractured, causing his death.

According to Chung Ark, Wong Bat had last been seen on November 1 at 10:30 pm, near a Chinese restaurant, carrying a bowl of chop suey; presumably he bought the food for his wife. As Wong was found dead a few steps inside the gate of his house, it was assumed that the assailant was hidden inside the fence, waiting for him to come home. Unfortunately, his assailant was not caught. Robbery was probably the motive for this ruthless murder. Apparently Wong Bat had the habit of carrying a huge roll of money bills with him, a convenience for him to pay for purchases in his extensive business dealings. It was believed that Wong had several hundred dollars with him when he was attacked. But less than $10.00 in loose change was found in his pocket when he was found dead. The crime remained unresolved although a coroner's inquest was held with a jury.[125]

After the death of Wong Bat, his wife was left alone to deal with his estate. Since she did not realize that she had to pay taxes for the assets left behind by her deceased husband, their property on the south side of Harvey Avenue between Abbott and Water streets was confiscated by the city.[126] And her late husband's business, the Kon Wo Company, was left in the hands of his business partners. Although she was not fluent in English, she was determined to make life work and raised her two daughters in the Chinatown.

Another suicide occurred. On December 22, 1932, Mah Leung, aged forty-seven, jumped into Okanagan Lake near the CPR wharf and drowned. Prior to his suicidal act, several people saw him walking from the Kon Wo Store (共和号) in Chinatown to the wharf, but no one expected him to leap into the water. His body was found naked under the wharf. His friends noticed that he was depressed, often worried over money matters. He had expected to receive a certain sum of money from his father-in-law, who lived in the United States. But the money did not arrive. Three or four days prior to his death, he starved himself, refusing to eat any food. No inquest was held. His relatives in Vancouver took care of his funeral.[127]

The Golden Pheasant Restaurant

This famous first-class restaurant on Bernard Avenue, outside of Chinatown, was established by Mar Jok. In 1927, Mar migrated to Kelowna from Revelstoke and started the Star Restaurant on Water Street. Three years later, with the help of his brother, Mar Fee, he opened the Golden Pheasant Restaurant. The main feature of this restaurant was the 40-cent cost of a three-course dinner with coffee. At the back of his restaurant, card games were regularly held to entertain his fellow countrymen and other customers. There was no fear of raids in this gaming facility, since one policeman was a frequent player.

At the age of eleven, Mar Jok had immigrated with his father and his brother, Mar Fee, to Canada from Guangdong and settled in Revelstoke, where his father set up and the family operated a laundry shop. He attended school and graduated from high school in Revelstoke. He was frequently hired as an interpreter in civil and criminal court cases involving Chinese people throughout the Kootenay and Okanagan regions as well as in Alberta. Even after he had moved to Kelowna, he continued to provide interpretation services to the courts for Chinese cases. During the Great Depression, he fed the hungry with hot soup prepared in the kitchen of the Golden Pheasant after business hours.[128]

During World War II, Mar joined the BC Dragoons militia and attained the rank of sergeant. He also briefly attended the Vernon Army Camp. He was not only a successful businessman but also a community activist throughout his life. He reached out to the mainstream community, started the first Kelowna Boy Scout troop, taught the youngsters gymnastics and sponsored a local basketball team. In the community, he was recognized as a sage whose counsel was widely sought by Chinese and white people alike.[129]

In 1968, Mar retired from the restaurant business to operate a farm on the west side of the city to grow and supply vegetables to the retail stores and local markets.[130] Yet he continued to volunteer his services in the Chinese-Canadian community. Together with the late Ben Lee and other Chinese Canadians, he founded the Kelowna Chinese Cultural Society, which advocated connecting the Chinese-Canadian community with the mainstream society and other ethnic groups, such as the Japanese and the Vietnamese, as well as the group of landed immigrants from Hong Kong and Guangdong in Kelowna. Mar passed away on August 21, 1983, but his deeds and contributions are remembered and recognized. An elementary school erected on his property was named the Mar Jok Elementary School.[131]

The Decline of the Chinese Population in Chinatown

By 1930, the Chinese population in Kelowna had reached its peak of 500 Chinese settlers in Chinatown. As the years went by, the Chinese population gradually declined. Mar Jok estimated the drop in Chinatown's population as follows:[132]

1930	400–500
1940	250–300
1950	100–160
1960	50–60

Mar said the decline of the Chinese population was primarily due to there being no replacements for men who died or returned to China. The head tax, leveraged solely on the Chinese, had affected the replacement of Chinese labourers in agriculture, because many Chinese people could not afford to pay the tax to immigrate to Canada, and thus it was challenging to find replacement for those labourers who either had left Kelowna to work elsewhere or returned home to Guangdong. In 1923, the federal government passed the infamous Chinese Exclusion Act that successfully stopped Chinese immigration to Canada. Without new immigrants coming into Kelowna, the labour contractors found it very difficult, if not impossible, to find or recruit Chinese labourers for the farms and the orchards to replace those who had left. Thus, many employment contractors retired from their businesses. In 1947, Lee Bon, the employment contractor, bid farewell to Kelowna and returned to China for his retirement.[133] As the Chinese population dwindled, some Chinese businesses also closed down. Kwong Lee Yuen, the Chinese general and grocery store, shut its doors in 1949.[134]

Furthermore, in the 1950s, local market gardening declined due to imports of American fruits and produce to British Columbia, which contributed to the sluggish wholesale and retailing of local fruits and vegetables. Packing houses and fruit canneries also reduced the numbers of labourers they employed. As a result, many Chinese labourers lost their jobs and left town.[135]

The City Park Café, commonly known as Quong's, was turned over to Jim and Won Quong by Tape Kwong (Quong) when he went back to China to retire in the early years. Both Jim and Won managed the café well and their business flourished. For more than twenty-five years, the café was a popular eatery for many people after going to a movie or to dance parties in town. After Jim passed on, Won carried on the business for a while. On January 1964, the café shut its doors. Later, the building was demolished, marking the disappearance of an important landmark in Chinatown. Many old-timers in Kelowna, however, still retain fond memories of the steak sandwiches, clam chowder and cream pies served at the City Park Café.[136]

Many young Chinese Canadians who were born and raised in Kelowna left home after they had graduated from high school. They went to the Lower Mainland and Vancouver Island for post-secondary education. After they graduated from college or university, many remained in the Lower Mainland or migrated to other growing and vibrant cities to seek job opportunities.[137] When they did not return to Kelowna, their parents usually followed them and moved away from Kelowna to Vancouver or Victoria where the Chinese communities were larger. Their departures compounded the reduction in Chinese population.

As time went by, many members of the Chinese Freemasons society and the Dart Coon Club passed on or left town. "In 1972, only six or seven senior members of these organizations were in town," said Tun Wong. "Wong Kim, one of the directors of the Chinese Freemasons society, asked me if I could sell the buildings for the organizations. I sold the buildings for them. And Wong Kim sent the proceeds to the society's headquarters in Vancouver." But the new owners did not take care of the buildings and left them unkempt, littered with torn-apart furniture, ancient bedding and garbage. The Dart Coon Club building deteriorated into a windowless wreck. Dr. Dave Clarke, the South Okanagan Health Officer, recommended to the city council that the building be torn down.[138] Eventually, in 1979, the building was demolished. By then, many buildings in Chinatown were also vacant and neglected and had fallen apart because their owners had left. The only house that survived was the single-storey brick building, the premises of Jung Shoe Repairs and the Kwong Sing Laundry at 265-269 Leon Avenue—but the owners of these businesses were long gone. Thereafter, Chinatown disappeared in Kelowna.

A Remarkable Woman

After Wong Bat was robbed and killed, his wife, Wong Lee Sue Ping (黃李淑萍), lost his assets but she remained in Kelowna and managed to put bread and butter on the table and raise their two daughters. "Being a single mother without education and not able to speak English, how she could make a living and raise the two daughters is beyond me," said Tun Wong.[139]

Sue Ping was indeed a strong and resourceful Chinese woman, a supportive wife and loving mother. She was born October 10, 1911, in a village in the Zhong Shan district (中山县), formerly known as Xinning (新宁), and arrived in Vancouver at the age of seven with her aunt, who went back to China later on. She was left behind and worked as a maid in the Wing Sang Company in Vancouver.

In 1930, through arrangement, she married Wong Bat Hong Suam, a man who was twenty-four years older than she was. They had two girls and lived in Chinatown. In 1937, five years after the death of Wong, she met Wong Ying (黃金英), a labourer, and married him. Wong Ying was fifteen years older. He worked in orchards and on farms near Kelowna and attempted to operate a restaurant twice. The couple lived in a sixty-five-square-metre (700-square-foot) house on 245 Leon Avenue in Chinatown. The house consisted of a living room, bedroom and kitchen. A few years later, the house was expanded to include a large stove for a wok and fryer, a large granite millstone and a one- by three-metre (three by eight feet) sink.

After her husband, Wong Bat, was murdered in a robbery, Wong Lee Sue Ping stayed in Kelowna to raise their two daughters. She later met and married Wong Ying and had nine more children with him. The family of thirteen lived together in a small one-bedroom house. Image courtesy of Tun Wong.

During the fourteen years of their marriage, they had nine children—five sons and four daughters. All thirteen members of the family, including the two girls from Sue Ping's previous marriage, slept in the single bedroom that was lined with beds from wall to wall. Wong Ying's nine children were born in this small house with his help in delivering the babies. When a baby arrived, the children were asked to leave the bedroom. The door of the bedroom would be draped with a piece of large cloth. Wong Ying then went to the kitchen to prepare a basin of boiling water, brought it to the room and helped his wife give birth to their child. "Giving birth to a baby really wasn't any big deal," wrote Tun Wong, her fifth son, in commemorating his mother.

When Wong Ying passed away in 1960, seven of his children had yet to complete their grade twelve education. Sue Ping continued sending them to school by making and selling tofu to the community as well as in Vernon. Apparently, an RCMP officer helped her to send her products to Vernon every day. Making tofu demanded hard work. The soya beans needed to be soaked overnight. Early the next morning, Sue Ping would get up around 4:00 am to grind the beans on the large granite millstone. It required great strength to push the top part of the millstone round and round to grind the beans into soya milk. The final procedure of lifting and placing a heavy rock onto racks containing the bean curd to squeeze out the liquid was most challenging for Sue Ping. It took her a couple of hours to produce eight dozen of tofu every day.

Besides this, Sue Ping did all her household chores and tended to her family's needs, including preparing meals and doing laundry. She made time to listen and give advice to her children, always emphasizing helping and caring for one another in the family: "all members were to stay in touch and assist one another whenever required to do so."[140] She put all her children through high school. When the children were able to work after-school hours or after they had graduated from high school, she wanted them to contribute their earnings to the family so that they could stay ahead.

After all her children were able to stand on their own feet, she stopped making tofu for retail. Tun Wong sold the house on Leon Avenue and built Sue Ping a large house in the Lakeview subdivision. "My mother was not happy with me when I sold her house and donated her granite millstone to the Centennial Museum," said Wong. "I thought she would never speak to me again. But she had worked so hard to raise us and make sure we all acquired a secondary school education. I wanted to give her a comfortable house for her retirement. She is my inspiration." He paused. With gratitude and a hint of remorse, he continued, "I am glad my mother lived long enough to see us, brothers and sisters, succeed in life. Unfortunately, my father did not have the chance to see our successful endeavours."

Sue Ping was also a compassionate and generous person and had never turned anyone away when the person needed financial help, though her ability to do so was rather limited. "Mother had a little book in which she recorded small loans to needy people," said Wong. "Needless to say, most of the people who borrowed money from her never paid back."

She was friendly and hospitable, always offered tea or snacks to friends, especially those of her children who came visiting or dropped by briefly. During World War II, she showed empathy towards the Japanese living in Kelowna who were alienated by the Chinese and the community at large.

She passed away on November 11, 1997, fondly remembered by her children and grandchildren. Many members in the Chinese community and the mainstream, including the employer of her late husband, Wong Ying, attended her funeral.[141]

Three Notable Chinese Canadians

After the early Chinese settlers and their descendants in Canada had regained their enfranchisement in 1947, they applied for Canadian citizenship and became Chinese Canadians. Prior to this year, the Chinese in Kelowna had made attempts to reach out and gave generously to the Red Cross and supported the victory bond drives and other national efforts, especially at the beginning of World War II. Meanwhile, the local Chinese Canadians took pride in looking after and assisting one another. Tom Hamilton, Kelowna's welfare administrator from 1946 to 1974, knew the residents of Chinatown well. He commented that no Chinese would ask for or be willing to receive welfare even when they were unemployed; only in rare cases of chronic illness would they accept assistance.

Although the Chinatown had disappeared from the landscape of Kelowna, the spirit of the Chinese-Canadian community remained alive. It was very fortunate that the late Ben Lee arrived in Kelowna in 1961. He had been born in Armstrong in 1930. After graduating from high school there, he went to Normal School in Victoria and then completed his bachelor of education degree at the University of British Columbia. In 1961, he took a teaching position in Rutland. While he was there, he became involved with the park society. In 1973, he entered politics and was elected as an alderman to Kelowna's city council; he served on the council for twenty-four years. He was instrumental in the assimilation of Rutland into the City of Kelowna when the city's boundaries expanded in that year, and he played a significant role in the development of Kelowna's Heritage Management Plan and Guisachan Heritage Park.[142] While on council, he served as a regional board director and chair of the regional parks committee for thirteen years and established the regional district park system. Over the years, his community involvement extended to his church, Kelowna General Hospital, the Athens Aquatic Centre and coaching youth sports.

In 1974, Ben Lee founded the Kelowna Multicultural Society with Mar Jok, Tun Wong, Dr. Lim Woh and a few young professionals to promote multiculturalism, and he spearheaded the Folkfest celebration on July 1, Canada Day, for many years. It was important to him for all Canadians to know their roots. "If we don't know our roots, we will lose our heritage," he said.[143] "Canada is a country that gives people the right to retain colourful traditions. We do not want to assimilate people and lose their identities. We want to maintain our multicultural diversity."

On Kelowna's seventy-fifth anniversary, he encouraged the Chinese community to participate in parades. They put up a float with participants dressed in traditional Chinese garments and re-enacted the past. "We need to inform the present and future generations of all Canadians about the difficult lives of our ancestors," said Lee.

In the early 1980s, many young Chinese professionals immigrated to Kelowna from the Lower Mainland and overseas. Some of the landed immigrants arrived in Kelowna from Hong Kong and Vietnam. The Kelowna Chinese Cultural Society became the centre for the new arrivals to get together, socialize with one another, participate in various multicultural activities and get to know Canada. For a number of years, the board members met in a room upstairs in the arena. Mar generously donated a lion's head with a colourful costume to the society to encourage young people to learn and perform the dance, especially for Chinese New Year celebrations.

"At the beginning, it was really terrific," said Lee. "We had about fifty young people interested in learning the lion dance. Unfortunately, we often could not find a teacher to continue teaching them!"

At one time, they celebrated the Chinese New Year with the lion dance, folk dances, music and songs in a community hall at Rutland. Many of the prominent citizens of the city and other guests, including Chinese, Japanese, Vietnamese and Euro-Canadians, were invited to the event.

There was no charge for admission except for food and drinks, which they had to purchase from some stores and restaurants.

Lee also felt it important to preserve Chinese culture. So, the society established a Chinese school to teach Chinese language two days after school hours and during the weekend.

"We held three classes—two in Cantonese and one in Mandarin in a public school," said Lee. "The school not only offered Chinese language to the Chinese people or descendants but also to other Canadians." Unfortunately, as time went by, it was not easy to find people to teach the Chinese languages. So the Chinese school became a thing of the past.

As our conversation continued, Lee appeared somewhat disappointed. He said, "Nowadays, it is difficult to find leaders to run the society. Many former directors are professionals who have limited time to volunteer their services. Also some of them were transferred away. For example, our treasurer, who was a vice-manager of the TD Bank, was transferred to Vancouver. The martial arts teacher, a controller at Sears who was responsible for teaching the younger ones kung fu and the lion dance, left for Vancouver. When these key members left town, it became difficult for the society to remain active. Young participants had their commitments in school. After graduating from high school, some of them left for university and other post-secondary institutions out of town."

In 1989, Lee received a public service award from the Vancouver Multicultural Society of BC for his invaluable contributions in preserving cultural heritage. It was the first recognition of anyone outside of the Lower Mainland. In 1996, the City of Kelowna named a new eight-hectare park in Rutland in his name, as recognition of his years of dedicated service in the city and its vicinity.

"Usually a park is named after a great person who had passed on," commented Mayor Doug Findlater of West Kelowna, a friend and associate of Lee. "It is quite a tribute for Ben Lee."

"The city wanted Ben to raise money and develop the park," remarked Tun Wong.

"I am honoured that the park is dedicated to me," said the late Ben Lee. "As the chairman of the park steering committee, I have started the fundraising campaign for creating the park."

Lee succeeded in his fundraising campaign, created with support and assistance from the city council, his family and many of his associates. The Ben Lee Park was officially opened on June 24, 2001.

In his sunset years, Lee suffered from and battled with cancer for a while. At the age of eighty-six, the honourable and admirable Ben Lee passed away in his sleep at home on March 21, 2016. He was survived by his wife, Joyce, and their two sons, John and Robert. The celebration of his life took place at the Ben Lee Park. His legacies will be remembered and treasured by his family, associates and friends and the community in Kelowna.

Tun Wong is another well-known Chinese Canadian in Kelowna. Wong was born in 1942, raised in Chinatown and lived with his parents and ten siblings in the small house at 245 Leon Avenue. His parents, Wong Ying and Lee Sue Ping, and all his siblings lived in the house when they were young. "Originally the house [the residence of Wong Bat] was on Harvey Avenue," explained Tun Wong. "When my mother lost the properties of Wong Bat, she was somehow allowed to retain the house and to drag it over to Leon later on." [144]

In his childhood, Tun Wong and his siblings were the only kids in the area. Mar Jok had a daughter, but they did not live in Chinatown.

In 1996, a park was named after Ben Lee for his contributions to the Multicultural Society of BC. Here, Ben Lee is pictured at the park in 2009. Image courtesy of Lily Chow.

Tun Wong's father, Wong Ying, was a seasonal labourer who worked at farms and orchards. In order to make ends meet, his mother produced and sold tofu to support the family. While his father was at work and his mother was making tofu, the older children, especially those who were not old enough to go to school, had to babysit the younger ones. They often went to the city park to play or read comic books. After making tofu, their mom would prepare meals and do the household chores. They returned home for meals and went back to the park again. The older siblings joined them in the park after school and stayed together until sunset. The city park was a safe place for children and adults then.

Tun Wong often saw his older siblings crying when they returned home from school. They were bullied, insulted and discriminated against in school. On his first day at school, his father dropped him at the door of the school. Before leaving him, his father said, "There is nothing much I can do for you in school as you know more English than I do. Behave yourself and learn well."

As he entered the school building, he saw a white man and a blond student talking together. The adult pointed at him and murmured to the young boy. Then the boy came up and sneered at him. "You're a Chink!" Obviously, the adult had taught the boy the racist language. Tun Wong got mad, punched the boy and started a fight. A teacher came by to stop them but did not make any attempt to find out the cause of the fighting. Racist slurs continued to be hurled at him in school, and he continued fighting back to retaliate against those who called him names and hurt his feelings.

One day, a group of students were playing soccer in the school field during lunch hour. One player missed the ball but Wong caught it and kicked it to the goal. The goalie missed catching the ball. The opposite team cheered. Then he was asked to play in the game. With his natural talent in sports, he excelled in soccer and gradually gained acceptance by many students. And his academic achievements in school astounded the teachers and students. Gradually, the prejudice and discrimination against him in school disappeared.

Although he gained acceptance and recognition in school, some other young adults in the community still gave the Wong family a hard time, especially at Hallowe'en. Because his mother needed firewood to make tofu, the Wong family stacked up at least four rows of firewood, each row about fifteen metres (fifty feet) deep, in front of the house. A few nights after Hallowe'en in one year, a group of eight or nine teenagers came into the yard and pushed down the rows of firewood in the dark. The following morning, the Wong kids piled the wood up again. This disturbing occurrence continued for a few years. Every time it happened, they called the police using the telephone of a neighbour, but the police never appeared. Finally, Wong told his four brothers that they had to do something to stop the disturbance. They decided to leave a space between the third and fourth rows where they kept boxes of fairly large stones. As the evening approached, they wore gloves and helmets that they used in sports, prepared slings with willow branches, and hid among the boxes of stones, ready to retaliate. When the culprits arrived to dismantle the rows of wood, they threw or flung stones at them. Many of the perpetrators got hurt and took flight. After that, no one came to push down the rows of firewood.

Participating in sports was bound to give the Wong boys cuts, bruises and sprains at times. When they came home with injuries, their mother always used her homemade Chinese medicated plaster (铁打膏药) to rub the injured areas strenuously. "Her treatments were usually more painful than the injury," commented Wong. "When we screamed with pain during her massaging, she smiled and said, 'The more it hurts, the better it is for you'! We always thought it was her way of getting even with us for not listening to her advice not to take part in sports. But her remedies and treatments worked and helped us to recover from the injuries."[145]

When he reached his preteen years, Wong went to work in an orchard as a casual after-school labourer. The owner of the orchard told him, "I pay your dad seventy-five cents a day, but I will only pay you fifty cents because you are young and inexperienced." He accepted the offer. After a few months, the owner raised his pay to seventy-five cents, because he was hard-working and did his jobs well. He continued working as a casual labourer in the orchard for nine years, although he still made time to participate in sports.

Every month Wong handed his wages to his mother, as did all his siblings when they were able to earn money. His mother told them that as members of the family they had to support and take care of one another, and must stay together in unity.

After he graduated from elementary school, Wong continued his secondary education at Kelowna Senior High School. He played soccer on the school team and won many tournaments for the school. He was a leader and elected as the president of the athletic council for five years. In 1960, he graduated from grade thirteen, senior matriculation, but could

Tun Wong (pictured in 2016), son of Wong Ying and Lee Sue Ping, was born in 1942 in Kelowna's Chinatown. He studied accounting through correspondence, and eventually became the finance manager at Kelowna City Hall. Image courtesy of Lily Chow.

not go to college or university because his dad had passed away that year, and his family could not afford to send him to a post-secondary school. But he continued studying accounting by correspondence and obtained a chartered accounting designation or diploma.

After obtaining the diploma, he applied for an accounting job in a sawmill. He was not accepted, since the position had been given to a white person. He went to work in the agricultural industry instead. In 1969, the City of Kelowna recruited him to work in its finance department. After a year or so, he was promoted to the position of finance manager at Kelowna City Hall. He remained in this position until he retired.[146]

In 1971, Wong married Kathy, a sweet lady with British and French ancestries. Wong and Kathy had two children, a boy and a girl. Grandma Lee often babysat the children when the young couple went to work and on vacations. "I am so happy to have married Kathy. She is a sweet woman and a loving wife," commented Wong. "And I am grateful that my mother was around when my children were born. My children have very fond memories of their grandmother."

Prior to his retirement, Wong volunteered to serve in many non-profit organizations, such as the Kelowna Football Club, the Junior Hockey Club, the Westside Minor Hockey Association and the Kelowna Triathlon, among others. In the 1980s, he assisted the late Ben Lee in organizing Folkfest on Canada Day. When Lee initiated the Kelowna Chinese Cultural Society, Wong became one of the founding members and served as treasurer of the society for two years. "We raised funds for the Kelowna Chinese Cultural Society by selling food in a booth at Folkfest on Canada Day. After twelve years of active performances and recognized achievements, the society began to show signs of fatigue, as quite a number of board members had left town," he commented. "The new members wanted to attend functions but did not want to serve the society. Ben Lee and his family and I and my family, including my brothers and sisters in town, kept it going for thirteen or more years. Then we dissolved the society. We had some funds left and donated them to the Central Okanagan Foundation to set up a legacy fund in the name of Ben Wah Lee. Ben Lee's two sons and I are the consulting directors of the legacy fund. We hope the legacy fund will grow and help to maintain the Ben Lee Park."

Besides these activities, Wong sat on the board of the Centennial Museum [now the Okanagan Heritage Museum], was elected as president of the Lakeview Recreation Commission, and was appointed as an organizer of the cemetery restoration by the Asian Heritage and Restoration Committee. He was a director of the Friends of Mission Creek that helped create a trail in the area. His deeds and contributions have been enormous and commendable.

Lee Shui Dong is a remarkable Chinese-Canadian in Kelowna, capable and resourceful. Lee is not a Canadian-born Chinese but was born in Guangdong. One month after his birth, the Lee family left home and took refuge in Hong Kong because of the land reform policy, a strategy Mao Zedong (毛泽东) implemented in the 1950s. In Hong Kong, his dad owned and operated a thriving laundry business. Lee attended school in Hong Kong for five years. While the family was in Hong Kong, they applied to immigrate to Canada. In 1969, Lee's great-grandfather, Lee Yick Wei (李奕伟), visited them in Hong Kong and returned with them to British Columbia, since their applications for immigration to Canada had been approved by then. They arrived in Vernon, where the Low or Lau (刘氏家族) family, the maternal grandparents of Lee, were living. The Low family was very wealthy, and had owned and operated Chinese herbal stores and a cloth-dying factory in China prior to their immigration to Canada. In Vernon, the Lows owned and cultivated farmland and operated restaurants. Lee and his brother, Shui Chor (李瑞楚) or Jay Lee, attended school in Vernon, but he only stayed in school for a year. He was then twelve years of age and Jay was eleven.

"In school, some white students called us 'chink', Chinaman and some other subordinate names," said Lee. "I was angry and frustrated, and felt that they were not only insulting me but also the Chinese people. As a young child, I felt degraded. They made me feel ashamed and inferior for being a Chinese person. I often wondered why I was not a white person but a person with yellow skin. If I was a white person, I would not have been bullied."

Then he talked about his experience learning English. "It was not easy for me to learn English. Fortunately, I met a Canadian girl in school who wrote me love letters that motivated me to reply to her in English. When I made mistakes

Lee Shui Dong moved to Canada from Guangdong as a young boy. He became the president of Kelowna's Chinese Freemasons society in 1995, and continues to hold the position at the time of publication. Image courtesy of Lee Shui Dong.

in my responses, she corrected me. This short-lived romantic fantasy enabled me to learn and communicate in English. In later years, I joined the cadre in Kelowna that helped me improve my spoken English too."[147]

After leaving school, Lee worked as a busboy in his uncle's restaurant in Vernon for two years. Once he noticed a group of ten persons who left after their meals without paying. He was asked to chase after them. He did, but was only able to catch one person. The customer paid what he owed but refused to pay for his peers. When Lee argued with him, the customer retorted, "Tough! If you don't like it, go back to Hong Kong."

The incident gave the owner of the restaurant a chance to scold and accuse him for not having caught all the runaways. "How could I?"

he asked, as he spread his arms and shook his head. "I was alone and smaller than most of them!" Then he sighed and continued, "In a way I do not blame my people, because the restaurant was losing money in such an instance."

Lee's experiences as an immigrant in the late 1960s reflect not only his personal struggles and challenges but also the hardship in his adopted country and the political instabilities in China that forced the Chinese to leave their homes, especially those in Guangdong.

In 1972, Lee helped out at a vegetable farm located on Old Camp Work Road or Indian Lane (红番巷) at harvest time. He picked up a large winter melon, not knowing that it had prickling tiny white hairs on the skin. The bristles hurt his palms and were difficult to remove. The farmers told him to wash his hands with lime juice or vinegar, which would remove the hairs from his palms. He took their advice and got the hairs removed. "But I could not forget the pain when I poured vinegar on my hands. It was just like pouring acid on a raw wound," he lamented and shook his head.

Working at the farm made him realize that farming was not easy. He had to get up at 4:45 am, take a bath and then go to the field to pick tomatoes, cucumbers and winter melons. The most challenging task was removing weeds from green onions with their tall leaves. He had to bend down to remove the weeds because if he was to squat down while pulling the weeds, his bottom might squash the green onions. Bending down like this took a toll on his back.

In 1972, his family bought the Seven Seas Restaurant on 275 Bernard Street. He stopped working at the farm and focussed instead on managing the restaurant business. Eventually he took over the restaurant and operated the business for more than twenty-six years. The restaurant business flourished. At the same time, he ventured into a tourist business. A tourist guide, Zhu Wei De (译音：朱怀德), from Vancouver encouraged him to introduce and promote Kelowna and its surrounding region to tourists from Hong Kong, Southeast Asia, Taiwan and China. As a tourism guide, he had to learn about tourist attractions in Kelowna as well as in the Okanagan region in general, and to make contacts with wineries, park supervisors, and museum managers and curators in these areas.

"At the beginning, I spoke mainly English to the visitors and tourists as a guide," said Lee. "Zhu then suggested that I should speak Mandarin and Cantonese to the Chinese guests. I am thankful to Zhu for the advice.

With practice, I am now fluent in speaking three languages—English, Mandarin and Cantonese."

In October 1997, the Seven Seas Restaurant took home the Award of the Decade for the best business with fewer than ten employees in Kelowna. This award was sponsored by the Kelowna *Capital News*.[148]

"He's definitely a bit of an ambassador," added Lynda Trudeau of the Okanagan-Similkameen Tourism Association. He is a good storyteller, often adds colour and humour to his narratives, which has enticed tourists and visitors into wanting to know more about the area."

In 1989, a golden opportunity presented itself when a Hong Kong reporter visited Kelowna to discover Ogopogo. Lee made himself available as a host and guide to the city. The resulting media coverage created a flood of tourists from Asia to Kelowna, and Lee's hospitality fanned the flames. After having engaged in the tourist business for two years, though only part-time, he earned an award from the Hong Kong Tourist Association for the Seven Seas Restaurant as the best restaurant in the Okanagan. During the summers from 1990 to 1995, at least five tour buses a day arrived in Kelowna and visited the Seven Seas Restaurant.

Although Lee's grandfather was a staunch member of the Chinese Freemasons society, he did not impart the history of the organization to his grandson. As stated earlier, the buildings of the Chinese Freemasons society and the Dart Coon Club had been demolished by 1979, but a few members still lived in Kelowna. These members often received information from the society headquarters and got together to share news with one another. Lee thought the old-timers were just socializing with one another on those occasions. One day, a couple of the society members asked him to join the organization. They said, "Since your older generations were members of the Chinese Freemasons society, you should join the organization and revitalize the society and the Dart Coon Club."

Then the old-timers related the history of the society to him. In China, it was formed when the Ming dynasty was conquered in 1644 by the Qing, the Manchurian people. The main objective of this organization was to overthrow the Qing dynasty and restore the Ming dynasty (反清复明). Originally the organization was known as the Heaven and Earth Association (天地会).

In 1995, Lee joined the Chinese Freemasons society and was elected president of the Kelowna chapter, becoming the youngest society leader in Canada. He continues to hold this position today. After eight years of great efforts and determination, plus the ability to recover the funds from the sale of the original buildings in Chinatown from the Chinese Freemasons society headquarters in Vancouver, he and a few dedicated members were able to purchase the building at 1433 Ethel Street. It took them eight years to achieve their goals. Both the Kelowna Chinese Freemasons society and the Dart Coon Club have been resurrected, and membership has increased and progressed under Lee's leadership.

In August 2003, a huge forest fire occurred at Okanagan Mountain Park that destroyed many homes and properties. The city accommodated the fire victims at the Parkinson Activity Centre. Lee and a group of Freemason members went around town gathering donations to provide subsidies and other aid to the fire victims and brought them food and clothing at the Parkinson Centre.[149] On October 10, 2003, the Honourable Adrienne Clarkson, the twenty-sixth Governor General of Canada (1999–2005) visited Kelowna and the disaster area. She met with and congratulated Lee for his efforts and achievements in leading the Kelowna Chinese Freemasons society and the Dart Coon Club.

Nowadays, the Kelowna society and club have a ladies' auxiliary and a lion and dragon dance group. These organizations observe and celebrate many Chinese festivals, such as Qing Ming, the mid-Autumn Moon Festival and the Chinese New Year, and participate in many community events. These two Chinese organizations have, indeed, revived, rising up like a phoenix from ashes under the leadership of Lee, commonly known as Shui Lee.

In January 2014, the Honourable Minister Teresa Wat of the Ministry of International Trade and Multiculturalism held a consultation forum in Kelowna, aimed at correcting the historical wrongs that had imposed hardship and suffering on the Chinese pioneers and investigating the need for an apology from the province of British Columbia. The late Ben Lee, Tun Wong and Shui Lee of the Kelowna Dart Coon Club attended the consultation. Shui Lee told the assembly that his great-grandfather had paid the $500.00 head tax to gain entry to Canada but the Chinese Exclusion Act prevented him from sponsoring his wife to come over to reunite with him. His grandfather could not see his immediate family until 1947, when the act was repealed. In November of the same year, Shui Lee was appointed by the ministry as a member of the Legacy Initiatives Advisory Council.

The Pavilion of Eternal Rest

About a hundred Chinese graves are found in the Asian section of the Kelowna Memorial Park Cemetery. The deceased were Chinese and Japanese people who lived in Kelowna between 1900 and 1960. This section was segregated from the burial ground of the mainstream pioneers. Some of the deceased were labourers who built the seventy-four-kilometre (forty-six-mile) CPR line from Sicamous south to Vernon, then eight kilometres (five miles) west to Okanagan Landing,[150] while the others were residents of Kelowna. Many of the deceased were members of the Chinese Freemasons society. Their graves were marked by wooden markers on which their names and birthplace were inscribed. The City of Kelowna has operated the cemetery, now known as Kelowna Memorial Park Cemetery, since 1911.[151] A few graves have been exhumed.

Over the years, people from Kelowna's Chinatown looked after the graves in the Chinese section. They lit candles, burnt paper money and offered sacrifices at the gravesites of their relatives and friends, and cleaned up their tombs during Qing Ming and Chong Yang, the Chinese festivals of the dead. As time went on, the writings on the markers became weathered and worn. In the 1950s, many Chinese families replaced the markers with new concrete headstones.

As the cemetery aged, the concrete headstones cracked and fell apart, and maintenance and safety issues began to surface, as the site is located on a slope at the back of the original cemetery site. In 2000, the city, the Kelowna Chinese Cultural Society and the Japanese Canadian Club initiated the rehabilitation for the old and unkempt Asian section and formed an Asian Heritage and Restoration Committee. In 2000, both Lee and Tun Wong, the key members of the committee, undertook the restoration of the Chinese and Japanese section in the cemetery. The committee also invited Donald Luxton and Associates along with Dr. David Chuenyan Lai to study and produce the Kelowna Cemetery Heritage Management Plan in 2001. It took a couple of years for these two gentlemen to complete the plan.

In this project, 150 headstones, inscribed with the names and the dates of birth and death of the deceased, were replaced with polished granite stones. The undertaking included restoration work around the graves and on the defined paths in the cemetery, and the construction of a gazebo, the Pavilion of Eternal Rest (永眠亭). This pavilion also serves as a place of repose and remembrance. The contributions of the early Asian community in Kelowna were documented and displayed inside the pavilion. With these efforts, the memory of the early Chinese people in Kelowna is being preserved and kept alive.

In 2015, the Kelowna Chinese Cemetery was recognized as a Chinese Canadian Heritage Site by the Ministry of International Trade and Multiculturalism, the Legacy Initiatives Advisory Council, and the Ministry of Forests, Lands and Natural Resources. On December 3, 2016, Shui Lee,

The Pavilion of Eternal Rest was erected to honour the memory of the early residents of Kelowna's Chinatown, many of whom died during the consruction of the CPR. Image courtesy of the author.

the president of the Kelowna Chinese Freemasons society and the Dart Coon Club, organized a ceremony for unveiling a large granite monument installed in the pioneer section of the Kelowna Memorial Park Cemetery. This commemorative plaque is a follow-up to the 2014 apology by the provincial government that recognized the hardships experienced by the Chinese in Canada in the past and honoured their contributions to the province.

Indeed, the Chinatown in Kelowna had its glorious days. Small businesses flourished and employment agencies found jobs and accommodation for the Chinese men. Because the population consisted mostly of men without their families, Chinese organizations provided them with recreation and information about the turbulent situations in their home villages, and made efforts to look after early Chinese settlers, helping to create an outstanding Chinese community. It was the differences in culture and language, and the disparities in social and economic conditions and political settings, that kept the Chinese community and the mainstream community apart. Prejudice and discrimination were the main factors that isolated the Chinese community in the early days. The personal narratives generously shared by the interviewees reflect the effects of political changes in Canada and China, and their effects on the lives of the Chinese pioneers and their descendants as well as those of Chinese Canadians.

ARMSTRONG: THE "CELERY CITY"

In 1885, William Charles Heaton-Armstrong, a private banker who successfully promoted and sold bonds for the construction of the Shuswap and Okanagan Railway, a subsidiary line of the Canadian Pacific Railway, visited the valley of Spallumcheen, the territory of the Splatsin First Nation, a member of the Shuswap Nation Tribal Council. Heaton-Armstrong found that a large portion of the area was covered with marshes. But years before, Alfred Postill had erected a sawmill on the 640 acres (259 hectares) he had pre-empted at the edge of the wetland. When the Shuswap and Okanagan Railway construction was completed in 1892, Heaton-Armstrong and other pioneers paid to drain the water from the swamps and remove the weeds (sphagnum and other weeds) so that the land could be used. After draining off the water and clearing out the weeds, a thick layer of loam was exposed. People called the land covered by loam the "bottom land."

Farmers then tilled the bottom land to grow oats, potatoes and vegetables. In 1904, E. R. Burnett harvested three hundred pounds of celery from his first crop; obviously celery would thrive in the bottom land.[152] This success story motivated Chinese farmers to migrate and cultivate celery and other vegetables in the bottom land. Lettuce, carrots, tomatoes and strawberries were also grown on the land where celery was not cultivated.

Within a few years, the excellent quality of the celery had created a great demand for it. As a result, the cultivation of celery became the primary industry in the bottom land, which produced four to five hundred tons of celery each year in the industry's heyday. The celery was shipped in forty-, fifty- and sixty-pound boxes each day from July to December to grocers in BC and other cities, provinces and states, including Toronto in the east, California in the south and Hawaii in the west. The production of celery, mainly by the Chinese gardeners, won fame for the municipality as the Celery City.

On March 26, 1913, the town was incorporated as the City of Armstrong in honour of William Charles Heaton-Armstrong. This city is located in the North Okanagan between Vernon and Enderby, about 482 kilometres (300 miles) away from Vancouver. Gone are the days when rows of celery in immaculate geometrical arrangements covered the landscape, but agriculture, ranching and logging still remain as the main industries in Armstrong.

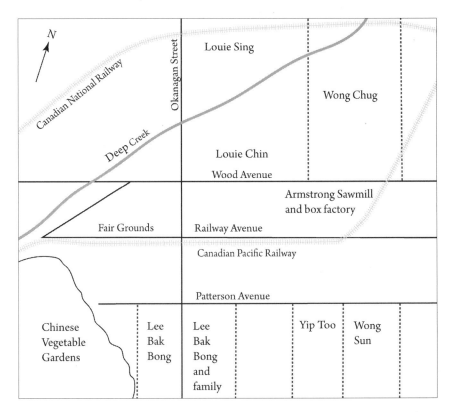

Armstrong's Chinatown began to form in the early twentieth century. The Chinese residents struggled against the prejudices of the town's white residents.

The Chinese Migrants and Laundries

It is not known when the first Chinese immigrants arrived in Armstrong, but their existence in town was noted in early newspapers. On October 15, 1903, the *Armstrong Advertiser* stated that "negotiations are under way to sell a place… in the heart of town to some Chinamen for erecting a laundry… the deal is almost completed. If such is the case it certainly throws discredit on the seller… it is a shame as a dirty Chinese laundry is most undesirable in the centre of our town. There is plenty of room… outside the town proper [for the laundry]."

Similar complaints and prejudice against the Chinese small businesses also surfaced. On January 12, 1906, the *Armstrong Advance* said that "… some places among the Chinese washee houses in town [carried] on gambling… among the Celestials… this is hardly the proper thing to be tolerated among people who enjoy the protection of civic courts of the country…"

Furthermore, in April 17, 1909, one person wrote the following letter to the editor of the *Armstrong Advertiser*:

Dear Sir,

The revelation of the Vernon Chinese laundries and the dwellings should make the ratepayers and the citizens of our own town pay attention to the Chinese question in... Armstrong... The very dirty habits of these people, no regard to sanitation, no sense of decency, make them extremely undesirable next door neighbours... land might be allotted to them on the outskirts, not on the principal street... In these days when prevention of disease is becoming as important as curing, we might help ourselves to get the filthy pest removed from our midst. [I] presume that our municipality with its energetic Reeve and Councillors will see fit to move "O Washee Me" and "Me too" to a breezy few acres with some natural drainage.

Signed: Ratepayer.

Whether the newspaper journalists and this "Ratepayer" in Armstrong had gone into these Chinese premises to investigate remains doubtful. Obviously, they became alarmed after having read the findings of Vernon's Health Committee about the poor conditions of the Chinese laundries in that city from the *Vernon News*. Those findings stated "the washing operations were conducted in an indescribably filthy condition... In Hong Suey laundry... clothes were found thrown in heaps on a very dirty floor, one pile being in the pool of dirty water... the clothes were dried in a yard in which there was an open drain."[153] This report of the Vernon Health Committee plus additional similar messages about two other Chinese laundries in Vernon might have stimulated the Ratepayer to make his distasteful remarks about the Chinese laundries in Armstrong.

Other complaints and resentment towards the Chinese immigrants also appeared in the newspapers. In March 1909, the *Armstrong Advertiser* stated that:

Night after night a hideous clatter is kept up at the Chinese den on Okanagan Street; gambling is constantly indulged, first class aromas constantly arise from these premises and a dope fiend finds shelter there… Residents in town living in Rosedale and Eastview pass [through] the Chinese premises many times a day… School children go up and down the street [Okanagan] four times daily… The present wash house should be removed… Their presence in town is an eyesore and will no longer to be tolerated.[154]

Indeed, the voices against the Chinese laundries and the desire to have them relocated to the outskirts of the townsite came out loud and clear.

On May 29, 1909, the editorial in the *Armstrong Advertiser* responded that Councillor Brett had brought up the issue of the Chinese laundry at a council meeting, and Reeve Daykin and Councillor Brett were given instructions to deal with the matter and to put a stop to the Chinese laundry businesses. The actions taken by Daykin and Brett to deal with the issue of the Chinese laundry businesses are not known.

But it is comforting to find a letter written by a reader to the *Armstrong Advertiser* editor in favour of the Chinese immigrants. The letter was published in the May 15, 1913, edition of the paper:

Editor, *Advertiser*,

[I write] to protest against the insinuation made about the Chinamen here. I have been dealing with the Chinamen for many years and have always found them easy to deal with, reasonable as to business, and prompt in delivering the produce ordered. As such I claim they are valuable citizens in the community… As to their shipping money out of the country, I presume they earn it or they would not get it and if they earn it is theirs to do what they like with… I agree with the man in the Kelowna Labour Commission. I would like to see ten times as many in here for the good of fruit growers and the Okanagan generally.

Signed: FAIR PLAY

Meanwhile, other Chinese activities were also noted in newspapers. For example, the *Armstrong Advance* stated that "the Chinese of this place were quite energetic… in celebrating their new year." A few months later, the same newspaper described a Chinese funeral in the Lansdowne Cemetery: "… the clothing of the deceased was burnt on the grave… a duck was roasted on top of the grave and left lying there as food for the spirit…"

And the *Armstrong Advertiser* reported that "Chung Yuen has bought out the Royal Café and will serve meals at all hours of the day or night…"

All the expressions in the news, positive and negative, suggested that the Chinese immigrants had arrived and begun to settle in Armstrong.

The Chinese Farmers

In 1911, W. A. Cuthbert, owner of the Fairfield Ranch on Wood Avenue, employed a full-time Chinese gardener, Louie Chin, and a few other Chinese workers to cultivate celery on his farm. He had two greenhouses for germinating celery seeds and nurturing the seedlings, which were transplanted into the fields in February each year. Chin tended the celery from seed to seedlings and from transplanting to harvesting. His job only ended when the produce was packed and shipped out. He continued to work at the farm even after Ted Poole took over the packing house from Cuthbert.

Chin was a likeable, happy-go-lucky person, always wearing a smile, and was able to read and write Chinese. "He used to come along with a little iron-wheeled wagon pulled by a horse to haul stuff from the farm to the packing house," said Mat Hansen Junior, a knowledgeable and long-time resident of Armstrong.

Many Chinese market gardeners and individual Chinese farmers also migrated to Armstrong around the same time that Chin arrived there. The Chinese market gardeners included John Hughie, Lee Bak Bong, Harry Lee, Wong Chug, Leon Sing, Hong Choy, Wong Soo and a few others. They were often referred to as the head gardeners. Since the Chinese farmers could not purchase property for farming, they leased land by the acre from white owners, Indigenous people and the owners of packing houses. In 1912, the farmland leased to the Chinese head gardeners caused fear and anxiety in some members of the Armstrong Board of Trade. Some of their concerns were expressed in the *Vernon News*:[155]

> By leasing for a cash rental, the Chinaman has the selling and disposal of all crops and as the immense increase in their production and shipping during the last two years proves, it is only a matter of a short time till they have control of the entire vegetable shipping industry of this valley… They are rapidly driving the white man out of this industry… Chinamen can pay a far higher rental than the white… his low standard of living can underbid the white man… Having leased say 10–20 acres, he secures his necessary

labour by forming a 2–3 or 4-man company… the renter [be-comes] the boss and the company are simply men working under him and get no pay till the crops are sold…

Obviously, members of the Armstrong Board of Trade were afraid that the Chinese gardeners would soon monopolize the farmland and take control of the vegetable business. The message, however, reveals the thrift-iness of the Chinese gardeners, who saved up their meagre earnings to pay higher rents to ensure they would have a piece of land for cultivating crops.

It was true that a few Chinese farmers had formed companies to cul-tivate their leased land. Wong Chug was one of these. He formed a com-pany under his name with his fellow workers on land leased from a white farmer. He did not pay wages regularly to his fellow workers until they har-vested and sold their crops. But he financed the company, including paying for and signing a lease for the land. He also provided food and shelter for his partners while the company was in operation. Perhaps having paid the initial expenses to establish the company, Wong might not have had the resources to pay his partners during the growing season. And operating the company required money to buy equipment and fertilizer. Besides, his partners might have agreed to accept the terms when the company was formed. In the early days, it was not easy for Chinese immigrants to find work in any field. Working together in a cooperative could help them earn a living and keep them going in a foreign land. In truth, forming this kind of cooperative was a common practice among the early Chinese settlers in both mining and farming. It was one way the Chinese immigrants could assist and support one another.

The Armstrong Board of Trade members also commented that the Chinese grocery stores in town advanced rice and provisions to the head of the company so he could feed his fellow workers. This only illustrates the mutual trust between the merchants and their customers. In the good old days, it was not easy for Chinese immigrants to obtain credit from financial institutions. And as credit cards were unknown at the time, obviously, the head of the Chinese company would be a reliable and trustworthy person, a man of good reputation. However, Wong was doing well, and bought a truck for the corporation to transport produce from the farmland to the packing houses.

In terms of protecting the Chinese farmers who appeared to have been unfairly treated by the head of such corporations, the voices of the members of the Armstrong Board of Trade showing their concern for the members in the cooperative should be appreciated. Unfortunately, the message projected more of their apprehension and fear of losing control over vegetable production and marketing than showing kindness and compassion towards the Chinese workers.

In 1912, a disturbing incident occurred in the Chinese community. Arthur Gee, a produce grower and shipper, was working with three Chinese farmers growing celery. These Chinese farmers felt that Gee had been unfair to them and attempted to take the issue into their own hands. They sold celery to Chong & Co. and collected payment contrary to Gee's instructions. So Gee stopped paying them for their products, which resulted in a conflict.

One day, Gee was pursued by two of these Chinese farmers. He quickly got away from them and went to A. Warner, a constable in town, for protection as well as assistance in resolving the matter. Warner then accompanied Gee uptown to meet with the Chinese farmers who again attempted to take Gee by force. A dispute occurred among them. Sing was one of the Chinese who verbally abused the constable and rushed at the policeman. At that instant, Warner pulled his revolver but could not intimidate Sing. Instead Sing challenged the constable, asking him to shoot. Warner put the gun in his pocket but gave Sing a black eye. In return the

Wong Sue built his home on the west side of Okanagan Street, north of Wood Avenue. Image courtesy of Ben McMahen.

constable also got a blow on his forehead. Warner left and returned with Geo. Wilson so that they could arrest Sing and put him into custody. At his trial, Justice of the Peace J. M. Wright and D. Graham imposed a penalty of $50.00 or six months in jail for Sing. The charge of assault laid by Gee against Sing was dismissed.[156]

In 1914, World War I began. Farmers grew potatoes instead of celery and other vegetables. A large dehydration plant was erected to dry the potatoes before they were sent to the troops in Europe. The cultivation of potatoes and the production of dehydrated potatoes attracted an influx of Chinese men to Armstrong. After World War I ended, the dehydration plant was closed down and the Chinese ventured into celery cultivation with the existing Chinese farmers. It was estimated that about a hundred acres (forty hectares) were devoted to celery production, one-third of which was cultivated by the Chinese farmers.[157] These Chinese farmers persevered in cultivating celery and lettuces, living and working in the fields season after season.

In 1918, Wong Sue arrived in Armstrong and built a shack on the farmland on the west side of Okanagan Street, north of Wood Avenue. He was a caring and generous person who always made an effort to help his countrymen in the Chinese community and donated as much money as he could to charity, especially to the Armstrong-Spallumcheen Hospital. He died at the age of seventy-eight in the hospital and was buried in the Chinese section of the Lansdowne Cemetery. He was survived by his wife in China.

Wong Sue's shack was left standing on the site for many years. It became the home of stray cats and mice. Old farm tools and two old wooden baskets along with stacks of crates as well as an old stove and chimney were left in the house. Old newspapers were found scattered on the floor. The windows had been permanently boarded up, but the door remained open.

It was well-known in town that Chin, another Chinese farmer, Wong Sue, and Limpy, an Indigenous woman from Enderby, had a kind of mutual understanding or rather a triangular relationship among them. Limpy and Wong Sue lived together in his shack. But whenever she had a fight with Wong, she went to Chin's, whose farmland was next to Wong's. Chin was gracious and generous to Limpy and allowed her to live with him. She lived with Chin until they too had a fight, and then she would leave and return to Wong across the street.[158] This state of affairs continued until Limpy left Armstrong later on.

Wong Sue's shack was abandoned after he died, but it stood for many years as a reminder of his generosity and contribution to the community. Image courtesy of Ban McMahen.

Leon Sing was the tallest Chinese man in the area, but very thin. He farmed on the land north of Okanagan Street. He and Wong Chug each lived in cabins in their fields to look after their vegetable crops. "Sing was an honest man," said Ralph Lockhart. "At one time, I wanted to take some lettuce to the coast. I went to his farm to get the lettuce. He asked me to pick any ones I wanted. I made my choice, showed him a box of lettuce that I had picked and wanted to pay him. He took a look at the lettuce, looked at me and laughed. He asked, 'Are you crazy picking this stuff?' Immediately, he took the box from me, threw away the lettuce and filled the box with the best ones. 'These are better ones for you, take them,' he said and offered the box to me."

Only two head gardeners, Lee Bak Bong and Hughie Jong, had their families with them. Both Lee and Jong brought their wives from China a few years after they had immigrated to BC and raised their families in Armstrong. The other Chinese farmers were single men who either worked for the head gardeners or as helpers on ranches or in the lumber industry. They lived in rooming houses on the top floor of the Chinese laundry buildings in Chinatown. During the growing season, the head gardeners cultivated many varieties of celery and lettuce in their fields, and practised crop rotation. In early spring, they planted celery on one part of the field and lettuce on the other. After harvesting the early celery, they grew lettuce in the same place where they had grown the celery. Similarly, after having harvested the early lettuce, they would plant the late celery crop there. The farmers used horse manure and other animal droppings to fertilize their crops.

These Chinese farmers started work early in the morning and toiled through the heat of the day. They worked harder than anyone, and didn't even stop to take time to eat together. Each of the men took turns cooking their meal on a tiny stove in the field, fuelled with dry firewood or branches that they had gathered in winter.

The Chinese Settlement: Chinatown

Chinatown was located at the corner of Okanagan Street and Patterson Avenue in the area where a red brick building, the Lee Bak Bong family house, once stood. In this Chinese settlement, small Chinese businesses, such as grocery stores, laundries, restaurants, cafés and rooming houses, were found. In the rooming houses, single Chinese men slept on bunk beds with pillows and blankets; a common kitchen at the back on the same floor was provided for them to do their own cooking. In winter, many of the farmers living in shacks in the fields returned to Chinatown and stayed in these rooming houses. Since they had no gardening work to do in winter, they often gambled on the upper floors of some of the laundry premises to pass the time. Some attempted to grubstake miners hoping to earn a couple of dollars. A few miners were found panning for gold around the three creeks that flow through the Spallumcheen Valley, the Fortune, Deep and Meighan creeks.

A disastrous occurrence took place in Chinatown in June 1922. Chinatown was almost burned to the ground by a blazing fire which started in an outbuilding. The flames spread to the wood-framed buildings of the Chinese and wiped out everything; even parts of a brick building in that location fell down. When the fire was out of control, a big fire engine came in from Vernon to help put out the fire. There was a lot of damage to the telephone and electric light poles, resulting in no services for half the city. The damage was estimated at about $25,000.00. It is unknown how much the Chinese lost in the blaze. Luckily, those Chinese farmers who lived in the rooming houses in Chinatown had gone to work in the field. Although this saved their lives, they lost their belongings and savings because they kept them in the rooming houses.[159] Reconstruction of some of the houses in Chinatown took place almost immediately. On September 7 of the same year, the *Armstrong Advertiser* stated that "work has been started on repairing the Chinese brick block next to the Fire Hall… The Yit Tong Co is the concern… the building is being repaired… The brick halls left standing after the fire appeared safe and no repair work was necessary but a certain amount of strengthening and bracing was deemed required… The interior of the building will be fixed up much the same as it was before… the job should be completed in about six weeks." The Sing Lung laundry at 3375 Okanagan Street was also affected by the fire; most of the building's interior was damaged. But major renovations and reconstruction of the building were carried out soon after the fire.

The Chinese community attempted to reach out and donated generously to the Armstrong-Spallumcheen Hospital. On December 18, 1947, the *Armstrong Advertiser* published a list of the Chinese donors and the amount that each donor had contributed. The list was as follows:

Number of Chinese Donors	Amount Donated
3	$10.00 x 3 = $30.00
18	$5.00 x 18 = $90.00
11	$2.00 x 11 = $22.00
4	$1.00 x 4 = $4.00
TOTAL	$146.00

The Cultivation of Celery

Around February each year, the farmers germinated celery seeds in hotbeds outside the house. After sowing the seeds in trays of soil, the Chinese farmers buried them in the ground and surrounded them with horse manure. Then they covered them with a piece of glass, on top of which they added a roll of tarpaper to keep heat inside as well to prevent excess water from slipping inside. These germination locations are referred to as the hotbeds. Gunny sacks were added on top of the two layers of insulation and pegs inserted on sides of the sacks to hold the insulators in place. These layers of coverings would be taken off in the morning so that the manure would absorb and keep the heat from sunlight. The layers of insulators would be replaced again at night.

After the seeds had germinated, the seedlings would be thinned out by hand to allow the selected seedlings to grow bigger and stronger, ready for

Celery fields by Willowdale Avenue in 1911–12, where many Chinese labourers worked. Courtesy of the Armstrong-Spallumcheen Museum and Art Society 935.

transplanting into the fields. Meanwhile, the Chinese farmers used horses to plough and create soil ridges in the field especially for cultivating celery crops. Many of the gardeners did not own horses or tractors to work in the field, except the Lee Bak Bong family, which owned a tractor. So they hired horses from either W. E. Warner or Dave Blackburn to do the ploughing. When the seedlings were ready for transplanting, the Chinese farmers would take them out to the ploughed field. They would take along with them sticks and strings and a device known as a "stamper." This apparatus was constructed from two pieces of light board separated by coil springs and twelve or more conical pegs attached to the lower surface of the bottom board. When the stamper was pressed down on the surface of the soil, the pegs would punch holes in the soil. In the field, the Chinese farmers would first line up strings with the sticks and then put the stamper parallel to the strings. When the stamper was in place, one farmer would press it into the soil to punch holes. Then he would lift up the device and place it in the next spot to repeat the same task. In this way, slowly but surely a row of holes would be punched into the small soil ridges in the ploughed field. Either the same farmer or another one following behind him would transfer the seedlings to the holes and cover the roots of the young plants firmly with soil. These two procedures of making holes and transplanting seedlings were done by hand until the whole field was planted with young

The celery fields north of town in 1946, with Okanagan Street to the left and the fairgrounds to the right. Courtesy of the Armstrong Spallumcheen Museum and Art Society 1420.

plants. The whole operation demanded energy, stamina, skill and patience from the farmers. Cultivating celery was a back-breaking task. This meticulous method of planting celery produced geometrical rows of celery in the field when they matured.[160] If two crops of celery were planted in one year, the procedure would be repeated again when they started planting the new crop.

During the growing season, the Chinese farmers would irrigate the field and kneel down to pull out weeds from the lengthy symmetrical rows of celery. They put the weeds in a pail or bucket and disposed of them away from the growing plants. Some of them practised hilling to keep the celery crops white or blanched, because the market preferred white and crispy celery. Hilling is a procedure of scooping up the soil to cover the lower stems of the celery so that the plants would not be able absorb sunlight and turn green. This procedure is another back-breaking task requiring farmers to bend over to scoop up the soil. At harvest time, they used a heavy knife to cut off the celery at the top of the root system and peeled off the outer layer before they packed the celery into boxes and sent them out to the packing houses for shipment.

In late fall, the head gardeners would gather all the receipts and calculate how much money they had earned for the year with an abacus, and would then go to local banks or the banks in Vernon to send money to agents in Hong Kong, who would in turn deliver their remittances to their families in Guangdong. Then they would buy gifts such as bottles of brandy or whisky, silk, lychee nuts (a dried fruit), lily bulbs or ginger candies for their landlords before Christmas. "When we were young, we often looked forward to receiving lychee and ginger candies from the Chinese gardeners," said Ralph Lockhart.

Packing Houses and a Declining Market

Many long-time residents claim that there were once eight packing houses in the community. J. Serra wrote that the packing house of R. W. MacDonald and Co. was the first one that shipped produce to Kenora, Ontario. Jackson's building, another packing house, stood by the CN railway line. Later, when Jackson partnered with Reeve Daykin, this packing house became Daykin and Jackson Co. but it was bought out by Ed P. Poole. Then it was amalgamated with Fairfield Ranch and Associated Growers to form Armstrong Packers. This company had ice storage in a log house with a steep ramp to help deliver blocks of ice from trucks to the storage house. The ice was cut and hauled by Josh Blackburn and Son from Otter Lake to the packing houses of this company. When the blocks of ice arrived, the haulers would deliver them to the ice crusher in the log house using a chain on the ramp. When the crusher was in operation, the noise could be heard in the city. The crushed ice was then kept in the storage house, ready to be used to preserve produce in crates as it was shipped to different outlets in BC as well as to other provinces and southwestern states in the United States.

Opposite the railway station stood another packing house, a brick building erected by William McNair.[161] Included were J. Tiltonson, the Ted Coolin Company and Tedfield Ranch packing houses. Lockhart said that the Tedfield Ranch used to take the bulk of the lettuce grown by the Chinese head gardeners, and then repack and ship it out in boxes by the carloads. T. W. Fletcher was one of the individual shippers who sent produce to the Kootenay and Slocan areas. The packing houses and individual shippers picked up produce from Chinese market gardeners and then packaged and shipped it out to various wholesale and retailing grocers. "Celery went from here to Toronto in the east and Hawaii in the west," said Mat Hassen Junior. "The packing houses shipped them out at different times, up to twenty-four carloads of vegetables a day. The growing of celery was all Chinese labour."

As time went by, the number of head gardeners decreased. J. H. Wilson Ltd., an accounting company, recorded the following numbers of head gardeners from various packers in the 1930s.

Chinese Gardeners in the 1930s

Year	Number of Chinese Gardeners
1929 (April)	34
1930 (February)	8
1931	8
1935	3
1936	1
1937	3

Challenges the Chinese Farmers Faced

In the 1930s, the Chinese market gardeners ran into problems for working on Sundays when a local Christian group agitated against the practice. The Chinese agreed to stop working on the Sabbath in the fields. But then on Monday morning, the packing houses in town could not operate because the employees had no vegetables to pack and ship out. Normally, Chinese market gardeners would send produce to the packing houses on Sunday so that the workers could pack and get it ready for shipping out on Monday to the wholesalers and retail grocers. Since no vegetables were delivered to the packing houses on Sunday, the employees stood idle, and that affected the grocery stores in town or nearby regions as they had no fresh vegetables for retailing. Finally, the western community agreed to allow the Chinese market gardeners to work on Sundays.

The Chinese farmers worked hard to make a living despite the inequality they faced. They were conscientious, honest and peaceful people. Depending on the weather and prices, some head gardeners might make on average $300 to $400 annually. Some years they earned barely a pittance for working and sweating in the fields for eighteen hours or so per day during the growing season. "Wong Duck had two acres of vegetable garden near the lagoons," said Mat Hassen Junior. "He used to have coffee at George Taylor's Gold Gate Café every morning. And George usually read for him the statements he received from packing houses. One day I learned from George that Wong had only earned $28.00 for the year working on his two acres!"

During World War II, the market for produce was poor; one crate of five dozen lettuces sold for 35 cents but a good sack of fertilizer cost $4.00 or $5.00 per ton. The great news for the Chinese settlers and their descendants in Canada was the repeal of the Chinese Exclusion Act and the recovery of enfranchisement after World War II. All Chinese settlers and their Canadian-born children could apply for Canadian citizenship and become Chinese Canadians with the same rights and privileges as other Canadians of different nationalities. In 1948, Louie Chin and many Chinese farmers became Chinese Canadians who could purchase or apply for Crown lands for farming in Armstrong. Chin then purchased four acres (1.6 hectares) of land at the corner between Okanagan Street and Wood Avenue, after which he went back to China and got married. He returned with his wife to Armstrong and continued to cultivate celery on his land. He did well in vegetable gardening and prospered.

Yet the vegetable market remained sluggish after World War II. "In 1952, Chinese market gardeners earned 9 cents a dozen for lettuce and the packing house sold it for $4.80 for three dozen in a pack," added Ralph Lockhart. The comments from Hassen earlier and Lockhart were referring to the wholesale prices the Chinese farmers received from packing houses and shippers. Yet many of the head gardeners and individual farmers were not allowed to sell their produce by themselves outside a fifteen-mile radius of their fields unless they had obtained retailing licences from the Vegetable Marketing Board.

"There were markets in Kelowna, Penticton, Kamloops and Revelstoke, but the Chinese farmers could not sell their produce directly to these cities because they are not within fifteen miles of their gardens," said Ben Lee. "This was the regulation of the Vegetable Marketing Board. But the Chinese gardeners cultivated mainly celery and lettuces, perishable produce that needed to be harvested when mature and sold within a week or so after harvesting; otherwise they would rot away. Some Chinese gardeners produced tons of celery and lettuces because they had ten to twenty acres cultivating these vegetables. They needed markets to sell the bulk of their produce before it perished. So they had no choice but to sell their produce to the packing houses and shippers at depressed prices. The packing houses and shippers had licences for retailing vegetables, whereas the Chinese farmers did not. Even the head gardeners found it very challenging to apply for licences for retailing in many instances. In short, the Vegetable Marketing Board controlled the marketing of all vegetables, including root crops like carrots, onions and potatoes, and protected the packing houses and the wholesalers, not the Chinese farmers who produced the vegetables."

Besides this, Chinese gardeners had to buy tags from the Vegetable Marketing Board before they could sell their produce to the packing houses. If the gardeners bought tags for selling onions, they had to attach the tags to the bags containing onions and not to other products. If the products did not match the tags, they would be confiscated! Sometimes, when prices dropped to the point that it cost more money to harvest and pack the products, the Chinese market gardeners simply ploughed them into the field. Especially in the late 1950s, the Vegetable Marketing Board could not find a ready market for celery and lettuce because other provinces and California were producing similar vegetables in competition with the farming industries in Armstrong. So the packing houses closed down. By the 1960s, many Chinese market gardeners and the individual farmers had gradually left Armstrong, except for the family of Jong Hughie, who remained and continued farming.

Two Notable Families of Chinese Head Gardeners

Like many of the early Chinese immigrants, the Chinese head gardeners and farmers came to Canada, the Gold Mountain, to seek a better life for themselves as well as for their families who were left behind in the villages of Guangdong. Lee Nye, the father of Lee Bak Bong, is an example.

During the 1870s, Lee, who came from Sun Wei County (新会县) in Guangdong Province, arrived in Victoria and worked in the lumber industry, clearing land and building cabins in Sooke. In the 1890s, he migrated to Armstrong and worked as a labourer clearing weeds and draining water from the bogs.

His son, Lee Bak Bong, came to Canada as a student on May 15, 1908. Because he was a student, he did not have to pay the head tax. Lee Junior met and stayed with his father, who had by then returned to Victoria from Armstrong. They continued working at odd jobs in Victoria. "My grandpa and dad could not get any employment in public works or in other professions," said Ben Lee. "They were like many early Chinese immigrants who were simply tied down to whatever labouring jobs they could get or to start their small businesses if they had enough resources."

In 1910, Lee Bak Bong went back home to Guangdong to get married, and then he returned to Canada without his new wife. "The head tax made it very difficult for the Chinese immigrants to bring their wives and families with them, because they could not afford to pay the $500.00 head tax for each family member to gain entry to this country," remarked Ben Lee. "Upon returning from China, my father and grandpa migrated to Armstrong to start market gardening in 1911. They worked very hard to save up $500.00 so that they could pay the head tax for my mom to come over and join them."

In 1920, Mrs. Lee Bak Bong arrived in Armstrong. She was the only Chinese woman in the Chinese community of a few hundred single men. She did not speak or understand English, so she had no female companions or friends in the community. Until the 1940s, Chinese people, including those living in western countries, were very conservative, hanging on to the traditional Chinese belief that Chinese women were not supposed to look at or take the initiative to talk to men other than their husbands. So Mrs. Lee Bak Bong was lonely and without friends. However, this couple had eleven children over the years. There were seven sons—Wing, Qoung, Jim, Bill, Ben, Howe and Don; and four daughters—Alice, Ann, Betty and May.

At the beginning, the Lee Bak Bong family lived in a house located at the corner of Okanagan Street and Patterson Avenue. It is unknown whether their house was affected by the huge fire of 1922 or not. By then, Lee was doing so well he was able to purchase farmland from a private owner and expand his market gardening. As time went by, the Lee family outgrew their home and moved to a large, rustic brick house at 3255 Okanagan Street. This red brick house was constructed by Mah Yick on the site of a wood building that had burned down in the huge fire of 1922. On August 10 of the same year, the construction was completed. Mah rented this new brick house to Kwong Wing On & Co. which operated a rooming house on the upper floor of the building.

After Lee bought the red brick house and moved his family into the building, he kept the rooming house in operation for some time. Then the Lee family ran a grocery store on the ground floor. On weekends, the Lee children worked in the fields with their father from early morning to late evening. "Everyone in our family had to help out at the farm and the store to keep the family going," said Ben Lee.

Lee Bak Bong, however, believed in education. He sent all his children to school and allowed them to participate in school activities. To him, education for his children came first and farm work came second. Both husband and wife taught their children to respect one another in the family as well as people in the community, especially the elderly people.

As time went by, the Lee family ventured into the vegetable wholesale business and shipped produce to various areas in the Okanagan. The wholesale operation was known as Wing Quong & Co., named after the two eldest sons of Lee Bak Bong. "When we started the wholesale business, my father hired several Indigenous people from Enderby to work on the farm; one of them operated the tractor. Flexis, another Indigenous person, drove the company truck for our wholesale business. And we children also got involved in the business operation," said Ben Lee. "For example, we needed ice to preserve the vegetables when the gardeners delivered them for shipment. We could not send the bulk of the produce out all at once, so we had to pack it with ice to preserve it before we shipped it out. In winter, we received blocks of ice from Otter Lake. We kept the ice with sawdust in a large storage building. When the produce arrived, we would take blocks of ice out, wash off the sawdust and break the ice blocks into chips with a machine. We used the ice chips to pack the vegetables, especially lettuce, into wood boxes. When the boxcar or truck arrived, we loaded the boxes on the truck and blew ice chips into the car. All this was needed to be done for shipping produce out."

Although Lee Bak Bong had acquired a retailing licence from the city for his store, he faced some challenges obtaining a licence from the Vegetable Marketing Board for his wholesale business. At the beginning, the board refused to issue the Lee family a licence for shipping vegetables to other regions. "My dad and my brothers brought the marketing board to court twice, and both times we won," stated Ben Lee. "At one time a member of the board stopped my brother just outside Penticton and told him he couldn't sell the produce in Penticton, a city not within our growing area. But my brother had an order from a grocer in Penticton. Regardless, the board member seized the produce and took us to court. We won in court because the Vegetable Marketing Board couldn't find a market for us."

Indeed, success in the vegetable business did not come easy. Besides all the hard work, the merchants had to face and overcome many challenges and obstacles before they could make a profit.

Lee Bak Bong was a well-known and liked businessman in Armstrong, whre he operated a packing and shipping house. Though he retired in 1961, the building stood until around 2014. Courtesy of the Armstrong Spallumcheen Museum and Society 5730.

Lee Bak Bong, however, was well respected in the Chinese community; many Chinese residents looked up to him as a leader and asked for his counsel and assistance when they ran into problems. He helped bail out many Chinese men who were caught gambling when police raided the premises on the upper floors of a couple of Chinese laundries.

By the 1950s, all his children were grown up and had left home for post-secondary education or to enter careers and professions other than farming. The vegetable growers were facing stiff competition from growers in California and other regions of BC that produced similar vegetables. In 1961, Lee retired from his gardening and wholesale businesses. He and his wife held their fiftieth wedding anniversary the same year, a grand occasion for the Lee family. That ended the epoch of the Lee family in Armstrong.

The red brick building was left vacant, but it was a landmark in Chinatown for more than thirty years. Although the building was still owned by the children of the Lee family, the Armstrong city council was instrumental in having it demolished around 2014. No complaint has been found, except Ben Lee lamented the loss. But he agreed that the building was too old to remain standing against the further challenges of time.

In 1912, Jong Hughie, the head of the Jong family, paid the head tax of $500.00 to gain entry into Canada. He was a Chinese scholar from San Way (新会), a county in Guangdong Province. When he arrived, he hoped to meet his father in Canada, but his father had gone to the United States. So they never met. After arriving in Victoria, he could not find a teaching job, so he worked as a bricklayer and cleared land for road construction in the capital city, including in the vicinity of Victoria's Chinatown. Later, he migrated to Armstrong and cleared lands for road construction there as well. When the Chinese Exclusion Act was repealed in 1948, he went back to China to marry. He returned from Guangdong without his wife and continued to work as a labourer, clearing land and building roads in the Okanagan. Eventually he settled in Armstrong. Since he did not speak much English, he could not get acquainted with many non-Chinese people. But he was well-known and respected in the Chinese community because he helped many Chinese old-timers correspond with their family members, since they could not read and write Chinese characters; they depended on Jong to read letters from home and to write replies for them to their families in Guangdong. He also read Chinese newspapers and shared news with folks living in Armstrong's Chinatown.

In 1954, Jong sent for his wife to join him in Armstrong. Then both husband and wife took up market gardening, did very well and bought a property on Pleasant Valley Road, where they erected a house in the 3800 block. Jong's wife and children still live on the same property today. His loving wife was his compatible and diligent partner in his market gardening enterprises. Her assistance and support for him not only encouraged him to advance and succeed in business but also stimulated their children to engage and believe in gardening. "My mother is the motivation behind the vegetable gardening," said Mary Jong, the eldest daughter. "She is in her nineties now, but she is still very active and instrumental in our planting and harvesting of the vegetables. Every spring, she was the first one out hoeing the garden and getting the patch ready for planting. When we [children] returned from work in the evening, we would go to the garden to help her out. It is her passion and love for vegetable gardening that keeps us going."

"Once, we farmed up to eighteen acres of vegetables and shipped them to the local packing houses," continued Mary. "When the California produce flooded the market, the packing houses shut down. When we could no longer supply our vegetables to the stores, we had to find another outlet. We helped Armstrong set up the first farmers' market in BC."

When it became challenging for the Jong family to find markets for their produce, they ventured into the Chinese restaurant business. In the 1960s, they erected a building downtown and established the Shanghai Chop Suey House. The interior decoration of the restaurant was finished with "striking amber elm and indirect fluorescent lighting behind matching Elmwood panels."[162] The restaurant opened on June 12, 1967, which was the fifth day of the fifth moon (month) in the Chinese calendar, an auspicious day for commemorating Qu Yuan, a poet and statesman in the Chu kingdom (楚国) during the latter part of the Warring States Period (476 BC–221 BC; 春秋战国末期). Chinese people the world over celebrate the Dragon Boat Festival on this date: the fifth day of the fifth moon in the Chinese calendar.

The night before the grand opening of the Shanghai Chop Suey House, Jong Hughie and his wife invited eighty business associates and guests to a banquet. On May 11, 1967, the *Armstrong Advertiser* stated that "the new and ultra-modern restaurant, located in the heart of the downtown business [district in the City of Armstrong] has attracted large crowds of patrons; many from neighbouring centers…[They] came to enjoy the specialized Chinese foods, as well as the unique and oriental atmosphere. The business is a tribute to the foresight and long-planning on the part of its owners, Mr. and Mrs. Jong Hughie." Their restaurant introduced the first taste of authentic Chinese food to many white, First Nations and other residents of different nationalities in the Spallumcheen Valley. Although the restaurant business was a family enterprise, they operated it for about twenty-eight years. In 1995, the restaurant was sold and the new owner changed its name to Great Wall Restaurant.

Although all the Jong children always helped out in the family market gardening business, even doing so today if they are at home, all of them have graduated from high school and embarked on good careers or professions. Mary graduated from the University of Victoria with a fine arts degree. She is an artist; her paintings are priceless and her lithographic prints put one in awe! Soon after her graduation from university, she taught ESL (English as a second language) at Simon Fraser University as well as in Hong Kong and China. Unfortunately, she had a very unpleasant experience when she first started elementary school in Armstrong.

Mary's Chinese name is Jong Enyit Guaw. Many non-Chinese people found her name difficult to pronounce, so her grade one teacher gave her the name Mary. For a long time, she did not realize that "Mary" referred to her. When the name Mary was called out, she did not answer or respond. After she comprehended that Mary was her English name, she attempted to respond or answer questions. But her voice cracked most of the time when she spoke up, making her feel awkward and embarrassed. So she chose to sit at the back of the class in silence and in apprehension that the teacher would call her, as she would not know how to answer or respond. "When she [the teacher] asked me a question, I would freeze," recalled Mary. "A deafening silence would fill the air and I could only hear my heart pounding louder and louder. At first the kids just stared at me; later they teased, pointed and laughed at me, and called me 'dumb chink'! And I could see the disgust on their faces." She paused and continued, "Every morning, the teacher would check our hands, our hair and our clothes. Then she would divide the class into rows, and gave stars to the row that had the cleanest students. My row always came in last because of me. Everyone blamed me for losing, and no one wanted me in the group. They didn't understand that I had to work in the vegetable garden every morning before going to school and didn't have time to clean up. Also, a star was given to those students who ate cereal, bacon, eggs, juice and milk for breakfast; that was considered a proper meal by the teacher. But I never had those meals. I ate congee or rice pudding for breakfast. So I never got a star!"

Mary's recollection of her first year in school was, indeed, unhappy and agonizing. It is unbelievable that racism still remained so glaring and awful in the 1960s. No wonder she felt isolated and miserable in school. Her inability to articulate in English as expected and her feeling of not belonging resulted in her failing grade one! However, she realized the importance of going to school, because she had the chance to get an education in Canada, whereas her parents did not. Despite the prejudice and challenges that she faced in school, she stayed on and worked hard. She completed elementary school, graduated from high school and eventually earned a university degree. And now she is an accomplished artist.

"There were about sixty Chinese families working at market gardening in this area," said Mrs. Jong. "Now we are the only gardening family in Armstrong."

"In 1998, we had the best crop of celery," added Mary. "We shipped at least 3,000 pounds [1361 kilograms] of the produce to Askew's store in town and in Salmon Arm, as well as to farmer's markets in the regions nearby."

As the last of the Chinese market gardeners, the Jongs still employ the old methods to cultivate celery, using a hotbed to germinate the seeds and stampers to transplant seedlings into the field. Jong Hughie has passed away but Allan, his son, took over his father's role as the vegetable gardener. As well, Mrs. Jong and Mary help perpetuate the legacy of Chinese market gardening in Armstrong.

Chinatown in Armstrong Today

Today, many buildings in the Armstrong Chinatown have disappeared, but the building of Sing Lung Laundry remains standing; it is occupied by a registered massage therapist. In 2015, the site of Chinatown was recognized as one of the Chinese-Canadian heritage sites in British Columbia (BC) by the Legacy Initiatives Advisory Council of the Ministry of International Trades and Multiculturalism and the Ministry of Forests, Lands, and Natural Resources Operations.

On December 23, 2016, the *Vernon News* reported that the Armstrong Heritage Committee had presented a plaque on behalf of the BC Labour Heritage Centre to the City of Armstrong at its regular council meeting to honour the Chinese market gardeners in Armstrong as well as to the municipality as the "Celery City" of BC. The plaque will be installed in the new Huculak Park in the near future. All these tributes recognize the deeds and contributions of the Chinese market gardeners that assisted the growth and the economic development of Armstrong, especially in its formative years.

AFTERWORD

The main focus of this book has been to examine and document the Chinese settlements and the ways of life of the Chinese settlers in the Fraser Canyon, the Okanagan and the Spallumcheen Valley region. Now it seems necessary to recapture the purposes of Chinese immigration to British Columbia and some of the events that led to or motivated the Chinese immigrants to migrate to these regions.

It was the allure of gold that stimulated the first influx of Chinese immigrants to BC during the Fraser gold rush. These Chinese immigrants were mainly Chinese gold miners and merchants who arrived either from California or from Guangdong Province through Hong Kong. They wanted to find wealth so that they could improve their lives as well as their families' lives back in China. When gold was depleted and they realized that gold mining was not necessarily a profitable enterprise, the Chinese gold miners changed their occupation, taking up various types of labouring jobs as helpers in pack trains and on farmlands and ranches or as domestic servants in private homes, and so on. Some of them pre-empted land from the Crown or leased land from the local Indigenous peoples and started cultivating vegetable and food crops. The Chinese merchants were doing well in the Fraser Canyon in the place where they first immigrated to and operated their businesses; they were able to make a comfortable living. Their success motivated their fellow countrymen to venture into small business. But these Chinese immigrants required a permanent residence, so they settled in places where they could make a living, hence the beginning of Chinese settlements and the formation of Chinatowns.

Similarly, construction of the Canadian Pacific Railway (1880–85) bought a second influx of Chinese immigrants to British Columbia. It was mainly the job opportunities that motivated them to emigrate from the various counties in Guangdong Province; they came mainly to work in the construction of the Canadian Pacific Railway. After the CPR was completed, these Chinese labourers were dismissed without compensation, despite their sacrifices and contributions, and were not provided with a return ticket home. The unemployed labourers left the different railway construction camps for various regions in the Interior as well as in the Lower Mainland of BC. In the Okanagan and the Spallumcheen Valley regions, they found work at ranches, orchards and farmlands, and they had opportunities to pan for gold in the various rivers, streams and creeks. Likewise, they settled in these two regions where they could make a living and created Chinatowns there.

While researching details about the Chinese settlements in the Fraser Canyon, the Okanagan and the Spallumcheen Valley, three characteristics of the Chinatowns were discovered. First, none of the Chinese settlers were employed in public works or in other professions. Second, the population in these Chinatowns consisted of very few, and often no, families. Third, the sites of the settlements were excluded from where the mainstream population carried on their lives. The following reasons might provide an explanation for these characteristics.

In the early days, white people were afraid that the Chinese immigrants, who were willing to work for lower wages, would take away their jobs. These concerns and fears were brought to the attention of both the federal and provincial governments, and motivated them to formulate and enforce regulations to restrict Chinese employment. In 1885, one of these restrictive regulations stated that government departments, industries, businesses, professional institutes, and firms such as hospitals and law offices could not hire Chinese immigrants unless they were unable to find white people to fill the positions. Consequently, the Chinese immigrants were tied down to whatever labouring jobs they could find or they had to start a small business in their own settlement. So no Chinese were found to be working in professional firms or government departments in the areas where they had established Chinatowns.

Again in 1885, the head tax was enacted. The unjust levy that applied only to Chinese immigrants was increased from $50.00 in 1885 to $500.00 by 1903. The main objective of this head tax was to stop Chinese immigration. The heavy levy had huge impacts on the Chinese immigrants. They could only earn a dollar or two a day in their work. Many of them could hardly make ends meet, let alone pay the head tax for their wives and children to come join them in this country; life was miserable and lonely for them living in a foreign land without their loved ones. In 1923, when the Chinese Exclusion Act was enacted, it became totally impossible for Chinese immigrants to be reunited with their families in Canada. Thus, the population of the various Chinatowns consisted predominantly of males.

At the beginning of the twentieth century, anti-Chinese sentiment simmered in British Columbia.[163] The Chinese immigrants were treated as

206 — Blossoms in the Gold Mountains

aliens, as inferior people. They often encountered name-calling, bullying, abuse and assault. To avoid humiliation, insults and physical harm, they opted to live apart from the white community. So these Chinese settlements were not located within the mainstream community.

In Canadian history, prejudice and discrimination against Chinese immigrants was evident; events related to racism were published in contemporary newspapers and documented in government records. Fortunately, some encouraging and heartening occurrences were noted in the Chinese settlements. To cite a few examples, Chan Ah Mee in Kamloops risked his life to save the house of a white person in a fire. The Chong family in Lytton established a lasting friendship with the Lytton First Nation people. Lee Shui Dong, president of the Chinese Freemasons society in Kelowna, led a group of members to fight against a forest fire. Many Chinese organizations in the past and present always invited prominent local citizens and other members of the mainstream community to their festivities and banquets. These instances demonstrated how the Chinese immigrants/settlers in the past and Chinese Canadians in the present had and have made efforts to reach out to the Canadian society at large.

The history of Chinese Canadians in these regions also indicates that many Canadian-born Chinese wanted to call this land home; they were eager to become Chinese Canadians. They made efforts to regain their enfranchisement. An obvious illustration was the willingness of the Canadian-born Chinese to enlist in the Canadian armed forces to fight for Canada in World War II; they were prepared to sacrifice their lives for a country that had rejected them. The late Bevan Jangze and the late Walter Joe were two of those Canadian-born Chinese who volunteered to serve in the Canadian forces during World War II. Besides this, many Chinese settlers and Chinese organizations donated money and goods to support the war efforts. After World War II, Chinese settlers and their descendants were recognized as Canadian citizens; they became Chinese Canadians.

A couple of these Chinese Canadians have participated in civic politics. In 1965, the late Peter Eng was elected mayor of Kamloops, the first Chinese Canadian to hold such an important position in Canada. In 1973, the late Ben Lee, who was born in Armstrong, was elected as an alderman/city councillor in Kelowna. He served on the council and on regional boards for many years, founded the Kelowna Multicultural Society and spearheaded the Kelowna Folkfest to celebrate Canada Day on July 1.

Another amazing finding has been the discovery of some remarkable women in the Chinese settlements. In Yale, Lena Leong raised and continued to support her children's education after the death of her husband. All her children were successful Chinese Canadians. In Lytton, Lily Chow Lai Kuan was not only a devoted wife and loving mother but also a capable business manager; she operated the Wah Chong general and grocery store while her husband expanded their grocery business elsewhere. She nurtured and encouraged her children to study hard in school and in university. All her children became professionals. She also helped poor, single Chinese men and took care of the sick and homeless. In Kelowna, Wong Lee Sue Pink was another remarkable widow who manufactured tofu so she could raise and educate her thirteen children after her husband passed away. She gained respect and admiration not only from her children and grandchildren but also from the Chinese community and the mainstream community. Apparently an RCMP officer volunteered to help her deliver tofu from Kelowna to Vernon.

Besides this, it has been wonderful to discover that many members of the mainstream community in these regions were not anti-Chinese. Alice Barrett Parke, the wife of a ranch manager, wrote in her diary that the government was wrong to impose a head tax on Chinese immigrants. She developed a wonderful friendship with her Chinese cook. George Bower, a rancher, donated a piece of land at the Hudson's Bay Trail to the Kamloops Chinese community for burying their dead. An understanding reader wrote a letter to the *Armstrong Advertiser* to support the Chinese immigrants when many white people insulted the Chinese laundry management. News reports in the past and present often stated that members of the mainstream community loved watching and participating in Chinese New Year celebrations and in other Chinese festivities. A few historical newspapers published descriptions of Chinese weddings and news about Chinese funeral rites and other ceremonies. These publications demonstrated that the Chinese settlers had not forgotten their roots and abandoned their culture.

Celebrations and ceremonies were carried out not only by individuals but also by Chinese organizations. These Chinese associations were gathering places for the Chinese settlers so that they could socialize with one another. The organizations also provided a channel for their members to communicate with their families at home and learn about the situation in China. And they gave the settlers a sense of acceptance, justice, security and protection.

After World War II, immigration policies were modified to allow Chinese Canadians to sponsor their wives and children under the age of eighteen to come to Canada and be reunited with them. When their family members arrived, the Chinese Canadians moved away from the China-towns and lived with their families in the suburbs of the cities. Gradually, the population in the Chinatowns decreased and few people maintained or upgraded the buildings there. Many buildings were left vacant, deteriorated and many fell apart. Hence, these Chinatowns became the landscape of the past and gradually disappeared.

But the spirit of the Chinese communities remains alive. Although the residences of the Chinese Canadians are scattered in the subdivisions of towns and cities, they continue to celebrate Chinese festivals, perform ceremonies according to their traditions and customs, and practise Chinese teachings, such as showing filial piety and respect to parents, grandparents, parents-in-law and Elders. In short, the Chinese Canadians of today have made efforts to perpetuate Chinese culture.

In 1967, the federal government introduced the point system in the immigration act, which provided opportunities for professionals of all nationalities to immigrate to Canada. Many relatives and friends of Chinese Canadians in Guangdong, Hong Kong and Southeast Asia were able to meet the requirements of the point system. Subsequently, these overseas Chinese immigrated to Canada and became Canadian citizens. These more recent Chinese immigrants contributed to and added colour to Chinese culture. Some of them established Chinese schools to teach the Chinese languages, music and art, calligraphy and painting to the younger Chinese Canadians. This has stimulated the younger generations of today to search for their roots, to learn about the Chinese-Canadian history and to recognize the Chinese-Canadian heritage sites in BC as well as across the country. Today, many Chinese Canadians make an effort to commemorate their Chinese ancestors in this land in Qing Ming and Zhong Yang, the remembrance days for Chinese ancestors.

Indeed, early Chinese settlers took root and sowed their seeds, especially in the regions mentioned in this book. These seeds have germinated and the plants have grown tall and produced colourful blossoms that symbolize the deeds and accomplishments of the Chinese Canadians of the past and in the present generation. These bright and beautiful blossoms have dotted the landscapes of the Gold Mountains.

ENDNOTES

1. *British Columbia Gazette*, July 25, 1858, 2.

2. Lily Chow, *Sojourners in the North* (Prince George, BC: Caitlin Press, 1996), 12.

3. "First Chinese Here in 1858," *Kamloops Daily Sentinel*, December 19, 1970, 9.

4. Chow, *Sojourners in the North*, 14.

5 Interview between Imbert Orchard and Arthur Urquhart, 1971.

6. *Victoria Gazette* (under "Indian Difficulties," a letter from Captain Snyder), 4.

7. *BC Tribune*, June 25, 1886, 3.

8. David Williams Higgins, *The Mystic Spring and Other Tales of Western Life* (Toronto: William Briggs, 1904), 45.

9. *British Colonist*, March 12, 1862, 3; April 30, 1862, 2; November 12, 1862, 2.

10. George Hills, Bishop of British Columbia, *Journal of George Hills, 1860*, Anglican Archives, University of British Columbia, 66–67.

11. *Colonist*, November 19, 1871, 3.

12. The CPR contracts included Section 60—29 miles between Emory to Boston Bar along the Fraser River; Section 61—29 miles from Boston Bar to Lytton; Section 62—28-1/2 miles from Lytton along the Thompson River to Junction Flat; Section 63—40-1/2 miles from Junction Flat to Savona's Ferry on Kamloops Lake; and Section 92 from Emory to Port Moody.

13. *Inland Sentinel*, May 29, 1880, 1.

14. Lei, M. Pan, G. Rong Yang, and J. Ping Jian, eds., *The 140 Anniversary Publication of the Chinese Freemasons Society* (Vancouver: Vancouver Chinese Freemasons society, 2003), 129.

15. Henry John Cambie, *Diary and Notes: Contract 60*, April 1880–April 1881, Vancouver Archives.

16. When Onderdonk signed the contracts with the Dominion Government in 1879–81, the anti-Chinese sentiment was at its height, especially in Victoria and Vancouver. So he committed not to hire Chinese or Indigenous peoples unless it was absolutely necessary.

17. Pierre Berton, *The Last Spike: The Great Railway, 1881–1885* (Toronto: McClelland & Stewart, 1971), 296.

18. The Lee Chuck Labourer Recruitment Agency sent representatives to various counties in Guangdong Province to recruit and sign contractual agreements with those who were willing to work as labourers on the CPR construction.

19. Lily Chow, *Blood and Sweat over the Railway Tracks* (Vancouver: Chinese Canadian Historical Society of BC and Initiative for Student Teaching and Research in Chinese Canadian Studies, UBC) 2014, 37.

20. *Inland Sentinel*, May 16, 1881, 2; *British Colonist*, May 17, 1881, 2.

21. *British Colonist*, August 30, 1882.

22. *Inland Sentinel*, February 22, 1883, 2.

23. Interview between Andrea Laforet and Annie York; interview between Imbert Orchard and Arthur Urquhart.

24. According to Linda Eversole, a researcher, there were no contemporary photographs of the early On Lee Store when she and Don Tarasoff undertook a physical examination of the building in November 1983. The description of the store was obtained from the memories of the late Walter Joe.

25. Linda Eversole, *The Gold Rush Town, On Lee House & Store—Documentary History* (Unpublished report, BC Heritage Branch, January 1984).

26. Interview with Bevan Jangze (Cheng) by Chris Lee and Douglas Quan, August 2, 1996. The pronunciation of Jangze is in the Toishan dialect. A similar account is also obtained from Irene Bjerky and Darla Dickson, "Chinese Merchants in Yale" (Unpublished manuscript, 2009).

27. BC Government Agency, Correspondence Lytton, May 10, 1860, BC Archives.

28. BC Government Agency, Correspondence, Lytton, July 4, 1860, BC Archives.

29. BC Government Agency, March 1, 1861, BC Archives.

30. BC Department of Lands and Works, Chief Commissioner Correspondence inward, BC Archives GR 868, box 2, file 13.

31. Ibid.

32. *Williams' British Columbia Directory* (Victoria, BC: R. T. Williams 1882), 290.

33. Ibid.

34. M. George Murray, "Gods in a Lytton Woodshed," *Vancouver Daily Province*, May 7, 1933.

35. *Inland Sentinel*, April 12, 1883.

36. *Inland Sentinel*, August 19,1880; June 2, 1881.

37. *Colonist*, May 18, 1883.

38. Lily Chow, *Chasing Their Dreams* (Halfmoon Bay, BC: Caitlin Press, 2000), xvi.

39. Graham Everett, "Signor Guise Taverna and the Lytton Joss Temple," Lytton tourist brochure, 2002.

40. Ibid.

41. Ibid.

42. Personal interview with Peter and David Chong in 2008.

43. Personal interview with the late Rita Haugen in 2008.

44. Extract from Kenny Glasgow's tribute to Peter Chong at Chong's 90th birthday in 2011.

45. *Vancouver Province* (magazine section), "Kamloops in History," August 5, 1944; personal interview with the late Peter Wing, in Vancouver, 1999.

46. BC Correspondence to Premier, BC Archives, GR 411, box 1, file 2.

47. Ruth Balf, *Kamloops 1914–1945* (Kamloops, BC: History Committee, Kamloops Museum, 1975), 120.

48. W. Norton, *Kamloops: The Hundred Years of Community, 1893–1993* (Merritt, BC: Sonotek Publishing, 1992).

49. *Kamloops Daily Sentinel*, August 28, 1971, 9.

50. *Inland Sentinel*, October 23, 1896, 1.

51. Ibid.

52. *Kamloops Sentinel*, July 3, 1926, 1; July 9, 1926, 1.

53. David Chuenyan Lai, *A Proposal for the Kamloops Chinese Cemetery Memorial Park* (Kamloops, BC: City of Kamloops, July 1987).

54. The visit of Dr. Sun Yat-sen in Kamloops was reported by Vancouver's *Chinese Times* (大汉公报), March 1, 1911.

55. The Three Principles are: 1. People's government (民族), the freedom from imperialist domination; 2. People's power or civil rights (民权); 3. People's livelihood (民生). These principles remain explicitly as the platform of the Kuomintang (中国国民党) then, and in the *Constitution of the Republic of China*, Taiwan, today.

56. *Kamloops Sentinel*, March 19, 1929, 3. 1928 marked the end of the Warlord Era in China.

57. A decision was made at the Paris Peace Conference, following World War I, to allow Japan to keep the German concession in Shangdong that had been seized during the war. This sparked a massive outcry in China. On May 4, 1919, students at Peking University protested against Japan. Their protests were soon joined by other student groups, merchants, labour

unions and writers, which led to a general strike in the country. This event is known as the May 4th Movement in Chinese history. Following scholars like Lu Xun (鲁迅), Hu Shi (胡适), Chen Duxiu (陈独秀) and others initiated the Literary Revolution (文学革命) to introduce vernacular language (白话文) in literature and communication. They also advocated human rights and freedom of speech for the people, and denounced the feudal system, hierarchy in family structure and other traditions that repressed individual freedom, especially that of women. For more information, see https://en.wikipedia.org/wiki/May_Fourth_Movement.

58. *Province*, December 13, 1965, 2; *Vancouver Sun*, December 13, 1965, 2.

59. T. Roth, *The Peasant's Gold: The Story of Peter Wing* (Kamloops, BC: Goss Publishing, 1998).

60. *A Proposal for the Kamloops Chinese Cemetery Memorial Park*, July 1987.

61. Mel Rothenburger is the owner and editor of "The Armchair Mayor" (column), https://armchairmayor.ca/2014/03/15/.

62. M. Ormsby, ed. *A Pioneer Gentlewoman in British Columbia* (Vancouver: UBC Press, 1976), 117.

63. Theresa Hurst, *An Illustrated History of Vernon and District* (Vernon: Okanagan Historical Society Report and Museum and Archives, 1967), 46.

64. N. L. Barlee, *Gold Creeks and Ghost Towns* (Surrey, BC: Hancock House, 1984), 173; H. J. Blurton, "The Placer Mines on Cherry and Mission Creeks," *Seventeenth Report of the Okanagan Historical Society*, 1953, 105; personal interview with the late Walter Joe, November 2, 1998.

65. *Colonist*, September 19, 1888.

66. Personal interviews with the late Walter Joe, Harry Low, and Loo Gim On in Vernon, November 2, 1998.

67. Alice Barrett Parke's diary, October 31, 1896.

68. Alice Barrett Parke's diary, November 8, 1896.

69. Alice Barrett Parke's diary, March 4, 1897.

70. Donna Wuest, *Coldstream: The Ranch Where It All Began* (Madeira Park, BC: Harbour Publishing, 2005), 89.

71. "Oriental Labor," *Vernon News*, January 11, 1917, 3.

72. Dorothy Christian is a professional filmmaker. Information is quoted from the article "Articulating a Silence," *Ricepaper* (Fall 2004): 22–31.

73. Theresa Gabriel, *Vernon, BC: A Brief History* (Vernon, BC: Vernon Centennial Committee, 1958).

74. *Vernon Daily News*, February 16, 1988, 8.

75. This general store was destroyed by fire in 1978.

76. Announcement in *Vernon News*, May 28, 1931. But Sing Lee Lung died in Canton on December 25, 1938.

77. Information from Walter Joe and Harry Low, then president of the Chinese Freemasons society.

78. These houses at 3302, 3304 and 3306 Ellison were marked on the Vernon map of 1920 and also recorded in the *BC Directory* for 1948.

79. Why Wah Yuen was marked as a grocery store and Sung Lee Lung Co. as a warehouse in the *BC Directory*, 1948. The top floor of these houses could be rooming houses for seasonal farm workers.

80. *Vernon News*, February 27, 1913, 3.

81. Sung Lee Lung, a well-respected Chinese Elder, spent forty-five years in Vernon but passed away on December 25, 1937, soon after he returned to China, as recorded in the files of the *Vernon News* on January 29, 1948.

82. *Vernon News*, October 2, 1947, 3.

83. M. Pan Lei, M. Pan, G. Rong Yang, and J. Ping Jian, eds., *Special Publication: The Chinese Freemasons Society of Vancouver, 100th Anniversary: 1888–1988* [Chinese text] (Vancouver: Vancouver Chinese Freemasons society, 1989), 4.

84. Chinese and English Secretariats, *Special Publication; The 34th National Convention of the Chinese Freemasons of Canada* [Chinese text] (Vancouver: Chinese Freemasons of Canada, 2001), 64.

85. *Vernon News*, August 12, 1919, 1.

86. Certificates of the national government of the Republic of China bonds can be found in the Greater Vernon Museum and Archives.

87. On September 18, 1931, a small quantity of dynamite was detonated by Lt. Kawamoto Suemori close to a railway owned by Japan's South Manchuria Railway near Mukden (now Shenyang). Although the explosion was so weak that it failed to destroy the lines and a train passed minutes later, the Imperial Japanese Army, accusing Chinese dissidents of the act, responded with a full invasion that led to the occupation of Manchuria.

88. *Vernon News*, November 1920.

89. *Vernon News*, November 6, 1924.

90. N. Lascelles Ward and H. A. Hellaby, *Oriental Missions in British Columbia* (London: Society for the Propagation of the Gospel in Foreign Parts, 1925), 86–90.

91. *Vernon Daily News*, April 19, 1945.

92. *Vancouver Sun*, July 26, 1943, 5.

93. See the entry of Larry Kwong in the Canadian Encyclopedia, http://www.thecanadianencyclopedia.ca/en/article/larry-kwong/.

94. Personal interview with Gillian Huang in the Appleton Restaurant, Vernon, November 3, 1998.

95. Personal interview with Chan Yue Juan in the Appleton Restaurant, Vernon, November 3, 1998.

96. Personal interview with Michael Wong at the Hong Kong Village, Vernon, July 27, 2004. Wong had lived in Vernon since 1969 but did not provide much personal detail.

97. Barry Bondar, *Okanagan: The Story and The Sights* (North Vancouver, BC: Whitecap Books, 1986), 23.

98. L. M. Buckland, "Settlement at L'Anse au Sable," *Second Annual Report of the Okanagan Historical and Natural History Society*, 1927, 19–21.

99. A. H. Mann, "Kelowna's Chinatown," *Forty-sixth Annual Report of the Okanagan Historical Society*, 1958, 20.

100. Adam, Ettie. "Kelowna's Chinese." *Thirty-first Report of the Okanagan Historical Society*, 1967, 45.

101. *Daily Courier*, February 22, 1964.

102. In 1901, the Eight-Nation Alliance formed by Japan, Russia, Britain, France, the United States, Germany, Italy and Austria-Hungary invaded China to suppress the Boxer Rebellion (1899–1901), a violent anti-foreign and anti-Christian uprising. The alliance succeeded in their campaign against the Boxers and defeated the imperial army of the Qing government. Meanwhile several revolutionary organizations were formed that attempted to overthrow the Qing government. China was then in a state of war and disturbance, and therefore many government officials and wealthy Chinese made efforts to send their children overseas for safety; for more information, see https://en.wikipedia.org/wiki/Eight-Nation_Alliance.

103. Michael Kluckner, *Vanishing British Columbia* (Vancouver and Seattle: UBC Press and University of Washington Press, 2008).

104. *Daily Courier* (e-edition), October 29, 2012.

105. *Living Landscapes: III. The Chinese: Early 1900s–1930s*, Royal BC Museum.

106. Clement, J. P. "Early Days in Kelowna." *Twenty-fourth Report of the Okanagan Historical Society*, 1960, 134–135.

107. In 1908, a public meeting was held with a proposal that no one should pay an Oriental more than $1.25 per day, which was seconded and adopted. *A Fruitful Century: The B.C. Fruit Growers' Association, 1889–1989* (Kelowna, BC: BCFGA, 1990), 39–40.

108. Adam, "Kelowna's Chinese," 46.

109. Mann, "Kelowna's Chinatown," 21–22; D.A. Ruffle, "The Greata Ranch," *Thirty-ninth Annual Report of the Okanagan Historical Society*, 1975, 143.

110. Personal interview with Mr. Shui Lee, the current chair of the Kelowna Chinese Freemasons society; Lee Yik Wai was the grandfather of Shui Lee.

111. The Chinese Freemasons in Canada Publication (1863–1983).

112. The B.C. Fruit Growers' Association, 1889–1989 (Kelowna: BCFGA, 1990), 39–40.

113. *Kelowna Record*, January 15, 1920, 1.

114. *Kelowna Record*, January 22, 1920, 1.

115. The Chinese Freemasons in Canada Publication (1863–1983).

116. *Kelowna Record*, January 22, 1914, 1.

117. *Kelowna Record*, February 12, 1914.

118. *Kelowna Record*, July 30, 1914; *Daily Courier*, July 30, 1914.

119. Robert Michael Hayes, "Chinatown Patriarch," *Kelowna Daily Courier*, updated March 26, 2014. Lum Lock passed away in December 1914. On August 16, 1927, Lum's remains were exhumed together with the remains of seventeen local Chinese residents from the Kelowna Pioneer Cemetery and sent back to their home villages in China.

120. *Kelowna Record*, August 5, 1920, 1; *Daily Courier*, August 2, 1920, 2.

121. *Daily Courier*, June 3, 1920, 1.

122. *Daily Courier*, March 2, 1924, 1.

123. *Daily Courier*, March 6 and 27, 1933; *Daily Courier*, April 24, 1933.

124. *Daily Courier*, November 26, 1931.

125. *Daily Courier*, November 3, 1932, 1; *Chinese Times*, November 2, 1932, 1.

126. Tun Wong, "Human Endeavour: Sue Lee Ping Wong," *Okanagan History: Sixty-third Report of the Okanagan Historical Society*, 1999, 156–159.

127. *Daily Courier*, December 22, 1932.

128. B. Hayman, "Mar Jok Always Feeds the Poor." *Forty-eighth Annual Report of the Okanagan Historical Society*, 1984, 91–94.

129. *Daily Courier*, November 12, 2012.

130. *Kelowna Courier*, December 14, 1968, 3.

131. *The Capital News*, July 5, 2012. Mar Jok Elementary School was built on the land that was once owned by Jok Mar in Kelowna and named in honour of Mar for his long history of helping others in the community helping others, both as a businessman and as a volunteer.

132. Mann, "Kelowna's Chinatown," 29.

133. *The Daily Courier*, February 27, 1947.

134. Mann, "Kelowna's Chinatown," 23.

135. *Living Landscapes: Ethnic Agricultural Labour,* Royal BC Museum, June 2010.

136. B. Johnston, "Exit 'Quong's,' " *Twenty-eighth Report of the Okanagan Historical Society*, 1964, 54–55; *Kelowna Capital News*, A7.

137. Prince George was one of those growing cities when the paper and pulp mills were established in the city in the mid-1960s. Similarly, Alcan in Kitimat also offered job opportunities.

138. *The Daily Courier*, 1977.

139. Personal interview with Tun Wong, December 4, 2016.

140. Wong, "Human Endeavour: Sue Lee Ping Wong."

141. Personal interview with Tun Wong in Kelowna, December 4, 2016.

142. *The Capital News; Daily Courier*, March 23, 2016.

143. Personal interview with Ben Lee in the Kelowna Museum, October 5, 1998.

144. Personal interview with Tun Wong, December 4, 2016.

145. Wong, "Human Endeavour: Sue Lee Ping Wong."

146. Tun Wong retired from Kelowna City Hall as a finance manager in 1999.

147. Personal interview with Lee Shui Dong at the Seven Seas Restaurant, Kelowna, October 1998.

148. *The Capital News*, October 24, 1997, A23.

149. *Singtao News*, August 12, 2003, A2.

150. *History of Rail in Kelowna: Beginning of the Mainline,* http://www.okanagan.net/ocarc/hamrail.html.

151. David Chuenyan Lai and Donald Luxton and Associates, "Kelowna Cemetery: Heritage Management Plan 2001," City of Kelowna, 2001, 2; *Capital News*, February 26, 2001.

152. Mat Hassen and Ralph Lockhart at the Armstrong-Enderby Branch of the Okanagan Society meeting on November 7, 1997; http://www.cityofarmstrong.bc.ca/content/history.

153. "Chinese Wash Houses," *Vernon News*, reprinted by the *Armstrong Advertiser*, April 10, 1909.

154. "The Chinese Wash House," *Armstrong Advertiser*, March 13, August 7, 1909.

155. J. H. Patton, "The Celery Industry in the Okanagan," *Vernon News, Special Holiday Issue,* January 1912, 2.

156. "Chinese Assault Cases," *Armstrong Advertiser,* November 7, 1912, 2.

157. Ronald Rupert Heal, "Farms and Enterprises in the North Okanagan," *Sixteenth Report of the Okanagan Historical Society*, 1952, 123.

158. Information provided by Ralph Lockhart and Ben McMahen.

159. "Chinatown Burned to Ground in Fire Early This Morning," *Armstrong Advertiser,* June 29, 1922, 1.

160. N. G. Kristensen, "Armstrong, the 'Celery City,' " *Okanagan History: Forty-ninth Report of the Okanagan Historical Society*, 1985, 115–119; "The Last of the Gardeners," *Armstrong Advertiser,* January 28, 1998, 6.

161. Johnny Serra, "Armstrong Packing Houses," *Twenty-eighth Report of the Okanagan Historical Society*, 1964, 42–45.

162. Peter Critchley, "The Chinese in Armstrong," *Okanagan History: Sixty-third Report of the Okanagan Historical Society*, 1999, 19.

163. The following were anti-Chinese organizations: in 1878, the Workingmen's Protective Association was formed at Fort Street, Victoria, followed by White Canada Crusade in 1920 and the Native Sons of British Columbia in 1930.

BIBLIOGRAPHY

Books and Articles

Adam, Ettie. "Kelowna's Chinese." *Thirty-first Report of the Okanagan Historical Society*, 1967, 45–47.

Arnold, A. J. "BC's Chinese Come of Age." *Colonist* (magazine section), March 16, 1958, 2.

Balf, Ruth. *Kamloops, 1914–1945*. Kamloops, BC: Kamloops Museum Association, History Committee, 1975.

Barlee, N. L. *Gold Creeks and Ghost Towns*. Surrey, BC: Hancock House, 1984.

Barman, Jean. *The West Beyond the West: A History of British Columbia*, rev. ed. Toronto: University of Toronto Press, 1995.

Berton, Pierre. *The National Dream: The Great Railway, 1871–1881*. Toronto: McClelland & Stewart, 1970.

———. *The Last Spike: The Great Railway*. Toronto: McClelland & Stewart, 1971.

Bjerky, Irene, and Darla Dickson. "Chinese Merchants of Yale." Unpublished manuscript, May 2009.

Blurton, H. J. "The Placer Mines on Cherry and Mission Creeks." *Seventeenth Report of the Okanagan Historical Society*, 1953, 105–106.

Bondar, Barry. *Okanagan: The Story and The Sights*. North Vancouver, BC: Whitecap Books, 1986.

British Columbia Directory. Victoria: R. T. Williams, 1882.

Buckland, L. M. "Settlement at L'Anse au Sable." *Second Annual Report of the Okanagan Historical and Natural History Society*, 1927, 19–21.

Cawston, A. H. "John Chinaman: Recollections of A. H. (Gint) Cawston." *Thirty-first Report of the Okanagan Historical Society*, 1967, 109–117.

Cheung, George and Elsie, eds. *Special Publication: The 31st National Convention of Chinese Freemasons in Canada, Kamloops Chinese Freemasons 104th anniversary, Dart Coon Club 76th Anniversary* (Chinese text). Kamloops, BC: Kamloops Chinese Freemasons society, 1998.

Chinese and English Secretariats. *Special Publication: The 34th National Convention of the Chinese Freemasons of Canada* (Chinese text). Vancouver: Chinese Freemasons of Canada, 2001.

Chow, Lily. *Sojourners in the North*. Halfmoon Bay, BC: Caitlin Press, 1996.

———. *Chasing Their Dreams.* Halfmoon Bay, BC: Caitlin Press, 2000.

———. *Blood and Sweat over the Railway Tracks.* Vancouver: Chinese Canadian Historical Society of BC and Initiative for Student Teaching and Research in Chinese Canadian Studies, UBC, 2014.

Christian, Dorothy. "Articulating a Silence." *Ricepaper* (Fall 2004), 22–31.

Clement, J. P. "Early Days in Kelowna." *Twenty-fourth Report of the Okanagan Historical Society*, 1960, 134–135.

Critchley, Peter. "The Chinese in Armstrong." *Okanagan History: Sixty-third Report of the Okanagan Historical Society*, 1999, 8–19.

Everett, Graham. "Signor Guise Taverna and The Lytton Joss Temple." Lytton tourist brochure, 2002.

Eversole, Linda J. *The Gold Rush Town, On Lee House & Store—Documentary History.* Unpublished report, BC Heritage Branch, January 1984.

Fisher, Agnes. "Armstrong Sixty Years Ago." *Sixteenth Report of the Okanagan Historical Society*, 1952, 82–88.

Gabriel, Theresa. *Vernon, BC: A Brief History.* Vernon, BC: Vernon Centennial Committee, 1958.

Glasgow, Kenny. "Tribute to Peter Chong's 90th Birthday." Unpublished manuscript, Lytton, 2011.

Gowen, Herbert H. *Church Work in British Columbia: Being a Memoir of the Episcopate of Acton Windeyer Sillitoe, D.D., D.C.L., First Bishop of New Westminster.* London and New York: Longmans, Green and Co., 1899.

Hall, R. O. "Early Days of Fruit Growing in the South Okanagan." *Twenty-fifth Report of the Okanagan Historical Society*, 1961, 105–122.

Hauka, Donald. *McGowan's War.* Vancouver: New Star Books, 2003.

Hayman, B. "Mar Jok Always Feeds the Poor." *Forty-eighth Annual Report of the Okanagan Historical Society*, 1984, 91–94.

Heal, Ronald Rupert. "Farms and Enterprises in the North Okanagan." *Sixteenth Report of the Okanagan Historical Society*, 1952, 121–127.

Higgins, David Williams. *The Mystic Spring & Other Tales of Western Life.* Toronto: William Briggs, 1904.

Hill, Douglas. *The Opening of the Canadian West.* London: Heinemann, 1967.

Howay, F. W. *The Early History of the Fraser River Mines.* Victoria: Charles F. Banfield, 1926.

Hurst, Theresa. *An Illustrated History of Vernon and District.* Vernon, BC: Okanagan Historical Society Report and Museum and Archives, 1967.

Johnston, B. "Exit 'Quong's.' " *Twenty-eighth Report of the Okanagan Historical Society*, 1964, 54–55.

Kluckner, Michael. *Vanishing British Columbia*. Vancouver and Seattle: UBC Press and University of Washington Press, 2008.

Kristensen, N. G. "Armstrong, the 'Celery City.'" *Okanagan History: Forty-ninth Report of the Okanagan Historical Society*, 1985, 115–119.

Lai, David Chuenyan, and Donald Luxton & Associates. "A Proposal for the Kamloops Chinese Cemetery Memorial Park." Kamloops, BC: City of Kamloops, July 1987.

———. "A Proposed Plan for the Kelowna Memorial Park Cemetery. Kelowna Cemetery Heritage Management Plan." Kelowna, BC: City of Kelowna, 2001.

———. "Kelowna Cemetery: Heritage Management Plan 2011." Kelowna, BC: City of Kelowna, 2011.

Lai, Him Mark, trans. and ed. "Reminiscences of an Old Chinese Railroad Worker." *East-West Chinese American Journal*, May 5, 1971.

Lee, Ben. "Mar Jok Memorial Service." *Forty-eighth Annual Report of the Okanagan Historical Society*, 1984, 95.

Lee, David. "Chinese Construction Workers on the Canadian Pacific." *Railroad History* no. 148 (Spring 1983): 42–57.

Lei, M. Pan, G. Rong Yang, and J. Ping Jian, eds. *Special Publication: The Chinese Freemasons Society of Vancouver, 100th Anniversary: 1888–1988* (Chinese text). Vancouver: Vancouver Chinese Freemasons society, 1989.

———. *The 140th Anniversary Publication of the Chinese Freemasons Society*. Vancouver: Vancouver Chinese Freemasons society, 2003.

Liu Jiyao (刘纪曜). "Chinese Contemporary History (Chinese text)." China Republic, Taiwan: Chung Hwa Correspondence School, 1989.

Mann, A. H. "Kelowna's Chinatown." *Forty-sixth Annual Report of the Okanagan Historical Society*, 1958, 20–28.

Moore, James. "The Discovery of Gold on Hill's Bar in 1858." *BC Historical Quarterly* 3, no. 3 (July 1939): 215–220.

Morse, J. J. *Kamloops: The Inland Capital, A Condensed History.* Kamloops, BC: Kamloops Museum Association, 1958.

Moseley, George. *China: Empire to People's Republic.* London: B. T. Batsford, 1968.

McIntyre, Joan, ed. *A Fruitful Century: The British Columbia Fruit Growers' Association, 1889–1989.* Kelowna: British Columbia Fruit Growers' Association, 1990.

Murray, M. George. "Gods in a Lytton Woodshed." *Vancouver Daily Province*, May 7, 1933.

Norris, L. "The Townsite of Vernon, BC." *First Annual Report of the Oka-nagan Historical and Natural History Society*, 1926, 29–30.

Norton, Wayne, and Wilf Schmidt, eds. *Kamloops: One Hundred Years of Com-munity, 1893–1993*. Merritt, BC: Sonotek Publishing, 1992.

Oram, Edna. *The History of Vernon, 1867–1937*. Kelowna, BC: Author, 1985.

Ormsby, Margaret, ed. *A Pioneer Gentlewoman in British Columbia: The Recol-lections of Susan Allison*. Vancouver: UBC Press, 1976.

Pearson, Anne. *An Early History of Coldstream and Lavington*. Victoria: Author, 1986.

Roth, Terrence. *The Peasant's Gold: The Story of Peter Wing*. Kamloops, BC: Goss Publishing, 1998.

Ruffle, A. D. "The Greata Ranch." *Thirty-ninth Annual Report of the Okanagan Historical Society*, 1975, 142–144.

Serra, Johnny. "Armstrong Packing Houses." *Twenty-eighth Report of the Oka-nagan Historical Society*, 1964, 42–45.

Sterne, Netta. *Fraser Gold, 1858!* Seattle: University of Washington Press, 1998.

Stewart, John. "The Kamloops Canneries: The Rise and Fall of a Local Industry, 1913–1990." *BC Studies* 93 (Spring 1992): 30.

Tan, Jin and Patricia Roy. *The Chinese in Canada*. Canada's Ethnic Groups. Booklet No. 9. Ottawa: Canadian Historical Association, 1985.

Tomkins, Janet. "Chinese-Canadians in Search of Immigrant Ancestors: Current and Potential Resources." Paper presented at the World Li-brary and Information Congress, Oslo, 2005.

Ward, N. Lascelles, and H. A. Hellaby. *Oriental Missions in British Columbia*. London: Society for the Propagation of the Gospel in Foreign Parts, 1925.

Wickberg, Edgar, ed. *From China to Canada*. Toronto: McClelland & Stew-art, 1982.

Williams' British Columbia Directory. Victoria, BC: R. T. Williams, 1882.

Woodward, Meredith B. *The Land of Dreams: A History in Photographs of the British Columbia Interior*. Banff, AB: Altitude Publishing, 1993.

Wuest, Donna. *Coldstream: The Ranch Where It All Began*. Madeira Park, BC: Harbour Publishing, 2005.

Wong, Tun. "Human Endeavour: Sue Lee Ping Wong." *Okanagan History: Sixty-third Report of the Okanagan Historical Society*, 1999, 156–159.

Archival Sources

Barrett Parke, Alice. Diary of Alice Barrett Parke. Vol. 20. October 22, 1896–December 25, 1896. Transcribed from the original by Jo Jones, 1996–97. Vernon Museum and Archives.

British Columbia Attorney General. Correspondence, 1872–1937, BC Archives, GR 0429, Box 1, file 10.

British Columbia Government Agency [Mining]. Correspondence. Yale— BC Gold Commission, Lytton.

BC Correspondence to Premier, BC Archives, GR 411, Box 1, file 2.

Correspondence outward from Provincial Mining Agency to Gold Commissions in Lytton, 1859–1863, BC Archives, GR 252, Vol. 1 and 2.

British Columbia Government Agency Correspondence [Mining], Lytton, 1860–61, BC Archives.

British Columbia Government Agency, Mining Record—Fort Yale, BC Archives, GR 252, Vol. 12, file 1.

BC Department of Lands and Works, Chief Commission Correspondence incoming, BC Archives, GR 868, Box 2, file 13.

Bureau of Statistics Correspondence, 1895–1898. Returns, A-M, BC Archives, Box 1, file 1; R. E. Gosnell, Correspondence inward and outward, 1895–98, BC Archives, GT 153.

Cambie, Henry John. *Diary & Notes: Contract 60,* Yale, BC, April 1880– April 1881. Vancouver Archives.

———. *Diary & Notes: Contract 60,* Spuzzum, BC, July 7 to December 14, 1883. Vancouver Archives.

———. *Memoir of Henry J. Cambie: Reminiscence,* MSS 34, file 15, Vancouver Archives.

Hills, George, Bishop of Columbia. *The Journal of George Hills, 1860.* Anglican Church Archives, University of British Columbia.

Hope Collectorate, BC Archives, GR 252, Vol. 33.

Living Landscapes: Nominal Census, records in Yale, 1891, Royal BC Museum and BC Archives, database 4001–4050.

Mining, trading and garden records, Lytton, BC Archives, GR 833.

Registration of Mining Certificates, BC Archives, GR 243, Vol. 1.

BC Government Agency [Mining], Correspondence with Gold Commissioner, Lytton, April 6, 1860; May 10, 1860; July 4, 1860; March 1, 1861.

Newspapers Consulted

Armstrong Advance, 1906
Armstrong Advertiser, 1909
British Colonist, 1862, 1871,1881–83
British Columbia Gazette, 1858
BC Tribune, 1886
Colonist, 1883, 1888
Chinese Times, 1911, 1932
Capital News, Kelowna, 1997, 2012, 2016
Daily Colonists
Daily Courier, Vernon, 1941, 1920, 1924, 1931–33, 1947, 1964,
　2012 (e-edition)
Daily Standard, 1880–81
Inland Sentinel, 1880–1885, 1896
Kamloops Sentinel, 1926, 1929
Kamloops Daily Sentinel, 1970–71
Kamloops This Week, 2011–14
Kelowna Capital News, 1964, 2014–16
Kelowna Records, 1914–1920
Singtao News, 2003
Province, 1933, 1965
Vancouver Daily Province, 1933.
Vancouver Sun, 1943, 1972
Vernon News, 1892, 1909, 1913, 1917, 1919, 1924, 1931, 1938, 1945,
　1947–48
Vernon Daily News, 1988
Victoria Gazette, 1858

Personal and Other Interviews

Interviewed by the author:
(1) the late Peter Wing of Kamloops at his residence, 2910 Ontario Street,
　Vancouver, May 10, 1999.
(2) the late Walter Joe, Harry Low and Loo Gim On, Vernon, November
　2, 1998.
(3) Gillian Huang in the Appleton Restaurant, Vernon, November 3, 1998.
(4) Chow Bing Yit in the Appleton Restaurant, Vernon, November 3, 1998.
(5) Michael Wong, Hong Kong Village, Vernon, July 27, 2004.

(6) Lee Shui Dong in Kelowna, 1998, 2004.
(7) the late Ben Lee in Kelowna, 1998, 2004.
(8) the late Walter Joe, July 2004.
(9) Ralph Lockhart in the Armstrong Spallumcheen Museum, 2004.
(10) Mrs. Hughei Jong and Mary Jong, in Armstrong, 1998, 2004.
(11) the late Rita Haugen in Lytton, 2008.
(12) the Chong family of Lytton, in Burnaby, 2008.
(13) Tun Wong in Kelowna, 2016.

Andrea Laforet interviewed Annie York in Spuzzum, March, April, 1973.

Chris Lee and Douglas Quan interviewed Bevan Jangzse for *An Oral History Project*, the Chinese Canadian Historical Society, Vancouver, August 2, 1996.

Imbert Orchard interviewed Annie York and Arthur Urquhart: Spuzzum, CBC Imbert Orchard Collection, #IH-BC. 1971. BC Archives.

———. Gus Milliken Talks about Yale, Hope and CPR Boats, 1964. T0 658:0001. BC Archives.